Disability Income Insurance

Group and
Worksite
Issues

This book is published by the Insurance Education Program of the Health Insurance Association of America (HIAA) in conjunction with the National Association of Health Underwriters (NAHU).

The Health Insurance Association of America
Washington, DC 20004-1204

ISBN 1-879143-81-X

Contents

Figures and Tables

The Health Insurance Association of America (HIAA)

HIAA is the nation's most prominent trade association representing the private health care system. Its more than 300 members provide health, long-term care, dental, disability, and supplemental coverage to more than 123 million Americans. It is the nation's premier provider of self-study courses on health insurance, managed care, long-term care, and related topics.

The mission of HIAA's Insurance Education Program includes the following goals:

- to provide tools for insurance company personnel to use in enhancing the quality and efficiency of services to the public;
- to provide a career development vehicle for insurer employees and other health care industry professionals; and
- to promote general understanding of the role and contribution of the health insurance industry in the financing, administration, and delivery of health care services.

The Insurance Education Program provides the following services:

- a comprehensive course of study in the fundamentals of health insurance, medical expense insurance, supplemental health insurance, long-term care insurance, disability income insurance, managed care, health insurance fraud, HIPAA, and customer service in the health care environment;
- certification of educational achievement by proctored examination for all courses;
- programs to recognize accomplishment in the industry and academic communities through course evaluation and certification, which enable participants to obtain academic or continuing education credits; and

- development of educational, instructional, training, and informational materials related to the health insurance and health care industries.

The Health Insurance Association of America (HIAA)
Insurance Education Program
1201 F Street NW, Suite 500
Washington, DC 20004-1204
800-509-4422
www.hiaa.org
Email: mgrant@hiaa.org

The National Association of Health Underwriters (NAHU)

The National Association of Health Underwriters (NAHU) serves qualified professionals who are trained and experienced in guiding individuals and employers through the complexities of choosing appropriate and affordable health plans.

NAHU believes that our 18,000 members hold a unique position as advocates for the health plan consumer and can be valuable players in the progress toward the right kind of health care reform. Our goal is to provide all Americans with affordable and high quality health care while promoting the activities and ethical conduct of insurance professionals through communication, education, and legislative representation. NAHU also educates the decision-makers about the value health insurance professionals deliver in helping consumers access the health care system, through education and association involvement, and increases members' ability to better serve consumers.

NAHU offers a wide range of resources as we strive to be the premier clearinghouse for a variety of health insurance education opportunities. Through NAHU's partnerships with government agencies, universities, associations, and education specialists, we offer premium educational products and services that are a valuable benefit to the professional growth of a NAHU member. Our continuing education conferences and Webview seminars present the industry's leading speakers addressing the most pressing topics in our field. Additionally, over 200 state and local chapters hold monthly meetings featuring speakers accredited for continuing education.

The National Association of Health Underwriters
Education Department
2000 North 14th Street, Suite 450
Arlington, VA 22201
703-276-3825
www.nahu.org
Email: education@nahu.org

Preface

Nearly one in three people will suffer a serious disability during their working lives. Without adequate disability income insurance coverage, the emotional and financial toll can be devastating. Increasingly, individuals look to their employers as the source of insurance benefits, and group disability income (DI) insurance continues to be the solution of choice for many employers. These plans typically cover most employees in the group and are paid for largely by the employer. Voluntary plans, paid for largely by the employee, may be offered in lieu of or in addition to group plans. Voluntary plans have gained popularity in recent years, as employers have looked for ways to shift benefit costs to plan participants.

Although government- and employer-sponsored programs, such as Social Security, state temporary disability income insurance, and workers' compensation, provide a baseline of protection, such programs fall woefully short for most individuals. Only individuals suffering from total and permanent disability qualify for Social Security coverage, and even for those who do qualify, the level of benefits is unlikely to meet more than basic needs. Workers' compensation benefits are limited to occupational illness or injury, and state temporary benefits are available in only a few states.

Group disability income insurance, typically distributed by insurance companies through a network of agents, brokers, and group representatives, is available not only to employer groups but also to association members, franchisees, and debtors. Although the requirements for these eligible groups differ from state to state, the common characteristics shared by the participating members are considered sufficient to allow the insurer to provide coverage to the group as a whole.

A key concept associated with group DI insurance is that coverage is guaranteed to plan participants. This does not mean, however, that coverage is guaranteed to a sponsor. In fact, the insurer's underwriters carefully assess the risk associated with a sponsor. In the case of employers, considerations such as financial stability, type of business, occupational duties of employees, and geographical dispersion are important considerations. Only those employers meeting the company's underwriting standards will be accepted for coverage.

Another important aspect of group DI coverage is pricing. In general, group premiums tend to reflect cost savings to the insurer in distribution, underwriting, and administration. Initially, premiums are often based on manual rates developed by the insurer's actuaries. These manual rates reflect certain assumptions about the employer, morbidity, and the economy, among other things. If the group is large enough, experience rating comes into play. With experience rating, prices are based on the actual claims experience of the group.

Group DI insurance products are characterized by many of the same features associated with individual disability products. Typically, the disability must persist for a specified period of time. The contract specifies the nature of the disability that must be suffered for benefits to be paid, and the duration of benefits is set forth. The level of benefits is usually based on a percentage of pre-disability salary or wages. Benefits received under the plan are generally coordinated with benefits received under other employer-sponsored and government-provided plans.

The last few years have seen a proliferation of new product features designed to meet market demand. Chief among these are features that reduce employer costs, provide cost-of-living increases, and allow for continuity of coverage through conversion to individual coverage in the event of a job change.

Major considerations with group DI coverage relate to claim adjudication and plan administration. Home office claims administrators must assess a claimant's eligibility both for coverage under the employer's plan and for benefits under the group contract. In today's world, claim adjudication is only the beginning. An increased emphasis is placed on returning disabled employees to work through a combination of partial disability benefits and rehabilitation.

State and federal regulation and taxation continue to impact group disability income insurance. State laws tend to regulate the types of groups eligible for coverage and the manner in which products are priced, marketed, and administered. Federal laws require non-discrimination in the provision of group disability benefits and protect participating employees by requiring adequate disclosure of plan features and benefits. Under current law, both employers and employees receive tax benefits for participating in group DI insurance plans.

This book is intended not only for insurance and health care professionals, but also for consumers and others interested in the disability field. It serves as the textbook for the third of three courses sponsored by HIAA and NAHU, which lead to the designation of Disability Income Associate.

This book has been written and organized to make its ideas easy to grasp and the information it presents easy to learn—and to facilitate study and review. Examples illustrating the practical application of concepts appear throughout the text. Key terms are in boldface and are marked in the margin with a key symbol. Focus questions and review questions draw attention to important points and engage the reader in active learning.

Finally, it should be kept in mind that the insurance industry is continuously changing and the information in this book may be superseded by the latest trends or innovations. For information on current developments, the reader should visit the Websites of HIAA (www.hiaa.org) and NAHU (www. nahu.org).

Gary V. Powell, JD, CLU, ChFC
President
Gary V. Powell and Associates

Gregory F. Dean, JD, CLU, ChFC, LTCP
Executive Director, Insurance Education
Health Insurance Association of America

About the Author

Gary V. Powell is President of Gary V. Powell and Associates. Located in Charlotte, North Carolina, the firm specializes in the design and development of customized instruction and other performance improvement tools for the financial services industry. Mr. Powell is a graduate of Indiana University School of Law and was formerly Assistant Director of Advanced Marketing for Northwestern Mutual Life and Managing Director, Personal Financial Planning, for KPMG Peat Marwick, Charlotte, North Carolina.

» Acknowledgments

Reviewers

Mark Andruss
Fortis Benefits Insurance Company

John A. Boni, RHU
Physicians Mutual Insurance Company

Winthrop Cashdollar
Health Insurance Association of America

Kevin Corcoran
National Association of Health Underwriters

Gregory F. Dean, JD, CLU, ChFC, LTCP
Health Insurance Association of America

Candida A. Friedman, ACS, AIAA, CSA
Guardian/CorPro

Arthur C. Jetter, Jr., CLU, CFP, RHU, FLMI, REBC, LTCP
Art Jetter & Company

Gerald Katz, MSPA, RHU, ALHC, DABFE
Disability Income Concepts, Inc.

Drew King
JHA, Inc.

Farren M. Ross
National Association of Health Underwriters

David A. Saltzman, RHU
D. A. Saltzman & Associates

Robert C. Tretter, CLU, ChFC, RHU
GroupLink, Inc.

Editor

Michael G. Bell
Consulting Editor

1 Introduction to Group Disability Income Insurance

- Overview
- The Definition of Group Disability Income Insurance
- Historical Background and Current Trends
- Socio-Economic Perspectives on Disability
- Summary

OVERVIEW

It is estimated that one out of three people between the ages of 35 and 65 will suffer a serious disability.[1] In the absence of disability income (DI) insurance coverage, when a worker becomes disabled the financial toll on her and her family can be devastating. Not only is the disabled worker's income lost, but expenses often increase because of the need for medication and specialized care. Even so, about 82 percent of U.S. workers either have no long-term disability income coverage, or they believe their coverage is inadequate, according to a joint survey commissioned by the Consumer Federation of America and the American Council of Life Insurance.[2]

Of those workers who are insured, a distinction is made between individual coverage and group coverage. Most, but not all, individual coverage is purchased and paid for by the individual insured. Group insurance, on the other hand, is typically sponsored by an employer that pays most or all of the premium. Not surprisingly, a recent survey from the Health Insurance Association of America (HIAA) shows that the primary reason employers offer disability income insurance is to attract and retain qualified employees.[3] The other side of the equation is that employees increasingly look to their employers to sponsor insurance and other benefits, and they make employment decisions based on the type and level of benefits offered.

Thus, the total number of workers protected by group long-term disability insurance has risen to 34 million.[4]

Although the large number of workers covered is encouraging, Department of Labor research reveals a more troubling picture. In 2000, significantly less than half of full-time employees had disability income coverage.

Table 1.1

Percentage of Employees with Disability Coverage[5]

Type of Program	All Employees	Professional, Technical, and Related Employees	Clerical and Sales Employees	Blue-Collar and Service Employees
Short-term disability coverage	39	54	38	32
Long-term disability coverage	31	56	31	17

Keep in mind that this survey included both large and small employers and that the authors report that the incidence of benefits among small employers (those with 100 or fewer employees) was significantly lower than with larger employers. On balance, one can conclude that even among professional and technical employees, there is a large and continuing need for group disability income coverage.

Focus Question #1

Although the number of workers covered by employer-sponsored DI insurance is growing, according to Department of Labor research the percentage of all full-time employees who are covered is less than
a) 10 percent.
b) 20 percent.
c) 30 percent.
d) 40 percent.

Scope of the Text

This text discusses group disability income insurance and to a lesser extent a related product, voluntary worksite disability insurance. One consideration in any discussion of DI insurance relates to the various sources of disability income and the extent to which Social Security, workers' compensation, state temporary disability income programs, other employer-sponsored benefits, and private resources offset the need for group DI insurance. This is discussed in Chapter 2.

Another consideration is how group DI insurance is marketed and sold. Chapters 3 and 4 address these issues. Chapter 5 identifies the various groups that are appropriate for group insurance. Although group insurance is often thought of in the employment context, associations, franchise owners, and creditors may also sponsor group DI insurance.

Chapters 6 and 7 discuss pricing and underwriting issues associated with group DI insurance. Included are the roles of the various players involved in pricing and underwriting, including the home office underwriter and actuary and the field representative.

More than any other product, with the possible exception of long-term care insurance, disability income insurance is feature-driven. A keen understanding of both basic and special product features is required for the marketing, sale, underwriting, and administration of group DI insurance. Chapters 8 and 9 discuss key product features, with an emphasis on how those features affect case design.

Chapters 10 and 11 explore an aspect of group DI insurance that affects all parties involved, including the employer, the employee/insured, and the insurer—claims administration. A threshold question is whether or not the insured is entitled to benefits. Assuming benefits are payable, a second question is how the claim will be managed during the disability. Increasingly, claims administration is geared to rehabilitation and financial incentives that encourage an insured's return to work.

In Chapter 12, the emphasis shifts to voluntary worksite programs. These plans enjoyed only limited popularity in the past, but recent compensation trends that offer employees greater choice in benefits and require greater employee participation in the cost of benefits have made them more common. It remains the case, however, that a high level of employee participation in the employer's plan is key to its profitability for the insurer and its value to the employer.

Group insurance, especially group DI insurance, remains subject to significant government regulation. Chapters 13 and 14 discuss both state and federal regulation, including income taxation of group DI insurance and voluntary worksite plans.

Objectives

After reading this chapter and completing the accompanying exercises, you will be able to:

- define group disability income insurance,
- describe the market for group disability income insurance,
- discuss the general characteristics of the group DI insurance product,
- discuss the historical background of group DI insurance and current issues associated with it, and
- explain the socio-economic impact of disability.

▶▶ THE DEFINITION OF GROUP DISABILITY INCOME INSURANCE

There are several approaches to defining group disability income insurance. One is to focus on the sponsor of the coverage. Employers are the most common sponsors of group DI insurance, and the ''group'' insured is typically full-time employees. There are, however, other types of sponsors, including associations (such as alumni and professional associations), franchisers, and lenders.

Another approach to defining group DI insurance is to consider the type of benefit provided. Group DI insurance benefits take two forms:

- short-term disability (STD) benefits and
- long-term disability (LTD) benefits.

In addition, many employers offer uninsured **sick leave plans**. Eligibility for sick leave plans is usually limited to full-time employees who have served a probationary period with the employer. Sick leave plans typically continue 100 percent of salary and all other benefits for a stated period of time, for instance 10 days per year. Group DI insurance plans typically come into play when these uninsured plans leave off.

Short-term disability (STD) benefits provide for salary replacement, most often at partial pay, for a period of three or six months. Benefits are paid either as a percentage of employee earnings (such as 60 percent of pre-disability earnings) or as a flat dollar amount. STD benefits can vary by the amount of pre-disability earnings, length of service with the firm, or length of disability.

Long-term disability (LTD) benefits provide a monthly income amount to eligible employees who, because of illness or injury, are unable to work for an extended period. Benefits are usually paid as a fixed percentage of pre-disability earnings up to a set limit. Most participants have a waiting period of three to six months, and benefits are usually coordinated to begin after sick leave and STD benefits end. LTD benefits generally continue until retirement or a specified age, or for a period that varies according to the employee's age at the time of disability.

The distinctions between STD and LTD are discussed more fully in Chapters 8 and 9.

Another approach to defining group DI insurance is to compare the way it is underwritten to the way individual DI insurance is underwritten. In general, individual DI insurance is underwritten by assessing the financial status and health of the individual applicant. By contrast, group insurance is characterized by guaranteed issue underwriting. With guaranteed issue, individual participants are guaranteed coverage at rates based on the insurer's standard manual rates or the characteristics and claims experience of the particular employee group. For example, the employer may require only that the participant be a full-time worker who is actively at work for at least 30 hours per week.

Yet another approach to defining group DI insurance is to distinguish it from other types of insurance, such as medical expense insurance, life insurance, and long-term care insurance. One major difference between disability income insurance and medical expense insurance is that DI insurance reimburses the insured for income lost as the result of an inability to work during a period of disability. By contrast, medical expense insurance reimburses the insured for the cost of covered health care, usually subject to co-pays, deductibles, internal limits for specific treatments, and overall maximum benefit limits.

Although there are other differences, a major distinction between life insurance and disability income insurance lies in the "trigger" for the payment of benefits. With DI insurance, disability as specifically defined in the policy is the trigger, and the definition may differ from policy to policy. Furthermore, there may be more than one occurrence of disability during the term of DI coverage. By contrast, the trigger for a life insurance death payment is death, and there can be only one death claim submitted under a life insurance policy (although policies with accelerated benefits may make payments before death in some circumstances).

The major difference between disability income insurance and long-term care insurance (LTCI) is that LTCI reimburses the insured for costs incurred for specified types of chronic care. Disability income insurance, on the other hand, replaces income lost because of a disability. In addition, while the triggering event for payment of benefits under a DI policy is disability as defined in the policy, the trigger for payment of LTCI benefits is the inability to perform a certain number of activities of daily living (ADLs) or a severe cognitive impairment.

Focus Question #2

Briefly explain key differences between STD and LTD.

_____

_____

_____

_____

_____

►► HISTORICAL BACKGROUND AND CURRENT TRENDS

Policies offered to employee groups or members of fraternal organizations were among the first modern disability income insurance policies to appear during the latter part of the 19th century. Driving forces credited with the emergence of employer-sponsored coverage include industrialization, the creation of the modern factory, and urbanization. People moved off of the farm, traditional family ties were broken, and employers increasingly became the center of social and economic life. Initially, paternalistic employers provided benefits to disabled, deceased, or retired employees out of benevolence.

The prevalence today of group benefits, including group DI insurance benefits, can be attributed to several key factors, described below:

- *Organized labor.* Two events formalized the need for employer-sponsored benefits. The first was the enactment in the early 1930s of the National Labor Relations Act, which gave labor unions the right to negotiate on behalf of their membership and strike if demands were not met. The second was a 1949 Supreme Court ruling that assured labor unions of the right to negotiate not only for working conditions and wages but also for benefits.

- *Wage freezes.* Government-imposed wage freezes during World War II did not include freezes on employee benefits. Employees who found their salaries and wages locked in place negotiated for more and better employer-sponsored benefits, including group DI insurance.

- *Cost advantages.* Savings arise from group rather than individual under-writing, from the issuance of a single master policy rather than many individual policies, and from the administration of standardized policy provisions rather than individually tailored policy provisions.

- *Tax incentives.* Since the codification of the 1954 Internal Revenue Code, employer premium payments have been deductible as ordinary and necessary business expenses. At the same time, employees are entitled to an exclusion from income for premium payments paid on their behalf by an employer. Only when group DI benefits are received by a disabled employee are they included in income for tax purposes (and not always then—see Chapter 14).

- *Inflation.* Although inflation has leveled off in recent years, wage infla-tion has contributed to the increase in demand for group DI benefits. Benefit levels are typically a percentage of wages, which are in turn increased with inflation. As will be discussed in more detail in Chapter 9, certain product features allow benefits to keep pace with both pre- and post-disability inflation. Furthermore, increases in the cost of living because of inflation erode family savings and second incomes, making any existing disability coverage all the more valuable.

- *State and federal legislation.* State laws have liberalized the definitions of the types of groups to which group insurance may be offered. Federal laws have been enacted that expand the scope of covered disabilities to include pregnancy, alcoholism, and drug abuse.

These factors combined to produce significant growth in group DI coverage during the 1960s, '70s, and '80s. Also contributing to sales growth, espe-cially in the 1980s, were innovative product development, creative pricing, and liberal claims and underwriting policies. Although growth slumped in the 1990s, by 2001 the aggregate group DI in-force premium had increased to $6.7 billion annually.[6]

Recent Changes

Unfortunately, the liberal policies, creative pricing, and product innovation that accounted for rapid sales growth in the 1980s also contributed to a downturn in insurer profitability in group DI insurance by the mid-1990s.

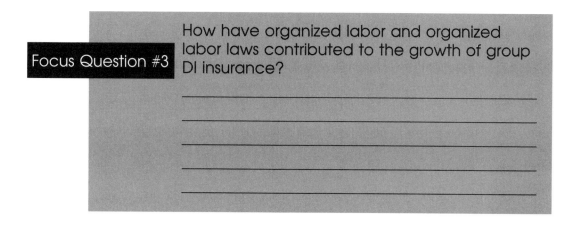

Focus Question #3

How have organized labor and organized labor laws contributed to the growth of group DI insurance?

In addition, other forces confronting the industry during the 1990s hurt insurers and led to changes that are still unfolding:

- *Slow market and customer growth.* Insurers misread the market opportunity, leading to misallocation of resources. While a study by JHA, Inc. shows that the LTD market was growing at only about 8 percent annually during the 1990s, DI insurance executives stubbornly and mistakenly targeted 15 percent growth, spending money and other resources on a market opportunity that simply was not there.[7] To make matters worse, insurers took the easy route of cannibalizing each other's business rather than focusing on creating new demand among first-time buyers. According to the study's author, "This lack of organic growth created havoc in the industry, as premium persistency levels plummeted to below 85 percent, from highs of 90 percent to 94 percent in the 1980s."[8]

- *Price-driven sales strategies.* As consumer demand declined during the 1990s, insurers slashed prices to remain more competitive. Unfortunately, revenues were declining at the same time that the problems associated with the liberal underwriting and claims practices of the 1980s were emerging. The net effect was a decline in insurer profits.

- *New disabilities and changing attitudes.* The 1990s also saw the recognition of new types of disabilities that had not been anticipated by pricing. The new disabilities included chronic fatigue syndrome, work-related stress, substance abuse, repetitive motion injury, sick building syndrome, and AIDS-related disabilities. Furthermore, changing attitudes in the workplace attached less of a stigma to disability and made it easier for an employee to file a claim. Adding to this change in attitude was an economic trend toward reorganization and consolidation, often accompanied by "downsizing" of older employees. In many cases, disability was viewed as an alternative to returning to work.

■ *Unfavorable economic conditions.* Although the 1990s saw a boom in productivity, conditions such as low inflation and low interest rates had a negative effect on group DI insurers. First, returns from fixed income investments used to fund reserves were lower than anticipated. Second, low wage inflation meant that DI benefits to disabled insureds retained most of their purchasing power, thus lowering the incentive to return to work.

■ *Changing demographics.* Two key demographic factors also contributed to declining group DI insurer profitability in the 1990s. The first of these we are all familiar with—the aging of the Baby Boom generation. Disability tends to increase with age, and as the first of the Boomers reached age 50, the proportion of them claiming disability nearly doubled in comparison to when they were in their 40s.[9] Another demographic consideration relates to the increasing number of two-income households. The ongoing income provided by a working spouse reduces the incentive for a disabled spouse to return to work and tends to lengthen the duration of disability claims.

The convergence of these factors has led to a major restructuring of the industry. Today, only a few carriers remain active in the business. Three major insurers, Provident Life and Accident, Paul Revere, and UNUM, have merged to become the UnumProvident Company. Also, those insurers remaining in the market have tightened underwriting, lowered policy benefits levels, and improved claims management. For example, most policies provide for partial benefits and rehabilitation and encourage the return to work.

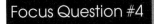

Focus Question #4

How did economic conditions during the 1990s contribute to lower profits for group DI insurers?

_____

_____

_____

_____

_____

Trends for the Future

Despite the tumultuous recent history of group DI insurance, there are some hopeful trends for a brighter future:

- Demand from smaller employers is on the rise, with groups of 1-50 employees expected to be a major market. Several companies have recently introduced products to this growing sector of the economy.

- Rising benefit costs and decreasing corporate profits have caused employers to shift part or all of the cost of benefit plans to employees. In the retirement arena, this has translated into an increase in profit-sharing and Section 401(k) plans and a decrease in defined benefit plans. In connection with employer-sponsored life and DI plans, the shift has been toward voluntary plans, where employees contribute part or all of the premium cost through payroll deduction. The challenge for disability income insurers, as always, is to emphasize the value of their voluntary products in a competitive marketplace.

- Changes in attitudes and in tax law have led to employee demand for greater flexibility in benefit choice. Increasingly, employees are interested in choosing how to allocate their benefit dollars. Tax laws, such as Internal Revenue Code (IRC) Section 125, allow employees to exclude the cost of many benefits from income, even though the employee can direct how those dollars are spent. To the extent that employees purchase disability income benefits with pre-tax dollars, those benefits are includible in the employee's income.

- Increasing financial demands on the Social Security system are likely to lead to legislative reform. Although no one can predict with certainty the direction such reform will take, growing government budget deficits make it a likely bet that more emphasis will be placed on the private sector. Certainly, the trend favors personal responsibility and private industry solutions over government welfare and social insurance.

In addition to these favorable trends for group disability income insurance, there are some concerns.

Government regulation at both the state and federal levels continues to require additional vigilance and compliance by the insurance industry. One key issue is the extent to which insurers will be required to provide coverage and benefits for mental illnesses. At the writing of this text, there is legislation pending in Congress that would require insurers to treat mental illness like any other illness for purposes of medical insurance, and it is possible that in the future such legislation could apply to disability income insurance. HIAA has taken the position that this "mental health parity legislation" is a misguided effort to provide additional coverage for a wide variety of "ill-defined and difficult-to-diagnose" mental disorders. According to HIAA, the legislation would drive up the cost of health insurance for everyone, and it will cause hundreds of thousands of Americans to lose their health coverage altogether.[10]

Another current issue facing the industry relates to disabilities resulting from acts of war and/or terrorism. Most group DI insurance policies contain an exclusion for a disability resulting from war, declared or undeclared, or any act of war. War is generally interpreted as involving hostilities between two or more governments or sovereign nations, so the war exclusion would generally not apply to acts of violence by individuals or political groups that are not employed by, or acting on behalf of, a sovereign government. The war exclusion could apply if a terrorist group is allied with or acting in concert with another nation in attacking the United States. For claims resulting from the terrorist acts of September 11, 2001, both life and DI insurers waived any right to deny benefits on the basis of the "war exclusion." But the question of how disabilities resulting from such acts will be treated by insurers in the future is currently unresolved.

Focus Question #5

What impact are anticipated strains on Social Security likely to have on the DI insurance industry?

_____

_____

_____

_____

_____

►►Socio-Economic Perspectives on Disability

Disability resulting in loss of income creates a huge socio-economic cost to our country. Based on a recent Census Bureau report, nearly one in five persons (53 million people) said they had some level of disability in 1997, while one in eight (33 million) reported they had a severe disability. The report found that the presence of a severe disability brings with it an increased likelihood of receiving welfare benefits, having low levels of income, and living in poverty. Also, individuals with a severe disability are less likely to be covered by health insurance than those with no disability. Among people 25 to 64 years of age having a severe disability, only 48 percent had health coverage, compared to 80 percent for people with a non-severe disability and 82 percent of those with no disability.[11]

A comprehensive study recently released by UnumProvident goes even further in demonstrating the cost of disability. According to this study, 10 percent of employees—those who file occupational or non-occupational disability claims—are responsible for 55 percent of employee medical costs and up to 66 percent of all medical, disability, and workers' compensation costs combined.[12] In recent years, the cost of health care in the United States has increased dramatically and has significantly outpaced inflation. U.S. health care expenditures totaled $73 billion (7 percent of GDP) in 1970. Today, those expenses top $1.3 trillion, more than 13 percent of GDP. As of this writing, health insurance premiums are expected to increase an average of 13 to 15 percent annually—the steepest increase in a decade.[13]

Ultimately, the cost of disability and associated medical care is borne by society as a whole. As will be discussed in more detail in later chapters, group insurance can do much to reduce the cost of disability. Claims management and employer return-to-work programs encourage disabled employees to return to productivity. Such programs can lead to higher income for disabled workers and lower medical costs for all.

⟫ Summary

Although the prevalence of group disability income insurance has increased significantly in recent years, still, fewer than 50 percent of employees have DI coverage. Reduced insurer profitability in the 1990s resulting from a number of factors has led to industry consolidation and a rethinking of the type of coverage offered, pricing, and claims administration. Even so, there are promising signs on the horizon. The strain on government-sponsored benefits, a workforce that demands greater choice in benefits, and an increased emphasis on tax incentives all point to increased demand for an important and much needed product.

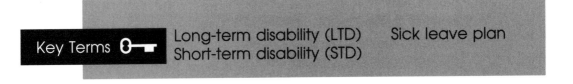

Key Terms

Long-term disability (LTD)   Sick leave plan
Short-term disability (STD)

⟫ REVIEW QUESTIONS

1. How does group disability income insurance differ from medical expense insurance, life insurance, and long-term care insurance?

2. List the key factors that have contributed to the growth of DI insurance over the last few decades.

3. What are the key market forces that led to a downturn in insurer profits during the 1990s?

4. What impact are rising benefit costs and decreasing employer profits likely to have on group DI insurance in the future?

5. What issues have recent terrorist attacks on U.S. citizens raised for the DI insurance industry?

►► ANSWERS TO FOCUS QUESTIONS

Focus Question #1—d

Focus Question #2—Short-term disability benefits provide for salary replacement, most often at partial pay, for a period of three or six months. Benefits are paid either as a percentage of employee earnings (such as 60 percent of pre-disability earnings), or as a flat dollar amount. STD benefits can vary by the amount of pre-disability earnings, length of service with the firm, or length of disability.

Long-term disability benefits provide a monthly cash amount to eligible employees who, as a result of illness or injury, are unable to work for an extended period. Benefits are usually paid as a fixed percentage of pre-disability earnings up to a set limit. Most participants have a waiting period of three to six months, or until sick leave and STD benefits end, before long-term benefit payments begin. LTD benefits generally continue until retirement or a specified age, or for a period that varies according to the employee's age at the time of disability.

Focus Question #3—Two events formalized the need for employer-sponsored benefits. The first was the enactment in the early 1930s of the National Labor Relations Act, which gave labor unions the right to negotiate on behalf of their membership and strike if demands were not met. The second was a 1949 Supreme Court ruling that assured labor unions of the right to negotiate not only for working conditions and wages but also for benefits.

Focus Question #4—Although the 1990s saw a boom in productivity, conditions such as low inflation and low interest rates had a negative effect on group DI insurers. First, returns from fixed income investments used to fund reserves were lower than anticipated. Second, low wage inflation meant that DI benefits to disabled insureds retained most of their purchasing power, thus lowering the incentive to return to work.

Focus Question #5—Increasing financial demands on the Social Security system are likely to lead to legislative reform. Although no one can predict with certainty the direction such reform will take, growing government budget deficits make it a likely bet that more emphasis will be placed on the private sector. Certainly, the trend favors personal responsibility and private industry solutions over government welfare and social insurance.

▸▸ ANSWERS TO REVIEW QUESTIONS

1. One major difference between disability income insurance and medical expense insurance is that DI insurance reimburses the insured for income lost as the result of an inability to work during a period of disability. By contrast, medical expense insurance reimburses the insured for the cost of covered health care, usually subject to co-pays,

deductibles, internal limits for specific treatments, and overall maximum benefit limits.

Although there are other differences, a major distinction between life insurance and disability income insurance lies in the ''trigger'' for the payment of benefits. With DI insurance, disability as specifically defined in the policy is the trigger, and the definition may differ from policy to policy. Furthermore, there may be more than one occurrence of disability during the term of a DI coverage. By contrast, the trigger for life insurance death payments is death, and there can be only one death claim submitted under a life insurance policy.

The major difference between disability income insurance and long-term care insurance is that LTCI reimburses the insured for costs incurred for specified types of chronic care. Disability income insurance, on the other hand, replaces income lost because of a disability. In addition, while the triggering event for payment of benefits under a DI policy is disability as defined in the policy, the trigger for payment of LTCI benefits is the inability to perform a certain number of activities of daily living (ADLs) or a severe cognitive impairment.

2. The key factors include:

- organized labor,
- wage freezes,
- cost advantages,
- tax incentives,
- inflation, and
- state and federal legislation.

3. These forces were:

- slow market and customer growth,
- price-driven sales strategies,
- new disabilities and changing attitudes,
- unfavorable economic conditions, and
- demographic changes.

4. Rising benefit costs and decreasing corporate profits have caused employers to shift part or all of the cost of all benefit plans to employees. In the retirement arena, this has translated into an increase in profit-sharing and Section 401(k) plans and a decrease in defined benefit

plans. In connection with employer-sponsored life and disability income plans, the shift has been toward voluntary plans where employees contribute part or all of the premium cost through payroll deduction. The challenge for disability income insurers, as always, is to emphasize the value of their voluntary products in a competitive marketplace.

5. Most group disability income insurance policies contain an exclusion for a disability resulting from war, declared or undeclared, or any act of war. War is generally interpreted as involving hostilities between two or more governments or sovereign nations, so the war exclusion would generally not apply to acts of violence by individuals or political groups that are not employed by or acting on behalf of a sovereign government. The war exclusion could apply if a terrorist group is allied with or acting in concert with another nation in attacking the United States. The question of how disabilities resulting from such acts will be treated by insurers in the future is currently unresolved.

NOTES

1 National Association of Insurance Commissioners Disability Table.

2 "Consumer, Insurer Groups Work to Inform Americans About Disability Income Insurance." *National Underwriter Online News Service,* The National Underwriter Company, Erlanger, KY, April 23, 2001.

3 Cashdollar, Winthrop, and Updike, Marcy. "Survey Probes Employer and Planner Attitudes Toward Disability Income Insurance." *National Underwriter,* The National Underwriter Company, Erlanger, KY, February 24, 2003.

4 Bell, Allison. "Group Disability Sales Rose in 2001." *National Underwriter,* April 15, 2002.

5 *National Compensation Survey: Employee Benefits in Private Industry in the United States, 2000.* U.S. Department of Labor, Bureau of Labor Statistics, Washington, DC, 2003.

6 Bell, Allison. "Group Disability Sales Rose in 2001." *National Underwriter,* April 15, 2002.

7 Taylor, Robert. "Group Long-Term Disability Income Insurance in the United States: At a Crossroads." *GeneralCologneRE Risk Insights,* 5(1):2, February 2001.

8 Ibid.

9 Ibid., p. 4.

10 Health Insurance Association of America. ''Health Insurers: Mental Health Mandates Misguided.'' *www.hiaa.org/search/content.cfm?ContentID=22528*, June 10, 2003.

11 ''Nearly 1 in 5 Americans Has Some Level of Disability, U.S. Census Bureau Reports.'' Housing and Household Economic Statistics Information Staff, U.S. Census Bureau Public Information Office, Washington, DC, April 3, 2001.

12 *UnumProvident Disability and Health Pareto Analyses 2001.* Sample size of 225,000 employees, of which 22,000 filed disability claims. Data provided by Options and Choices, Inc., a UnumProvident subsidiary that specializes in disability reporting and analysis.

13 ''Can Consumerism Slow the Rate of Health Benefit Cost Increases?'' *Issue Brief,* Employee Benefit Research Institute, July 2002.

2
Sources of Disability Income

›› OVERVIEW

Individuals have traditionally looked to three sources for replacement of income lost as a result of disability. These are:

- government programs,
- employer-sponsored plans, and
- private resources.

Government programs include Social Security and the short-term disability income programs provided by a few states. Employer-sponsored plans, in addition to group DI insurance and voluntary worksite plans, include workers' compensation, pension and profit-sharing plans, non-qualified retirement plans that offer incidental disability benefits, and executive bonus and salary continuation plans. Private resources include individual disability income insurance, savings, and other investments. While some or all of these resources may come into play when an individual is disabled, it is only in rare cases that any one of them or any combination eliminates the need for group disability income insurance.

Objectives

After reading this chapter and completing the accompanying exercises, you will be able to:

- describe the disability income benefits provided under government programs, including Social Security and state temporary disability income plans;
- describe the disability income benefits provided by employer-sponsored plans other than group DI insurance and voluntary worksite plans;
- describe private resources available to replace income lost as a result of disability; and
- explain the drawbacks to these sources of disability income that lead to a continuing need for group disability income insurance.

▸▸SOCIAL SECURITY

The two government-sponsored plans that replace income in the event of disability are Social Security and state temporary disability income plans. Many people mistakenly believe that these plans eliminate the need for group DI insurance. As we will see in this section and the following one, while the total dollar amount of benefits paid by these programs can be large, the benefits are available only to relatively few disabled workers.

Social Security refers to several programs sponsored by the federal government. Originally enacted in response to the Great Depression, the Social Security Act of 1935 established four distinct programs:

- old-age insurance;
- unemployment insurance;
- federal grants to certain needy groups, including the aged, the blind, and children; and
- federal grants for maternal and child welfare, public health work, and vocational rehabilitation.

Disability income insurance was added to Social Security in 1956. The programs that provide old-age, survivors', and disability income benefits are often called **OASDI**, or simply Social Security. The programs providing hospitalization and medical insurance are commonly referred to as **Medicare**. This section focuses on OASDI, or Social Security, benefits. Although Medicare provides valuable health care benefits to many people, it does not replace income lost because of disability and is not covered here.

Although Social Security disability benefits are usually considered inadequate to fully address the disability income insurance needs of middle-income and more affluent individuals, the volume of benefits paid is significant. In 2002, the Social Security Administration (SSA) paid $65.6 billion in disability benefits—$59.9 billion to disabled workers and $5.7 billion to their children, widows, or widowers. The number of disabled workers to whom benefits were payable under the programs, including all approved claimants since the program's inception in 1956, was 7.1 million.[1] But as valuable as Social Security benefits are to those individuals who depend on them, a concern is that many more people apply for these benefits than are approved. In fact, about 65 percent of Social Security disability income claims are declined.[2]

Eligibility

To be eligible for Social Security disability benefits, an individual must meet two criteria: He must be **disability insured**, and he must be disabled as defined in the Social Security Act.

An individual becomes disability insured under Social Security by earning **work credits**. Social Security work credits are based on an individual's total yearly wages or self-employment income. Up to four credits may be earned each year. The amount needed for a credit varies from year to year. In 2003, for example, one credit is earned for each $890 of wages or self-employment income. When an individual earns $3,560, four credits are earned for the year.

The number of work credits needed to qualify for disability benefits depends on an individual's age when she becomes disabled. Generally, 40 work credits, 20 of which were earned in the 10 years ending with the year the individual becomes disabled, are required for disability insured status.

However, younger workers may qualify with fewer credits, as described below:

- *Before age 24.* Individuals may qualify if they have six credits earned in the three-year period ending when disability starts.

- *Age 24 to 31.* Individuals may qualify if they have credit for working half the time between age 21 and the time they become disabled. For example, if an individual becomes disabled at age 27, she would need credit for three years of work out of the past six years (between ages 21 and 27).

- *Age 31 or older.* The number of required work credits is shown in Table 2.1. Unless an individual is blind, at least 20 of the credits must be earned in the 10 years immediately before she becomes disabled.

Table 2.1

Work Credits Needed for Disability Insured Status Under Social Security

Born After 1929, Becomes Disabled at Age	Number of Credits Needed
31 through 42	20
44	22
46	24
48	26
50	28
52	30
54	32
56	34
58	36
60	38
62 or older	40

The definition of disability under Social Security is very restrictive. To be disabled under Social Security, an individual must have a physical or mental impairment that prevents him from engaging in *any* substantially gainful activity. Furthermore, the disability must last or be expected to last at least 12 months or be expected to result in death.

Focus Question #1

What is the general rule for determining whether an individual is disability insured under Social Security?

_____

_____

_____

_____

_____

Thus, Social Security pays only for total and permanent disability. The Social Security program rules assume that working families have access to other resources to provide support during periods of short-term disabilities, including workers' compensation, insurance, savings, and investments.

To help individuals determine whether they meet the Social Security definition of disability, SSA offers a five-step, question-based process:

- *Step One—Is the individual working?* In 2002, if an individual was working and earnings averaged more than $780 a month, she generally cannot be considered disabled. If the individual is not working, she can proceed to Step Two.

- *Step Two—Is the condition "severe"?* The condition must interfere with basic work-related activities for the claim to be considered. If this is the case, the individual can proceed to Step Three.

- *Step Three—Is the condition in SSA's list of disabling conditions?* For each of the major body systems, SSA maintains a list of medical conditions that are so severe they automatically mean that an individual is disabled. If the condition is not on the list, SSA decides if it is of equal severity to a medical condition that is on the list. If it is, SSA will find that the individual is disabled. If it is not, the individual proceeds to Step Four.

- *Step Four—Can the individual do the work she did previously?* If the condition is severe but not at the same or equal level of severity as a medical condition on the list, then SSA determines if it interferes with the individual's ability to do the work she did previously. If it does not, the claim will be denied. If it does, the individual proceeds to Step Five.

- *Step Five—Can the individual do any other type of work?* If the individual cannot do the work she did in the past, SSA determines whether she is able to adjust to other work. SSA considers the individual's medical condition as well as her age, education, and past work experience, and also any transferable skills she may possess. If the individual cannot adjust to other work, the claim will be approved. If the individual can adjust to other work, the claim will be denied. SSA also does not distinguish whether the work the individual could do is available where she lives, or whether an opening for such a job is currently available.

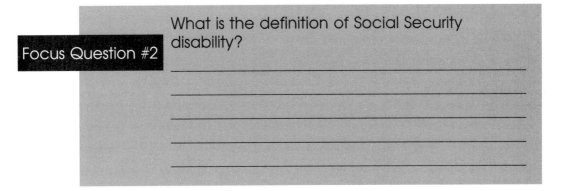

Focus Question #2

What is the definition of Social Security disability?

Benefits

Assuming an individual is eligible for Social Security disability benefits, there is a waiting period before payments begin. An individual can expect to receive his first benefit payment for the sixth full month after the date the disability began, and this payment will likely not be received until the seventh month.

For example, if an individual's disability began on June 15, 2003, the first benefit would be paid for the month of December 2003, the sixth full month of disability. Social Security benefits are paid in the month following the month for which they are due. This means that the benefit due for December 2003 would be paid in January 2004.

The amount of an individual's monthly disability benefit is based on the **primary insurance amount (PIA)**. Essentially, the PIA is determined by indexing lifetime average earnings covered by Social Security to current wage levels.

As a guideline to the amount of benefits available, SSA reports that a covered worker who had worked continuously at low wages (45 percent of average national wages) and who claimed benefits in January 2000 would have received a monthly benefit of $518. A person with earnings at or above the maximum amount subject to Social Security taxes would have received about $1,400 in monthly benefits.[3]

As mentioned above, Social Security disability benefits are typically inadequate to meet the needs of higher-income workers. This is because the benefits replace a smaller percentage of a high-income worker's lost salary than that of a lower-paid worker. For example, the $518 monthly benefit replaces about 17 percent of the monthly wages of a worker earning $3,000 per month. By contrast, the $1,400 in benefits replaces only about 11.2 percent of the earnings of an individual earning $12,500 per month. This aspect of Social Security, along with its restrictive definition, opens the door for private insurance to make up the shortfall.

As a general rule, disability payments from other sources do not affect Social Security disability benefits. However, if an individual receives a disability payment from workers' compensation or certain government-sponsored programs, Social Security benefits may be reduced. The following payments do *not* reduce Social Security:

■ Veterans Administration benefits;

■ federal benefits, if the work the individual did to earn them was covered by Social Security;

■ state and local government benefits, if the work the individual did to earn them was covered by Social Security;

■ private pensions or insurance benefits; and

■ Supplemental Security Income (SSI) payments.

If an individual receives a payment such as workers' compensation that reduces Social Security disability benefits, the amount of the reduction is determined by a simple formula. The combined amount of the Social Security benefit received plus any workers' compensation payment may not exceed 80 percent of the individual's **average current earnings**. For purposes of calculating the reduction, average current earnings mean the highest of the following:

- average monthly earnings (PIA) used to figure the individual's Social Security disability benefit;

- average monthly earnings from any work (including self-employment) covered by Social Security during the five highest consecutive months after 1950; or

- average monthly earnings from work or a business during the year the individual becomes disabled or in the highest year of earnings during the five-year period just before he became disabled.

Any reduction in benefits will last until the month the individual reaches age 65 or the month workers' compensation and/or government-sponsored disability payments stop, whichever comes first.

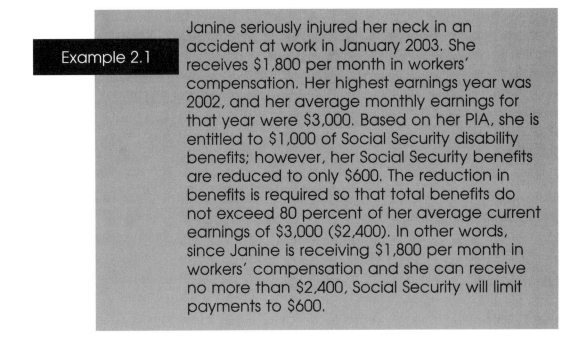

Example 2.1

Janine seriously injured her neck in an accident at work in January 2003. She receives $1,800 per month in workers' compensation. Her highest earnings year was 2002, and her average monthly earnings for that year were $3,000. Based on her PIA, she is entitled to $1,000 of Social Security disability benefits; however, her Social Security benefits are reduced to only $600. The reduction in benefits is required so that total benefits do not exceed 80 percent of her average current earnings of $3,000 ($2,400). In other words, since Janine is receiving $1,800 per month in workers' compensation and she can receive no more than $2,400, Social Security will limit payments to $600.

Social Security disability benefits terminate with death or retirement. However, termination of benefits as a result of either of these events results in commencement of Social Security survivor benefits or retirement benefits. In most instances, survivors can expect to receive benefits comparable to disability benefits following the disabled individual's death, and a disabled

individual who qualifies for Social Security retirement benefits can expe
to receive retirement benefits that are comparable to the disability benefits
he was receiving.

Taxation

Like Social Security retirement benefits, Social Security disability payments
are subject to federal income tax if **modified adjusted gross income**—
adjusted gross income (AGI) plus any non-taxable interest income and half
of Social Security benefits—exceeds certain limits. Single individuals may
have to pay income tax on 50 percent of Social Security disability payments
if modified AGI is between $25,000 and $34,000. If modified AGI is
greater than $34,000, 85 percent of benefit payments are subject to income
tax. Joint filers with modified AGI between $32,000 and $44,000 may
have to pay taxes on 50 percent of Social Security disability benefits, and
if modified AGI exceeds $44,000, 85 percent of benefit payments are
subject to income tax.

Working While Disabled

Helping people with disabilities to lead independent and fuller lives is a
national policy affecting both the government and the private sector. A
combination of laws passed in 1980 and 1987, the Americans with Disabilities Act of 1990, and most recently the Ticket to Work and Work Incentives
Improvement Act of 1999 encourage individuals to return to work following
a disability. These work incentives include:

- cash benefits while working,
- Medicare and/or Medicaid while working,
- help with any extra work expenses resulting from disability, and
- help with education, training, and rehabilitation needed to start a new
  line of work.

Following is a brief description of the rules that allow individuals to receive
Social Security disability benefits while working:[4]

- *Trial work period.* The trial work period allows an individual to test
  her ability to work for at least nine months. During the trial work
  period, the claimant will receive full disability benefits regardless of

uch she earns, as long as she continues to be disabled. The nine
need not be consecutive, and the trial work period continues
until the claimant accumulates nine months within a rolling 60-month
period. Certain other rules apply.

- *Extended period of eligibility.* For at least 36 months after a successful
  trial work period, if a disabled individual continues to work, he may
  receive a benefit for any month that earnings fall below the **substantial
  gainful activity level** (in 2003, $800 a month for people with disabilities,
  $1,330 a month for the blind). Usually, earnings of more than $800 a
  month are considered substantial, and if average earnings exceed $800
  a month, this is considered an indication of one's ability to work. If
  earnings average less than $800 a month, benefits generally continue
  indefinitely.

- *Expedited reinstatement of benefits.* If an individual becomes unable
  to work again because of her medical condition within 60 months after
  the extended period of eligibility has ended, and benefits were stopped
  because of earnings, she may request reinstatement of benefits without
  filing a new disability application.

- *Continuation of Medicare.* If a disabled individual has premium-free
  Medicare hospital insurance and then begins working, the free Medicare
  benefit continues for at least $8\frac{1}{2}$ years of extended coverage (including
  the nine-month trial work period). After that, the individual can buy
  Medicare coverage by paying a monthly premium.

- *Impairment-related work expenses.* Certain work-related expenses may
  be deducted when counting earnings to determine whether an individual
  is performing substantial work. These expenses may include the cost
  of any item or service needed to work, even if the item or service also
  is useful in one's daily living. Examples include a seeing-eye dog,
  prescription drugs, transportation to and from work (under certain conditions), a personal attendant or job coach, a wheelchair, and any specialized work equipment.

- *Recovery during vocational rehabilitation.* If an individual is likely to
  benefit from rehabilitation, she is referred to a state rehabilitation agency
  or private organization for rehabilitation services. Social Security pays
  for the services if there is a successful rehabilitation. If the individual
  recovers from disability while in an approved rehabilitation or training

program that is likely to result in her becoming self-supporting, benefits will continue until the program is over.

Example 2.2

Missy Watson, age 24, was receiving Social Security disability benefits of $557 a month based on a childhood condition that made it difficult for her to walk. She wanted to work but was afraid of losing her benefits and Medicare. After learning about Social Security's return-to-work incentives, Missy started working in a local laundry part-time and earned $850 a month. Her gross earnings, including Social Security and wages, increased to $1,407 per month.

At the end of Missy's nine-month trial work period, Social Security determined that her work was substantial, since she was earning more than $800 a month. Therefore, her benefits stopped after three more months. However, because she was still disabled, her benefits could be reinstated anytime during the next 36 months if her earnings dropped below $800.

During the first year after her trial work period, Missy's employer relocated outside the city, where there were no bus lines. She hired a neighbor to drive her to work and paid a co-worker to take her home. Her transportation expenses totaled $120 a month. In addition, Missy purchased a special motorized wheelchair so she could get around the new suburban plant. This cost $75 a month. Consequently her "countable earnings" were the $850 she earned working, reduced by her work-related expenses of $195, or $655 monthly.

Because her countable earnings are less than $800, Missy's Social Security disability payments were reinstated. Her total net income now was the $655 plus $557 in Social Security benefits, or $1,212.

After a year, she paid off the motorized chair, so her monthly work-related expenses went down to $120. She also received a $140 raise, so her earnings rose to $990 a month. Her countable earnings now are $990, minus $120, or $870.Because her countable earnings now exceed the "substantial" level ($800), her Social Security benefits will stop. As you can see, at each point in her working life, Missy's income was greater than it would have been if she had not worked. In addition, her Medicare coverage continued for 93 months following the trial work period.

Focus Question #3

List the incentives that encourage disabled individuals receiving Social Security benefits to return to work.

_____

_____

_____

_____

_____

>> STATE TEMPORARY DISABILITY PLANS

While all states provide unemployment insurance to employees who are involuntarily laid off, five states (California, Hawaii, New Jersey, New York, and Rhode Island) and Puerto Rico have gone further by enacting temporary disability laws. Under these statutes, individuals are entitled to temporary disability benefits whether employed or unemployed. Effectively, these plans supplement Social Security, because as we have seen, Social Security does not pay benefits until the sixth full month of disability. (The New York plan is commonly known as NYSDBL.)

All five states and Puerto Rico allow employers to opt out of the state plan and make employee contributions to a private plan. The private plan must meet state requirements.

Eligibility

Eligibility depends on a showing that the disabled individual has worked for a specified period of time and earned a minimum amount of wages. Both the time period and the minimum wage requirement vary from state to state.

Benefits

Following the usual waiting period of seven days, the disabled individual is entitled to benefits that are a percentage of average weekly earnings. The benefits vary significantly by state. For example, as of October 2002, Hawaii provides for 58 percent of average weekly wages with a cap of $378. New York provides 50 percent of average weekly wages with a maximum of $170. Benefits typically continue for no longer than 26 weeks, although California allows a maximum of 52 weeks.

Taxation

The income taxation of these plans varies from state to state. As a general rule, employer and employee contributions to a state plan are deductible. To the extent benefits are attributable to deductible employee contributions or employer contributions that are excludible from income, the benefits are subject to income tax when received.

►► WORKERS' COMPENSATION

Employers sponsor a variety of benefits through which disability income may be provided. The most obvious, of course, is group disability income insurance. The next few sections discuss employer plans *other than* group DI insurance, including workers' compensation, retirement plans, and executive bonus and salary continuation plans.

Workers' compensation laws evolved in response to the failure of the civil law system to adequately address the financial losses suffered by employees who became ill or were injured on the job. Before the enactment of these laws, an injured employee's only recourse was to sue his employer. Workers' compensation laws shift the financial loss resulting from a disability caused by injury or illness incurred on the job to the employer. Although most jobs are covered, some states exclude agricultural, domestic, and casual employees. Most states allow employers to either self-insure for workers' compensation benefits or purchase workers' compensation insurance. Employers who choose to self-insure are required to secure promised benefits with a performance bond.

Eligibility

Workers' compensation laws require no showing of fault on the employer's part. Eligibility for workers' compensation hinges solely on a showing of an **occupational disease or injury** arising out of and in the course of employment. Although some states continue to cover only those diseases listed in the statute, there is a trend toward full coverage of all occupational diseases.

It should be emphasized that eligibility is limited to those with *occupational* illness or injury—non-work-related disabilities are not covered. And according to the National Safety Council's October 2001 *Report on Injuries in America*, in 2000 only about 40 percent of disabling injuries suffered by American workers occurred on the job.

Benefits

If an individual is eligible, benefits under workers' compensation can be generous. First, employer-provided health insurance benefits typically continue without interruption. Also, most states provide limited survivor benefits, both burial expenses and cash income payments to survivors. Furthermore, all workers' compensation laws pay for the cost of rehabilitative and vocational services with the goal of making the employee productive again.

Most importantly, however, workers' compensation provides disability income benefits. Following a waiting period of between two and seven days, benefits for total disability are typically a percentage (commonly $66^2/_3$ percent) of an employee's average weekly wage over the 13 or 26 weeks prior to the disability. These benefits are subject to maximums and minimums that vary significantly from state to state. Benefits for total disability tend to continue for life in most states, while benefits for temporary disability are available until the employee returns to work.

Partial disability is also covered, and benefits are calculated as a percentage of the difference between the employee's wages before and after the disability. In some states, lump-sum benefits are paid to employees who suffer permanent partial disabilities such as the loss of a limb or an eye.

Taxation

Amounts received under workers' compensation are includible in the employee's income.

▸▸ TAX-QUALIFIED RETIREMENT PLANS

Tax-qualified retirement plans provide both tax and non-tax incentives to both employers and participating employees. From the employer's perspective, there are two important incentives to tax qualification. First, within limits, employer contributions to tax-qualified retirement plans are income tax-deductible. Second, employers are not taxed on the earnings and gains associated with plan contributions. The tax benefits to the employee include:

- Within limits, any employer and employee contributions are excluded from the employee's income.

- Plan earnings and gains are not currently taxable to the employee.

- Although plan distributions are taxable to the employee or her designated beneficiary when received, distributions may be stretched out over the life of the employee or the joint lives of the employee and her beneficiary.

- Within limits, tax-qualified retirement plans may provide both disability income and life insurance benefits to participants in addition to retirement benefits.

One way to categorize tax-qualified plans is to distinguish between **pension plans** and **profit-sharing plans**. Pension plans are primarily designed to provide participants with a retirement benefit. Profit-sharing plans, on the other hand, are primarily designed to accumulate employer profits on a tax-advantaged basis with provision of retirement benefits being only a secondary consideration.

Another common distinction is that made between **defined benefit plans** and **defined contribution plans**:

- A defined benefit plan specifies the benefit the employee will receive at retirement. The benefit is usually stated as a percentage of final average salary. Employer contributions vary and depend on the annual funding determined by the plan's actuary.

- By contrast, a defined contribution plan calls for recurring employer contributions that are allocated among individual employee accounts under a formula. The amount of a participant's benefit depends on the amount of contributions and investment performance. Some plans, for example 401(k) plans, allow for employee contributions, while other plans do not.

With all of these plans, employer and employee contributions are held and invested by a plan trustee for the benefit of participants. Benefits are normally payable at retirement, although profit-sharing plans allow earlier access to employee account balances, and most plans allow for early and deferred retirement. Incidental benefits are also often payable in the event of death prior to retirement. Although both pension and profit-sharing plans may provide disability benefits, there are limitations on the use of plan funds for this purpose.

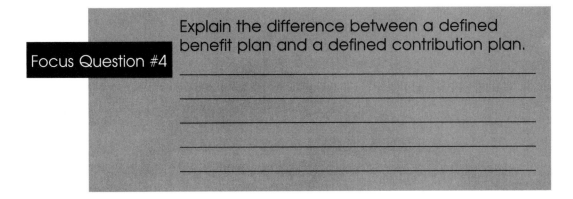

Focus Question #4

Explain the difference between a defined benefit plan and a defined contribution plan.

Eligibility

In general, eligibility for a tax-qualified retirement plan is determined by the **21 and one rule**. Under this rule, minimum age and service requirements for participation in an employer's tax-qualified plan are age 21 and one year of service.

Benefits

Unless a pension plan makes specific provision for disability benefits, the disability of a plan participant will not usually result in a plan distribution. (The only exception is a *de minimus* exception, which allows the trustee to distribute accrued benefits of less than $5,000 in cash in the event of termination of employment.) Even if the employee's disability is severe enough to result in a termination of service, no benefits are currently payable to the employee. Instead, when the disabled employee has a vested accrued benefit, he will not receive benefits until the plan's normal retirement age, or its early retirement age if the plan allows for early retirement.

Given these restrictions on access to plan accruals, it is increasingly common for pension plans to offer disability income benefits. However, because pension plans are intended primarily for the provision of retirement benefits, disability income benefits may be no more than incidental to the retirement benefits provided. Although there is little authority on this matter, it appears that a pension plan that allows employees to receive their vested accrued benefit in the event of disability does not violate the incidental rule.

Where employers provide disability income benefits through the pension plan, coordinating retirement benefits with disability income benefits may be a concern. One problem with paying disability income benefits through the pension plan is that once payments begin, retirement benefits do not continue to accrue. For many, a better solution is to design the pension plan not to pay disability income benefits, but rather to continue to accrue retirement benefits during a period of a disability.

Example 2.3

Tim is a participant in a defined benefit pension plan. The benefit formula provides a monthly retirement benefit equal to 2 percent multiplied by years of service, multiplied by final average salary. Tim becomes disabled after ten years of service. Although the plan does not provide payments to him in the event of disability, the plan does count years of disability as years of service. If Tim is disabled for three years before returning to work, he gets credit in the pension benefit formula for the three years of lost work.

This provision is especially attractive in cases in which the employer provides group disability benefits in addition to pension benefits. The employee continues to receive an income during a period of disability and also continues to build retirement benefits. Of course, providing both retirement and disability income benefits can be an expensive proposition for an employer. To address this problem, several insurers offer policies that are designed to cover the cost of ongoing employer retirement plan contributions during a period of employee disability.

Another way of protecting employee retirement benefits is for the pension plan to **vest** plan participants in the event of disability—that is, grant them rights to the benefits they have accrued. Although this does not completely solve the employee's retirement income problem, it protects the employee from loss of accrued benefits should she become disabled.

As with a pension plan, unless a profit-sharing plan makes specific provision for disability benefits, the disability of a plan participant will not necessarily result in a plan distribution. Only if the employee's disability is severe enough to result in a termination of service is it likely that the employee will be able to receive a distribution of his vested account balance.

However, it is common for profit-sharing plans to allow plan loans, subject to certain limitations. Furthermore, stand-alone profit-sharing plans allow for "in service withdrawals" of **seasoned funds**, funds that have been in the employee's account for at least two years. Section 401(k) plans even grant employees access to plan funds in the event of **financial hardship**, which includes hardship due to the following:

- medical expenses;
- the purchase of a principal residence;
- payment of tuition for college education of the participant, the participant's spouse, or the participant's children; and
- payment of expenses necessary to prevent eviction or foreclosure of a mortgage on the participant's principal residence.

Although payments for disability are not specified, medical expenses and home mortgage payments are, and these can make up a significant portion of a disabled individual's post-disability expenses.

As discussed in connection with pension plans, even if no disability benefits are available under a profit-sharing plan, the plan should continue to accrue retirement benefits during a period of disability or, at a minimum, immediately vest account balances in the event of disability. Without such a provision, the disabled employee is likely to find that his retirement benefits are far from adequate.

Taxation

As a general rule, benefits received because of an employee's disability are includible in income.

➤➤NON-QUALIFIED RETIREMENT PLANS

Unlike tax-qualified plans, which must meet non-discriminatory and vesting requirements and which are subject to contribution and benefit limits, non-qualified retirement plans may be offered only to selected individuals, vesting requirements are nonexistent, and there is no limit on the amount of the benefit or the contribution. The exclusivity of the plan ensures that the employer gets the most ''bang for its benefit buck'' by providing the maximum benefit to those key people who are most responsible for the business's success.

A distinguishing characteristic of non-qualified plans is that, unlike tax-qualified plans, non-qualified plan assets are not segregated from the employer's general assets. Tax-qualified plans are typically administered through a trust, and the trustee is under a fiduciary responsibility to hold, invest, and distribute plan assets solely for the participants' benefit. In contrast, non-qualified plan assets are available to the employer as working capital and may be reached by general creditors of the company. The obligation of the employer to pay promised benefits is backed only by the faith and credit of the company itself. If the company falters or if management squanders non-qualified plan assets and is unable to pay promised benefits, the executive's only recourse is to bring a lawsuit based on violation of the plan agreement. If the employer is insolvent, the executive stands in line with other general creditors of the company and is likely to receive only pennies on the dollar promised.

The implication is that non-qualified plans are not appropriate for all employers. In general, such plans are only appropriate for employers with sound financial standing and good prospects for the foreseeable future.

One common approach to providing disability income benefits through a non-qualified plan involves informal funding, with a life insurance policy insuring the executive's life, and with a disability waiver-of-premium provision attached to this policy.

Example 2.4

General Textiles, Inc. wishes to provide supplemental retirement benefits of $100,000 per year for 10 years to its CEO, Walter Fischer. To informally fund the benefits, it purchases a life insurance policy on Walter's life with a face value of $600,000 and a $24,000 annual premium including the cost of a disability income waiver-of-premium benefit. General Textiles is the owner and beneficiary of the policy. When Walter retires, the company can borrow or withdraw accumulated cash values to pay promised retirement benefits. If Walter dies before retirement, the policy death benefit provides cash for survivor benefits.

If Walter becomes disabled and the premium is waived, General Textiles will have the cash to pay him a disability benefit of $2,000 per month. Interestingly, its after-tax cost of doing so in a 40 percent bracket is $1,200 per month—$2,000 times 0.60 (1 minus 0.40).

If the company were willing to spend the same $2,000 after-tax outlay it was paying for the life insurance policy, it could pay Walter an even larger disability benefit. In fact, the company could pay Walter a monthly disability benefit of $3,333.33. ($3,333.33 times 0.60 equals $2,000.)

An alternative to informally funding disability benefits under a non-qualified plan with the disability waiver-of-premium provision offered by life insurance is for the company to insure such benefits with an individual disability income insurance policy. The benefits provided under this policy may be in lieu of or in addition to benefits provided under a group plan sponsored by the employer. This approach is especially attractive when the employer wishes to target only a very few select executives for long-term or supplemental long-term disability benefits.

When a disability income insurance policy is used to fund disability benefits under a non-qualified plan, the company should own the policy, because it is the company that has the obligation to pay the benefits. Also, care should be taken to coordinate the definition of disability under the individual DI insurance policy with the definition of disability under the plan. Unless definitions of disability are coordinated, it is possible that the company could become obligated to pay benefits under one definition of disability, yet not receive benefits from the insurer under another definition of disability. A common approach to resolving this issue is to simply use the same definition of disability contained in the individual DI insurance policy in the non-qualified plan.

Disability benefits are subject to employee income taxes in the year received (see Chapter 14 for details).

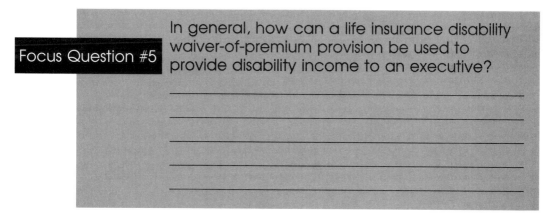

Focus Question #5

In general, how can a life insurance disability waiver-of-premium provision be used to provide disability income to an executive?

➤➤ EXECUTIVE BONUS AND SALARY CONTINUATION PLANS

Even as popular as group DI insurance benefits have become, there are situations in which an employer may wish to offer disability benefits only to selected executives. For example, a small business may decide that it can afford to offer only short-term disability benefits to all of its employees, but it wishes to provide long-term benefits to a select group of executives. Typically, such benefits are provided through an individual DI insurance policy for the executive.

Under an **executive bonus plan**, the employer increases the selected executives' salaries or pays them bonuses that they may use to acquire individual DI insurance policies. As a general rule, the salary increase or bonus is deductible to the employer and includible in the executive's income. When benefits are received, they are not taxable to the executive.

Under an **executive salary continuation plan**, a written agreement is entered into between the executive and the employer to provide disability benefits to the executive. Under the terms of the plan, the employer agrees to make plan contributions that must be devoted solely to the insurance premiums or to a fund for self-insuring promised benefits. In the typical situation, the plan contributions are applied to the purchase of an individual DI insurance policy owned by the executive.

The written plan assures the employer of a deduction for plan contribution. In addition, the executive is allowed to exclude the contributions (premium payments) from current income. If and when benefits become payable under the policy, the benefits are generally included in the executive's income.

›› PRIVATE RESOURCES

Another way that individuals make up for income lost as a result of disability is to rely on private savings and investments. These resources include:

- checking and savings accounts,
- certificates of deposit and treasury bills,
- mutual funds,
- corporate and government bonds,
- stocks,
- precious metals, and
- commodities.

One concern about tapping into these resources when a disability strikes is that they are often earmarked for other financial goals such as retirement and children's education. Diversion of these resources to supplement income during a period of disability can frustrate these other financial goals. Another concern is that these private resources are typically handled on a "dollar-for-dollar" basis, as opposed to the "pennies-on-the-dollar" concept used by insurance policies.

Another source of private funds is individual disability income insurance. Individual DI insurance is discussed in detail in another HIAA Insurance Education book, *Disability Income Insurance: A Primer.* Unlike group disability income insurance, individual insurance is usually paid for by the insured and is individually underwritten. Also unlike group DI insurance, individual insurance can be tailored to meet the specific needs of the insured. For example, there is considerable flexibility in choosing the elimination period, the amount of the benefit, and the duration of the benefit period.

On the other hand, for most people individual DI insurance is not an alternative to group insurance. Many blue-collar workers may find that they are not eligible for individual coverage or that the cost of the coverage is beyond their means. For these individuals, group DI insurance is a better solution. For white-collar and professional workers, the traditional market for individual DI insurance, individual coverage is usually not the sole answer to their disability income insurance needs. In many cases, individual DI insurance is purchased as a supplement, not an alternative, to group coverage.

▶▶ IMPLICATIONS FOR GROUP DI INSURANCE

Although there are many alternative sources of disability income, none of them is an adequate replacement for group disability income insurance.

Social Security

There are several drawbacks to Social Security as a sole resource for disability income benefits:

- The definition of disability is restrictive—to be disabled under Social Security, an individual must have a physical or mental impairment that prevents him from engaging in any substantially gainful activity. Furthermore, the disability must last or be expected to last at least 12 months or be expected to result in death. Thus, Social Security pays only for total and permanent disability. There are many disabilities that will prevent a person from working in her current occupation and/or earning anywhere near her current level of income, but that will not qualify her for Social Security benefits.

■ Even if one qualifies for Social Security benefits, these benefits can begin no earlier than six months following the onset of disability. Moreover, the Social Security Administration can take several months to make a decision on a claim, so that an individual can wait as long as 12 or 13 months before receiving his first Social Security check. And although benefits are retroactive until the sixth month of disability, bills must still be paid along the way, and many individuals will have run through their savings well before Social Security is available.

■ Even if one qualifies for Social Security benefits and can wait to receive them, the benefits are likely to be inadequate to sustain a middle-income lifestyle. For example, an individual with annual earnings of $100,000 could probably expect to receive no more than about $16,800 annually in Social Security disability income benefits.

State Temporary Disability Benefits

The major drawback to these plans, in the relatively few places where they are available, is that they last for only a short term—26 weeks is common.

Workers' Compensation

Although the benefits under workers' compensation can be generous, reliance solely on workers' compensation is inadvisable. Workers' compensation covers only illness or injury arising in the course of work. Disabilities that occur from non-work-related illness or injury are ineligible for benefits.

Tax-Qualified Retirement Plans

Even if disability income benefits are provided through a tax-qualified retirement plan, an employer may wish to supplement these benefits with a group DI insurance plan. Group disability income benefits will be available even to those employees who lack vested benefits under the retirement plan, while disability income benefits through the retirement plan are likely to be available only to those participants with vested benefits.

Furthermore, it is common for the definition of disability in tax-qualified retirement plans to be as restrictive as that of Social Security. If the administrator relies on the very restrictive Social Security definition of disability, only employees who qualify for Social Security disability income benefits will also receive retirement plan disability income benefits. A group LTD plan that supplements disability income benefits in a tax-qualified retirement plan ensures that employees who are disabled under the group plan definition of disability (which will be less restrictive than the Social Security definition), but not under the pension plan definition, will receive a disability income benefit.

Non-Qualified Retirement, Executive Bonus, and Salary Continuation Plans

These plans are, by definition, designed for a few select executives. They are very advantageous for the executives covered, but they are not intended to meet the needs of the larger employee group—only a group DI insurance plan can do this. Furthermore, these plans are usually designed not to replace group DI insurance plans, but rather to supplement them. As will be discussed in greater detail in Chapter 8, group plans are often capped. The dollar amount cap may be below the amount of disability income sought by executives. These supplementary plans can be designed to provide benefits over and above that provided by the group DI plan. In addition, as we will see, the definition of disability under group plans may be more restrictive than is desired for executives. Plans tailored just for an executive group can include less restrictive definitions of disability.

Private Resources

As pointed out earlier, while private resources must often be relied on to replace income during a waiting period and to supplement DI insurance benefits, they are rarely adequate to fully replace income and cover medical costs during a prolonged period of disability. And even if private savings are adequate to address disability income needs, consuming assets in this way makes them unavailable for other important financial objectives such as retirement and children's education.

Supporting the conclusion that these alternatives to group disability income insurance are inadequate to replace income during disability is a recent study by HIAA and John Hewitt Associates (JHA) of Portland, Maine. According to this important study, 86 percent of employers acknowledged that workers' compensation and Social Security are not adequate to provide the disability coverage their employees need.[5]

▸▸ SUMMARY

Disability income derives from a variety of sources, including government programs, employer-sponsored plans, and private resources.

Government programs, such as Social Security and state temporary disability income laws, provide a safety net in the event of disability. However, Social Security's restrictive definition of disability and the short duration of state disability income plans limit the effectiveness of these programs.

Employer-sponsored pension and profit-sharing plans and non-qualified retirement plans sometimes provide incidental disability benefits, but these plans are best when combined with group DI insurance. Executive bonus and executive salary continuation plans are also best viewed as supplements to an executive's underlying group disability income insurance. Workers' compensation, while a valuable employer benefit, only protects against occupational injury—employees who are injured or who become ill off the job need additional protection.

Finally, most people simply lack the personal resources to self-insure a long-term disability. In most instances, private resources should remain devoted to other financial objectives, while the risk of disability insurance should be insured.

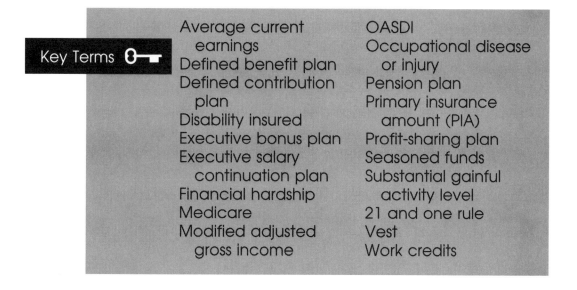

Key Terms

Average current
  earnings
Defined benefit plan
Defined contribution
  plan
Disability insured
Executive bonus plan
Executive salary
  continuation plan
Financial hardship
Medicare
Modified adjusted
  gross income

OASDI
Occupational disease
  or injury
Pension plan
Primary insurance
  amount (PIA)
Profit-sharing plan
Seasoned funds
Substantial gainful
  activity level
21 and one rule
Vest
Work credits

▶▶ REVIEW QUESTIONS

1. How does one become eligible for Social Security disability income coverage? What must be demonstrated in order for an individual to receive disability benefits under Social Security?

2. Lacy's disability began on June 10, 2003. When is the earliest that she can expect a Social Security disability benefit payment?

3. Ralph, a joint filer, is receiving Social Security disability income benefits of $1,000 per month. His modified AGI for the year is $60,000. How much of his Social Security benefits are subject to income tax, if any? Explain.

4. Describe the benefits of workers' compensation.

5. Jason's employer sponsors a defined benefit pension plan. In addition to providing an incidental disability income benefit under the plan, what other things can the employer do to protect disabled employees?

6. Cindy is a single mother with two young children. She is convinced that her private resources will be adequate to meet her long-term disability income needs. She earns $9,000 per month, has $50,000 in a mutual fund (received through an inheritance), and $20,000 in a savings account that is earmarked for college education expenses. She spends her monthly after-tax income each month and sometimes has a shortfall. What would you say to encourage her to insure her disability income needs?

▸▸ ANSWERS TO FOCUS QUESTIONS

Focus Question #1—An individual becomes disability insured under Social Security by earning work credits. Social Security work credits are based on an individual's total yearly wages or self-employment income. Up to four credits may be earned each year. The amount needed for a credit varies from year to year. In 2003, for example, one credit is earned for each $890 of wages or self-employment income. The number of work credits needed to qualify for disability benefits depends on an individual's age when he becomes disabled. Generally, 40 work credits, 20 of which were earned in the 10 years ending the year an individual becomes disabled are required for disability insured status. However, younger workers may qualify with fewer credits.

Focus Question #2—To be disabled under Social Security, an individual must have a physical or mental impairment that prevents him from engaging in any substantially gainful activity. Furthermore, the disability must last or be expected to last at least 12 months or be expected to result in death.

Focus Question #3—These work incentives include:

- cash benefits while working,
- Medicare and/or Medicaid while working,
- help with any extra work expenses resulting from disability, and
- help with education, training, and rehabilitation needed to start a new line of work.

Focus Question #4—A defined benefit plan specifies the benefit the employee will receive at retirement. The benefit is usually stated as a percentage of final average salary. Employer contributions vary and depend on the annual funding determined by the plan's actuary. By contrast, a defined contribution plan calls for recurring employer contributions that are allocated among individual employee accounts under a formula. The amount of a participant's benefit depends on the amount of contributions and investment performance. Some plans—for example, 401(k) plans—allow for employee contributions, while other plans do not.

Focus Question #5—Basically, the employer applies for a life insurance policy on the executive's life. The employer is the owner and beneficiary of the policy and intends to use the policy to informally fund the promised retirement and survivor benefits under the non-qualified retirement plan. In addition, the employer requests a disability waiver-of-premium rider on the life insurance policy. In the event the executive becomes disabled, the employer is no longer liable for premium payments. The amount of cash that would have been used for the life insurance premiums may instead be paid to the disabled executive as a disability income benefit.

▶▶ ANSWERS TO REVIEW QUESTIONS

1. An individual becomes disability insured under Social Security by earning work credits. Social Security work credits are based on an individual's total yearly wages or self-employment income. Up to four credits may be earned each year. The amount needed for a credit varies from year to year. In 2003, for example, one credit is earned for each $890 of wages or self-employment income.

   The number of work credits needed to qualify for disability benefits depends on an individual's age when she becomes disabled. Generally, 40 work credits, 20 of which were earned in the 10 years ending with the year the individual becomes disabled, are required for disability insured status. However, younger workers may qualify with fewer credits.

   To be disabled under Social Security, an individual must have a physical or mental impairment that prevents her from engaging in any substantially gainful activity. Furthermore, the disability must last or be expected to last at least 12 months or be expected to result in death.

2. She won't receive her first payment until January 2004. The benefit first becomes payable in the sixth full month following the disability—December of 2003. However, benefits are not actually paid until the following month.

3. Of Ralph's Social Security benefits, 85 percent, or $850 per month, is subject to income tax. Like Social Security retirement benefits, Social Security disability payments are subject to federal income tax if modified adjusted gross income (adjusted gross income plus any

non-taxable interest income and half of Social Security benefits) exceeds certain limits. Joint filers with modified AGI between $32,000 and $44,000 may have to pay taxes on 50 percent of Social Security disability benefits. If modified AGI exceeds $44,000, then 85 percent of benefit payments are subject to income tax.

4. If an individual is eligible, benefits under workers' compensation can be generous. First, employer-provided health insurance benefits typically continue without interruption. Also, most states provide limited survivor benefits, both burial expenses and cash income payments to survivors. Furthermore, all workers' compensation laws pay for the cost of rehabilitative and vocational services with the goal of making the employee productive again.

Most importantly, however, workers' compensation provides disability income benefits. Following a waiting period of between two and seven days, benefits for total disability are typically a percentage ($66^2/_3$ percent is common) of an employee's average weekly wage over the 13 or 26 weeks prior to the disability. These benefits are subject to maximums and minimums that vary significantly from state to state. Benefits for total disability tend to continue for life in most states, while benefits for temporary disability are available until the employee returns to work.

Partial disability is also covered, and benefits are calculated as a percentage of the difference between the employee's wages before and after the disability. In some states, lump-sum benefits are paid to employees who suffer permanent partial disabilities such as the loss of a limb or an eye.

5. The pension plan can be designed so that participants continue to accrue retirement benefits during a period of disability. Several insurers have recently introduced policies that are designed to cover the cost of ongoing employer retirement plan contributions during a period of employee disability. Another solution is for the pension plan to vest plan participants in the event of disability. This solution protects the employee from loss of accrued benefits in the event of disability.

6. First, Cindy's assets are sufficient to carry her for only six months to a year in the event of a disability. Second, if she taps into her current

resources in the event of a disability they won't be available for retirement and college education expenses.

Notes

1 Social Security Administration, *www.ssa.gov*, June 13, 2003.

2 *Social Security Forum,* 21(5), May 1999 (for fiscal year 1998).

3 Ibid., p. 16.

4 Detailed Work Incentives Information, Social Security Administration, *www.govern-mentguide.com/govsite.adp?bread=*Main&url=http%3A//www.governmentguide.com/ams/clickThruRedirect.adp%3F55076483%2C16920155%2Chttp%3A//www.ssa.gov/* June 10, 2003.

5 Cashdollar, Winthrop, and Updike, Marcy. "Survey Probes Employer and Planner Attitudes Toward Disability Income Insurance." *National Underwriter,* February 24, 2003.

≫ 3
Marketing and Distribution

≫ OVERVIEW

In today's customer-driven world, it is appropriate to include in a discussion of group disability income insurance a look at the market and the ways insurance companies reach it. The market for employee benefits remains competitive, as many employers continue to provide benefits as a way to get and keep top-notch workers. In fact, a recent study shows that 60 percent of employers that provide group DI benefits do so to recruit and retain employees.[1]

Although associations and franchisers are buyers of group DI insurance, private employers remain the largest market. Private employers can be segmented by industry, size (in terms of number of employees and/or revenues), and business type (sole proprietorship, partnership, or corporation). Marketers of group insurance often find it useful to segment on the basis of business size, because the size of a business has implications for how it is best approached, who makes employee benefit decisions, what cross-sell and up-sell opportunities exist, and how the case should be underwritten and priced.

Census Bureau statistics show that the largest number of employers have 100 employees or fewer. These businesses are usually closely held instead of publicly traded, meaning that they are owned by a handful of individuals. Often the owner is also a key employee in the business and can be found on the premises. Also, the owner or owners are the decision-makers when it comes to employee benefits.

One benefit of marketing to the small business market is the salesperson's direct access to the decision-maker. Another benefit is that there are many opportunities for cross-sales and up-sales. Small businesses need not only group disability income insurance, but also other group coverages, such as life, medical, and dental. Furthermore, the executives and business owners are prime targets for individual life, disability income, and long-term care insurance. Other sales opportunities include annuities and other investment products.

These small to mid-size businesses remain a largely untapped market. As Figure 3.1 illustrates, over three-quarters of employees in these businesses lack LTD coverage.

Figure 3.1

Percentage of Employees Without LTD Insurance

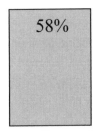

78%	58%
Smaller Companies (100 or Fewer Employees)	Larger Companies (More than 100 Employees)

Source: Robert Taylor.[2]

Larger companies are also targets for group DI insurance. While employers with over 100 employees make up a smaller percentage of the employer population, they are a significant source of premium. The decision-making process of these companies is much more complex. In many instances, a senior executive delegates the decision-making authority to a team or a human resource department head. Large companies are also good prospects for cross-selling and up-selling, but a challenge is that decisions are based less on personal relationships between salespeople and decision-makers and more on cost-benefit analysis. Thus, an insurer that wants to sell multiple products will have to offer competitive features, benefits, and pricing in all product lines. Furthermore, decision-making in these large organizations is likely to be more protracted than in closely held businesses, and product selections are usually subject to annual review.

Although large businesses are more likely to provide a broad range of benefits to employees, nearly 60 percent of them do not offer LTD coverage, as Figure 3.1 illustrates. The challenge for insurers is to reach these employers for initial sales and keep them as satisfied customers.

Insurance companies typically distribute their products and services through several different channels. These include:

- agents,
- brokers and consultants,
- group representatives,
- third-party administrators, and
- direct distribution.

Objectives

After reading this chapter and completing the accompanying exercises, you will be able to:

- identify the various distribution channels for disability income insurance, and
- describe characteristics of the various distribution channels.

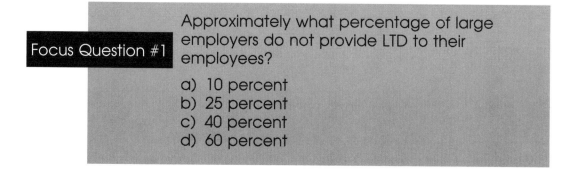

Focus Question #1

Approximately what percentage of large employers do not provide LTD to their employees?

a) 10 percent
b) 25 percent
c) 40 percent
d) 60 percent

▸▸ AGENTS

Insurance company **agents** have traditionally been an important distribution channel for both group and individual products. An agent is contracted by an insurance company to represent its products and services in the marketplace. Agents are typically housed in a local office under the leadership and supervision of a manager or general agent. Agents are responsible for all aspects of the sales process, from prospecting to close. They are usually compensated by commission only (although early in their careers they commonly receive a base salary plus commissions).

Agents rarely specialize in group disability income insurance. Instead, they typically call on many prospects in both the personal and business markets. Most companies train agents to ask business prospects about their employee benefit programs. Companies often supply agents with data-gathering tools that guide them in following up with specific questions about how satisfied the employer is with its benefits program, how many employees participate, whether the employer would consider a DI insurance plan, etc. Brochures and other marketing materials may be available to support the agent's efforts.

For small employers, the agent is likely to handle the case from start to finish. If the case is larger and more complicated, the agent may seek the assistance of an insurer's group representative or a broker or consultant who specializes in group DI insurance.

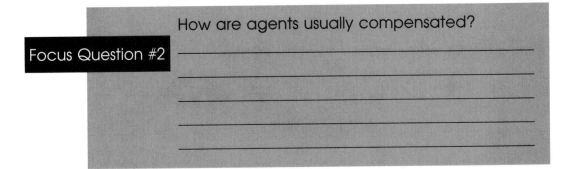

How are agents usually compensated?

Focus Question #2

▸▸ BROKERS AND CONSULTANTS

In recent years, many insurers that had previously distributed their products solely through a captive agency force have shifted to brokerages and other alternatives. Some companies have abandoned the agency system entirely, while others distribute their products through both brokerage and career (agent) systems. The rationale for brokerage and other alternative distribution is that it is less expensive to operate and more efficient than a career system.

Proponents of brokerage systems point out that independent brokers, unlike captive agents, need not be recruited, trained, housed, and supervised. Instead, the company simply contracts with a brokerage general agent (or employs a brokerage manager) to market its products and services to insurance agents, financial planners, and other licensed salespeople. The cost savings associated with a less expensive distribution system can be used to enhance the product and/or contribute to the insurer's bottom line. On the other hand, advocates of the career system argue that career agents are more loyal and that their business has greater persistency than that submitted by independent brokers. But particularly in the group DI insurance arena, distribution through brokers and consultants has carried the day over distribution through a career agency system.

Some **brokers** and **consultants** specialize in group disability income insurance. These specialists tend to focus on larger employers and employee groups and are often experts in employee compensation and benefits. A major distinction between brokers and consultants on one hand and agents on the other is that agents are contracted by an insurer to act on its behalf, while brokers and consultants represent the interests of the buyer. Consequently, brokers and consultants have access to the products of many insurers and will "shop" the employer's case, searching for the best pricing and coverage.

Traditionally, a distinction has been made between brokers and consultants, but the line has become blurred. A broker was someone whose compensation was based on sales commissions, while a consultant's compensation was based on fees. Brokers marketed their expertise and objectivity by stressing their ability to place the case with the insurer who made the best offer. Consultants also marketed their expertise and objectivity, but emphasized that their objectivity resulted from the fact that their compensation derived solely from fees.

In today's world, however, it is not uncommon for brokers to charge fees for case design and/or ongoing service. Many brokers contend that fees are necessary to maintain profitability in the face of increasing operational expenses and decreasing commissions. And although some consulting firms continue to operate on a fee-only basis, many more receive both fee and commission compensation. In some instances, an arrangement is made with the customer whereby fees are offset by any commissions earned through product sales. In other instances, fees are charged for specified services, and any commissions earned are considered additional compensation to the consultant.

Brokers and consultants specializing in group DI insurance usually prospect for business on their own and are able to carry the sale through to fruition. In addition, it is common for these specialists to work with agents and brokers who do not specialize in group DI insurance.

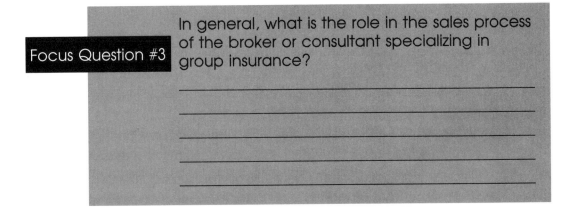

Focus Question #3

In general, what is the role in the sales process of the broker or consultant specializing in group insurance?

▸▸ GROUP REPRESENTATIVES

Most group insurers employ **group representatives** to market products to other producers such as agents, brokers, and consultants. Group "reps" can be viewed as **wholesalers**. Their job is to bring the insurer's product to retail sellers who have contacts and relationships with employers. In this role, they are involved in initiating relationships with sellers, training sellers on product features and benefits, and assisting sellers in all phases of the sales process, including prospecting, case design, and ongoing service.

Group representatives are usually compensated through a combination of salary and bonus, based on the sales generated by their agents, brokers, and consultants.

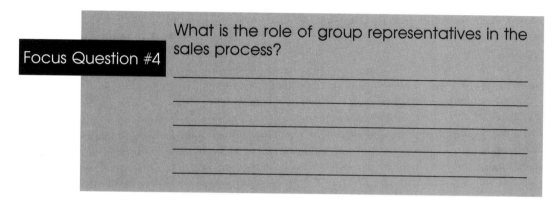

Focus Question #4

What is the role of group representatives in the sales process?

►► THIRD-PARTY ADMINISTRATORS

Third-party administrators (TPAs) are individuals or organizations specializing in the administration of employee benefit plans, including group DI insurance. While insurance companies and brokers and consultants may offer administrative services for smaller plans, employers may look to a TPA to handle the administration of larger plans. The kinds of services provided by TPAs include:

- enrollment of employees,
- preparation and dissemination of employee reports,
- collection of payroll deductions and payment of premiums,
- certification of eligibility of a participant for a claim,
- submission of claim forms to the insurer, and
- resolution of employee complaints and grievances.

TPAs are paid fees for these services, based on a fee schedule or a negotiated amount.

Because of their product and marketing expertise, it is not uncommon for TPAs to also act as brokers and/or consultants. These firms are involved in both the sale and the ongoing service of group DI insurance plans.

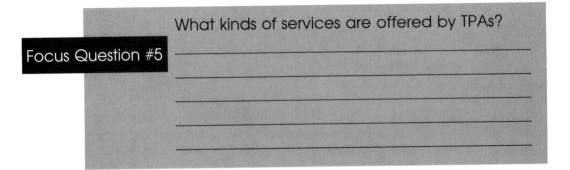

Focus Question #5

What kinds of services are offered by TPAs?

▸▸ DIRECT SALES

Home offices of group insurance companies develop products and bring them to market through their wholesalers, the group representatives. The home office is also engaged in administrative functions, such as underwriting, premium collection, and claims administration. In addition, in a few instances a home office may place a large group case directly with a buyer, thus minimizing distribution costs such as commissions and fees. In these cases, the home office personnel, including group representatives, underwriters, and claims handlers, interface directly with the customer's employees.

▸▸ SUMMARY

As the marketplace for group disability income insurance has become more sophisticated, insurers have responded with increasingly creative ways to market and distribute their products. Many career agency systems have been replaced with broker and third-party distribution. In addition, brokers, consultants, and TPAs specializing in group DI insurance play an important role, especially in larger cases. Group DI insurers continue to rely on group representatives to create shelf space among retail sellers.

Key Terms

Agent
Broker
Consultant
Group representative

Third-party
administrator (TPA)
Wholesaler

▸▸ REVIEW QUESTIONS

1. What is the difference between a broker and an agent? A broker and a consultant?

2. What arguments can be made in favor of brokerage distribution versus distribution solely through a career agency system?

3. What are the advantages to a company of placing a case directly?

▸▸ ANSWERS TO FOCUS QUESTIONS

Focus Question #1—d

Focus Question #2—Agents are usually compensated solely by commission.

Focus Question #3—Brokers and consultants specializing in group DI insurance usually prospect for business on their own and are able to carry the sale through to fruition. In addition, it is common for these specialists to work with agents and brokers who do not specialize in group DI insurance.

Focus Question #4—Group "reps" can be viewed as wholesalers. Their job is to bring the insurer's product to retail sellers who have contacts and relationships with employers. In this role, they are involved in initiating relationships with sellers, training sellers on product features and benefits, and assisting sellers in all phases of the sales process, including prospecting, case design, and ongoing service.

Focus Question #5—The kinds of services provided by TPAs include:

- enrollment of employees,
- preparation and dissemination of employee reports,
- collection of payroll deductions and payment of premiums,
- certification of eligibility of a participant for a claim,
- submission of claim forms to the insurer, and
- resolution of employee complaints and grievances.

▶▶ ANSWERS TO REVIEW QUESTIONS

1. Agents are contracted by the insurer to act on its behalf, while brokers and consultants represent the interests of the buyer. Traditionally, a broker's compensation was based on sales commissions, while a consultant's compensation was based on fees, but today many brokers and consultants receive both commissions and fees.

2. Proponents of brokerage systems point out that independent brokers, unlike captive agents, need not be recruited, trained, housed, and supervised. Instead, the company simply contracts with a brokerage general agent (or employs a brokerage manager) to market its products and services to insurance agents, financial planners, and other licensed salespeople. The cost savings associated with a less expensive distribution system can be used to enhance the product and/or contribute to the insurer's bottom line.

3. Doing so minimizes distribution costs such as commissions and fees.

NOTES

1 Cashdollar, Winthrop, and Updike, Marcy. "Survey Probes Employer and Planner Attitudes Toward Disability Income Insurance." *National Underwriter,* February 24, 2003.

2 Taylor, Robert. "Group Long-Term Disability Income Insurance in the United States: At a Crossroads." *GeneralCologneRE Risk Insights,* 5 (1):3, February 2001.

4
The Sales Process

▶▶ OVERVIEW

The sales process for group disability income insurance parallels that of other financial products. In this chapter, the sales process is explored in depth, with an emphasis on sales to employers. (A similar process is used for sales to other groups such as associations and franchisers.)

The sales process involves the following steps:

- **prospecting** for qualified buyers, usually employers;
- the **approach**, the first contact with the employer;
- the **sales interview**—the salesperson explores the prospect's concerns, educates the prospect on the group DI insurance product, and acquires information about the employer's business and the employee group;
- development of the proposal—product features are matched to employer and employee objectives, and tentative pricing and underwriting take place;
- presentation—the salesperson presents the proposal to the employer and responds to any objections the employer may raise;
- employee enrollment—the salesperson meets with employees to sign them up for plan participation; and
- continuing service—the salesperson focuses on re-enrollment, responds to service requests, and turns service requests into marketing opportunities for add-on sales, cross-sales, and referrals.

As a general rule, agents and brokers who do not specialize in group DI insurance generate prospects among small to mid-size businesses. These businesses are abundant, the decision-maker is usually accessible on the premises, and the agent or broker is better positioned to establish a personal relationship with the decision-maker that can only facilitate the sale. Also, there is likely to be less competition in the small to mid-size business market, and small businesses are less likely to "shop" their coverage each year.

The larger the employer, the greater the likelihood that the agent or broker will look to a specialist or group representative for assistance. The specialist or group representative can provide help at each stage of the sales cycle, from prospecting to case design to the presentation and the close.

Brokers and consultants who specialize in group DI insurance are more likely to focus their sales activities on larger employers. The larger group size and potential sales commission compensates these individuals for their expertise. Also, group representatives are likely to allocate a significant amount of their efforts to establishing relationships with these specialists.

Objectives

After reading this chapter and completing the accompanying exercises, you will be able to:

- identify the steps in the sales process, and
- describe the significance of each step in the sales process.

►► PROSPECTING

The lifeblood of the insurance business is the generation of new qualified prospects. Prospecting is the step in the sales process in which salespeople find and qualify individuals and businesses that are likely buyers of their products and services. Some salespeople view all individuals and businesses as prospects, using a "shotgun" approach in their prospecting. With this approach the salesperson calls on a wide variety of individuals and businesses, seeking appointments with nearly anyone who will agree to meet. In fact, most agents and brokers start out in the business this way.

Other salespeople use a more targeted approach in their prospecting. With **target marketing**, the salesperson focuses on segments of the marketplace made up of prospects that have certain things in common. Because the salesperson's targeted prospects share these commonalities, the entire sales process is more efficient and the salesperson's business is more profitable. Common market segmenters include business size, industry, geographical location, and years of operation.

A **target market** has the following characteristics:

- *Definition.* The prospects in the target market can be described by reference to their business, location, or what they call themselves.
- *Common characteristics.* The prospects in the target market share similarities of interests, hobbies, and/or occupations.
- *Common needs.* Because the prospects in the target market share common characteristics, they have common needs that can be met by the agent or broker's products.
- *Communication.* Because of the commonalities they share, prospects in a target market communicate among themselves. This sharing of information works in the salesperson's favor and can lead to the best advertising there is—word-of-mouth advertising among prospects and clients.

Another characteristic often cited with respect to target markets is that prospects within them are compatible with the salesperson's temperament, abilities, and likes and dislikes. For example, a salesperson who grew up in a family of entrepreneurs may relate well with entrepreneurial prospects, while a salesperson who has a background in engineering may work well with engineers and other professionals.

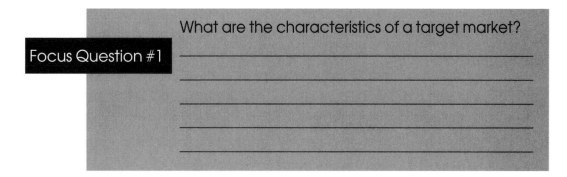

What are the characteristics of a target market?

Focus Question #1

Whether the salesperson uses a shotgun approach or a target marketing approach, there are several tried and true prospecting techniques, including the following:

- combing existing client files for qualified prospects,
- using lists and directories,
- seeking referrals from existing clients and centers of influence, and
- observing qualified prospects in day-to-day activities.

Existing Client Files

Many agents and brokers break into the group DI market by first developing a solid client base of individuals. Chances are that some of these clients are employed by businesses that are good prospects for group insurance. Some of these clients are professionals, such as attorneys and accountants, who provide services to qualified business prospects. Even if a salesperson's clients do not fall within one of these categories, it is a good bet that she has a client who knows professionals or people in business.

Lists

Another prospecting technique involves the use of lists. There are a variety of lists available for businesses. Salespeople using a targeted approach to prospecting often segment the lists to obtain names of businesses in industries with which they are familiar, businesses of a certain size, or businesses in a particular geographical area. By targeting prospects that the salesperson is comfortable calling on and that are nearby, the salesperson is able to maximize the time and energy devoted to prospecting.

Some of the lists available to salespeople are described below:

- Dun's Direct Access (DDA) allows access to Dun and Bradstreet's business digital database of over 10 million names. Each business name record includes the name of the business owner, address, telephone number, number of employees, sales volume, and the year the business was established.
- Thomas' Register of American Manufacturers lists businesses by product.

- Standard and Poor's Register of Corporations, Directors, and Executives provides information about corporations in all types of industries.

- Criss-cross or reverse directories are similar to telephone directories, but list businesses by street and telephone number instead of alphabetically by name.

- Other resources include local chambers of commerce, membership lists of manufacturers' and trade associations, state and local industrial directories, and the Yellow Pages.

In today's electronic world, nearly all businesses maintain Websites, some of which contain a wealth of information about the company, its owners, its products and services, and its staff. In addition, the Internet provides a great deal of additional information about both large and small businesses. For example, on the Website of the Securities and Exchange Commission (SEC), *www.SEC.gov*, annual statements and other reports can be accessed online. At the other end of the spectrum, the Small Business Administration Website, *www.SBA.gov*, contains reports, trend information, and other information about small businesses. Search engines such as Google and online Yellow Pages make finding phone numbers, names, and addresses easier than ever.

Referrals

A distinction is usually made between **cold lead prospecting** and **warm lead prospecting**. Cold lead prospecting involves calling on individuals and businesses with which the salesperson has no prior relationship. Although some agents and brokers make cold lead prospecting a regular part of their sales and marketing efforts, most prefer to pursue warm leads. Warm leads most often are the result of **referrals**.

Salespeople who count business owners or professional **centers of influence** (attorneys and accountants) among their existing clients should be able to obtain referrals to businesses that are good prospects for group DI insurance. One proven way to obtain referrals is to approach business owners and centers of influence with a list already prepared from a review of client files and/or directories. The salesperson asks whether the client is familiar with any of the names on the list. If so, the agent of broker asks whether the **nominator** would be willing to provide an introduction.

Successful salespeople who have won the trust and respect of existing clients and centers of influence have little trouble obtaining referrals. The relationship the nominator shares with the referral carries over to the salesperson, making it easier to obtain the first interview and serving as the basis for the relationship that secures the sale.

Personal Observation

Personal observation simply involves being alert to businesses that may be good prospects for group DI insurance. For example, a salesperson might jot down the names of businesses in an office park adjacent to the office of a business or professional client. The salesperson might develop a database of prospects gleaned from reading the local business journal. Or the salesperson could go through his own personal checkbook and note all the businesses he visits on a periodic basis.

The following guidelines are helpful in qualifying prospects obtained through personal observation:

- *Financial stability.* The business should have a proven track record of financial success. Because of the high failure rate of new business start-ups, many insurers require a business to operate successfully for at least three years to qualify for guaranteed issue underwriting for group products.

- *Relatively well-paid workers.* The business should have a group of well-paid workers who stand to suffer financial setbacks in the event of a disability. A poorly paid workforce is evidence of an employer that may be unwilling to invest in its most important resources—its human resources—and for which employee benefits are likely to be a low priority. Also, low-paid employees are more likely to have their disability income needs met by government programs and/or workers' compensation than are highly paid employees.

- *A full-time staff with low turnover.* The business should have a stable workforce. Part-time, seasonal, temporary, and transient employees are usually ineligible for group guaranteed issue underwriting.

- *No dangerous activities.* The type of business and the occupations of the employee group affect underwriting and pricing. As will be discussed in greater detail in later chapters, insurers are likely to exclude businesses engaged in hazardous activities (for example, nuclear waste removal) and certain occupations (such as agricultural and waste removal workers).

- *Accessibility.* Most agents and brokers are more successful focusing on small to mid-size businesses, where they can speak directly to the decision-maker. Although there are ''jumbo'' sales opportunities in the marketplace, these big sales are most often made by brokers and consultants specializing in group DI insurance and by group representatives working with these specialists, and they usually take a longer time to bring to fruition.

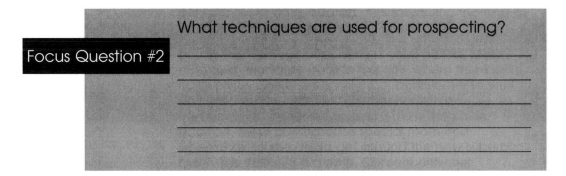

What techniques are used for prospecting?

Focus Question #2

▶▶ THE APPROACH

The primary goal of the approach is to schedule a face-to-face appointment with the employer to discuss employee benefits. In most instances, the salesperson will not focus specifically on group disability income insurance, because she is unlikely to know the prospect's specific needs. Instead, the idea at this stage is to obtain an appointment for a sales interview to address a wide range of employer needs and possible solutions.

There are several techniques for getting that first appointment. Each technique has its advantages and disadvantages, and some salespeople are more comfortable with some techniques than with others. The most common techniques are:

- direct mail,
- telephone, and
- face-to face interview.

Although the techniques for gaining a sales interview vary, each technique shares four essential elements:

- a brief introduction, including mention of a referral if the salesperson has been referred to the prospect by an existing client or center of influence;
- a brief description of how the salesperson can address employer needs;
- a request for an appointment to assess the employer's specific needs; and
- a preliminary needs assessment prior to the sales interview.

What is the goal of the approach step?

Focus Question #3

_____

_____

_____

_____

_____

Direct Mail

Approach direct mail introduces the agent or broker, as well as the group disability income insurance concept, to the employer and sets up the all important follow-up telephone call. The following guidelines apply to the use of direct mail to make an initial contact with a prospect:

- Letters should be addressed to the business owner or decision-maker by name.
- Letters should be mailed first class in time to be received mid-week. (Studies show that letters received at this time get the most attention.)
- Letters should be followed up with a phone call to make an appointment. Phone calls should occur within three to five days of the prospect's receipt of the letter.

Furthermore, an approach letter is more likely to be favorably received if it:

- contains a referral from another client in the salesperson's target market or from a center of influence (a professional adviser such as an attorney or accountant);

- indicates that the salesperson is familiar with the nature of the employer's business and has a general knowledge of the employee benefit needs of employers;

- includes an enclosure discussing a common business problem and solutions (for example, the importance of returning disabled employees to work and the way group DI insurance facilitates meeting this objective); and

- states that the salesperson will follow up with a phone call within three to five days.

Telephone

Many agents and brokers prefer a telephone call to prospects without the benefit of an approach letter. Keep in mind that the sole purpose of the phone call is to get an appointment for a sales interview. Some recommended guidelines for salespeople are listed below. The salesperson should:

- make her own calls (telemarketers and telephone solicitations are not well received),
- be well-prepared and well-informed both about the group DI insurance product and about the prospect,
- focus on the prospect's needs,
- convey a sense of urgency,
- be sincere but assertive,
- be an attentive listener,
- speak clearly,
- be brief and to the point, and
- avoid selling over the phone.

Generally, it is best to phone business owners early in the morning or late in the afternoon, before their day begins or as it is winding down. Experience suggests that the best days to call are Tuesday, Wednesday, and Thursday.

Face-to-Face

Many salespeople believe they are at their best when they are in front of a prospect, face-to-face. Because most group DI sales occur in the small to mid-size business market, where business owners or decision-makers are likely to be on-site, face-to-face interviews are quite feasible. A common technique is for a salesperson to call on a prospect unannounced, in the hope of getting a short time with the prospect to discuss needs and solutions.

►► THE SALES INTERVIEW

The sales interview is usually the salesperson's first face-to-face contact with the prospect. The objectives of the sales interview include the following:

- exploring the prospect's needs and concerns,
- educating the prospect about the features and benefits of group DI insurance, and
- gathering the data necessary to prepare a proposal tailored to the prospect's needs.

Although this sounds like a rigid, structured interview, nothing could be further from the truth. A good sales interview is marked by give-and-take, and most salespeople would agree that their job at this stage is to ask questions and listen. The prospect should do most of the talking.

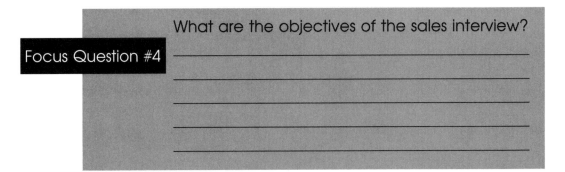

Focus Question #4

What are the objectives of the sales interview?

Exploring Needs and Concerns

Chances are, since the prospect agreed to an appointment, he has some underlying concerns. If the prospect already has a group DI plan, he may have an interest in shopping for better pricing or better service. A good agent or broker may be able to restructure the plan to reduce the cost or better address the prospect's service concerns.

For those prospects that do not yet have a group DI insurance plan, a major concern is that their employee benefit package be competitive. In today's environment, compensation is only part of the package. Most employers offer benefit packages that include life insurance, medical insurance, dental insurance, and retirement plans.

Another important factor is the sense of social responsibility many employers feel toward their employees. As we have learned, disability can be devastating for an employee and her family. At this stage of the sales process, the salesperson may provide the prospect with an illustration of how loss of income can affect a family.

If the prospect is going to buy, the salesperson has to do a good job of creating a sense of concern. One disturbing image the salesperson can bring to mind is that of prospective employees going to work for a competitor because the prospect's benefits package is inadequate. Another disturbing image is that of a hard-working employee having to change his lifestyle because of a disability.

Educating the Prospect

A good salesperson knows that once the prospect's concerns have been highlighted, it is important to educate the prospect about the solution.

In most cases, the education process begins with an explanation of why other employer-sponsored benefit plans, government programs, and personal savings are likely to be inadequate when compared to group DI insurance. This explanation should include all the reasons discussed in Chapter 2 of this text. For example, many prospects will be amazed to learn just how restrictive Social Security is when it comes to disability. And many employers are often surprised to discover that the disability income plan they currently have in place only covers sick-days or short-term disability.

The education process continues with an explanation of the features and benefits of the group DI product (discussed in detail in Chapters 8 and 9). However, at this point in the sales process, the salesperson is not trying to overwhelm the prospect with detail—instead the aim is to present product highlights and tantalize the prospect.

The salesperson may also want to describe the claim process and how an employee can expect to be treated during the benefit period. Many group DI insurance contracts contain provisions designed to encourage employees to return to work, and prospects may not be familiar with these provisions and how effective they are in helping them keep in the workforce qualified and experienced employees who have suffered a disability.

At this stage of the process, the prospect may ask about premium costs. Some salespeople are comfortable providing a ballpark estimate, based on what they have learned in the interview. Others prefer deferring a discussion of premiums until more information has been obtained. They may simply respond that the premium varies so significantly with case design that it is meaningless to talk about cost at this point.

Gathering Data

A good salesperson begins gathering information about a prospect from the time she first identifies the business as a potential buyer. Many important facts are learned through the give-and-take of conversation. In fact, a good icebreaker, after the salesperson has introduced herself, is to ask the prospect about the nature of the business, when it was founded, and how it has grown. Few if any business owners can resist the invitation to talk about their business, and for the skillful salesperson these questions can lead to more formal **data gathering**.

Most insurers provide agents and brokers with data-gathering forms that serve as guides to the type of information necessary for case design, pricing, and underwriting. Although these forms vary from company to company, some key considerations are:

- other benefit plans already offered by the employer, including existing DI plans;

- details about the employee group to be covered, typically contained in what is known as an **employee census**, which includes each employee's name, occupation, date of birth, date of hire, and compensation; and

- information about the employer, such as the nature of the business, its financial status, when it began operations, and its ownership (whether it is a closely held business or publicly traded).

If the prospect has an existing DI plan that it is considering transferring, additional data become important. The insurer is likely to request information about changes in the employee population; whether the existing plan is contributory and, if so, how much the employer contributes; and whether the plan is covered under a collective bargaining agreement. The insurer will also want copies of current plan information (for example, benefit booklets) as well as information on premium rates and renewal history.

▸▸ PROPOSAL DEVELOPMENT

On completion of the sales interview, the agent or broker should have sufficient information to create a proposal. In this next stage (often referred to as **case design**), the case is priced and underwritten based on the features and benefits selected. If the group is small and the case is straightforward, the agent or broker may be able to handle case design on his own, but for larger cases, the services of a specialist or group representative may come into play.

At this stage we see a major difference in the sales process for group as opposed to individual DI insurance. With individual insurance, the agent or broker typically creates a computer-generated proposal that reflects a selected benefit level, elimination period, and benefit period, among other policy features. Only after the proposal is presented to the prospect is a formal application taken and submitted. The insurer underwrites the policy based on the individual's gender, age, financial situation, and health. The computer-generated proposal is merely an illustration of what the policy might look like. The actual policy features and benefits might differ, based on the insurer's assessment of the risk. For example, the insurer might determine that the applicant is in a higher risk class than applied for, or that her income does not warrant the amount of benefit applied for.

In contrast, the group insurance proposal constitutes the insurer's offer to insure, and if that offer is accepted by the prospect, the group contract becomes effective. However, the insurer's offer is usually conditional, so the insurer has a certain amount of "wiggle room." For example, in most instances, preliminary pricing and underwriting take place in field offices, and the insurer's proposal is conditional on home office approval. Also, the proposal may be conditioned on other factors, such as verification of the employer's credit rating and a certain level of employee participation. Furthermore, premium rates quoted in the proposal are typically based on the employee census acquired by the agent or broker at the time of the sales interview; the final rates will reflect the employee census when the plan is installed.

Although there are differences among insurers, the group proposal is likely to contain the following:

- a description of the coverage, including the amount and duration of benefits and the elimination period;
- the tentative premium rates;
- a description of eligible participants;
- a description of the claim process; and
- general information about the insurer.

If the case is relatively small, there is likely to be little flexibility in the plans offered by the insurer. In fact, the insurer may simply provide the agent or broker with a "kit" that includes a standard brochure or information packet describing the coverage and a tentative premium quote.

Larger cases involving brokers, consultants, or group representatives are likely to be tailored to the employer's specific needs, and premium rates are more likely to be negotiated. After working with the employer to design the plan specifications, a broker or consultant creates a **request for proposals (RFP)** that is submitted to several insurers. Typically, the insurers are given a limited period to submit their bids (for example, until 60 days before the date coverage is to begin). The bid is based on certain specifications contained in the RFP. These ''specs'' include:

- a description of the coverage requested,
- an employee census,
- information about existing coverage, and
- employer information, such as financial stability, type of industry, and employee turnover.

The RFP usually requests information about the insurer's financial stability, including its financial rating by third-party rating services such as Standard and Poor's and Moody's. The RFP may also inquire about:

- the insurer's claim procedures and overall claims experience,
- the insurer's approach to rate changes,
- the background and experience of the insurer's management team, and
- the date on which coverage will become effective (that is, the date of delivery of the master contract and the individual participant certificates of insurance).

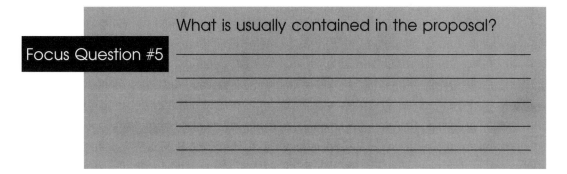

Focus Question #5

What is usually contained in the proposal?

➤➤ THE PRESENTATION

The objective of the presentation is to obtain a signed application and the first premium payment from the employer. If the salesperson has done her job up this point, the presentation usually goes smoothly. In fact, most experienced salespeople recognize that the sale is really made during the sales interview—that is when the salesperson establishes the trust and rapport with the prospect that opens the way to a successful presentation and close.

In smaller cases, the agent is likely to conduct the presentation alone. In larger cases, a broker or consultant specializing in group DI insurance or a group representative will either assist the agent or conduct the presentation alone. Also, while in the smaller case the presentation and close usually mark the end of the sales process, larger cases are often more involved. Rather than presenting just one proposal, the broker, consultant, or group representative may present several proposals, and the prospect, usually a large employer, may ask for modifications. The initial presentation is better viewed as one more step in a process that may require several iterations.

Regardless of the size of the case, a successful presentation usually contains four distinct steps:

- *Reviewing objectives.* A successful presentation often begins with a review of the prospect's objectives. By proceeding in this way, the salesperson demonstrates a commitment to serving the prospect and rewards the prospect's trust.

- *Observing discrepancies.* To recreate the urgency of the initial sales interview, salespeople often revisit the prospect's current situation and observe discrepancies between the prospect's stated objectives and where the prospect currently stands.

- *Matching objectives to the proposal.* The features and benefits of the proposal are matched to the prospect's objectives. The key is to show how the proposed solution addresses each and every one of the prospect's concerns.

- *Obtaining a signed application and collecting the check.* In most instances, the prospect will not offer to complete the sale—it is up to the salesperson to ask the prospect to sign the application and write a check. Many salespeople use what is referred to as an **assumed close**. After reviewing the proposal with the prospect, a skilled salesperson might simply slide the application across the table and hand the prospect a pen. The assumption is that the prospect is ready to go forward.

▸▸ ENROLLMENT AND SERVICE

Enrollment is the process by which plan participants are signed up for coverage. If the plan is non-contributory (the employer pays the entire premium), the employer typically provides the insurer with a list of employees to be covered and certification that they have met **eligibility requirements**. Employees typically must be actively at work (usually 30 or more hours per week) and have satisfied the eligibility period. In such cases, enrollment is a straightforward administrative task.

If a plan is contributory, requiring employees to pay part of the premium, enrollment actually involves additional sales—sales to employees. If the prospect is a large employer with a large employee population, chances are this step involves a group presentation followed by a brief enrollment meeting with each employee. The emphasis is on performing the administrative function of collecting applications and obtaining employees' consent to a payroll deduction arrangement. The employer often agrees to on-site presentations to employees and provides solicitation materials such as posters, brochures, and booklets.

If the employer/prospect is a small business with a relatively small employee population, the administrative task of enrollment must be carried out, but often the salesperson's emphasis shifts to building relationships with selected employees, with an eye toward bridging to sales of individual DI and life policies in addition to the group DI insurance coverage.

Following enrollment, the actual premium rate is calculated and a master contract and individual certificates are issued. The agent or broker (in larger cases assisted by a group representative) delivers these items. Skilled salespeople use the installation and delivery of documents as an opportunity to reinforce the value of the sale with the prospect. This is accomplished by reviewing, once again, how the features and benefits of the plan address the prospect's needs and objectives.

Once the case is installed, there are likely to be numerous opportunities for ongoing service. In small cases, the agent or broker who sold the case is responsible for ongoing service. In larger cases, the service obligation typically falls on the group representative or home office employees.

Common service requests relate to the payment of premiums, the enrollment of new employees, the termination of employees, and the handling of claims. Particularly with larger cases, the group representative should proactively keep the employer informed of the group's claims experience or other trends that might cause a rate increase.

The service provided following the sale is often a determining factor at the time of contract **renewal**. This is especially true if the renewal is accompanied by a rate increase. The salesperson should review the employer's experience to date and thoroughly explain the reasons for any rate increase. If the employer is considering a change of insurers because of a rate increase or dissatisfaction with service, the salesperson should remind the employer that a change may lead to additional administrative fees or loss of benefits for some employees. It should also be pointed out that changing insurers is no guarantee of lower premiums.

▶▶ SUMMARY

The sales process for group DI insurance can be broken down into distinct steps, from prospecting to enrollment and ongoing service. The most successful salespeople are those who develop centers of influence and obtain referrals to new qualified prospects. Once a qualified prospect is identified, the salesperson makes the initial contact, usually by letter or by phone, to set up a meeting. In the sales interview, the salesperson explores needs and concerns, educates the prospect, and gathers data needed to prepare a proposal. Case design involves tentative pricing and underwriting based on characteristics of the employer and the employee group. Following preparation of the proposal, it is presented to the employer, and any questions or objections are addressed. Once the employer has agreed to proceed, the process of enrollment can begin. Even after the sale is closed and employees are enrolled, the salesperson will face a variety of service opportunities.

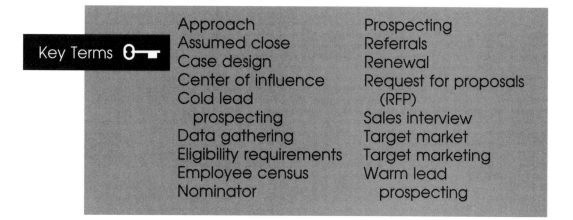

Key Terms		
Approach	Prospecting
Assumed close	Referrals
Case design	Renewal
Center of influence	Request for proposals
Cold lead	(RFP)
prospecting	Sales interview
Data gathering	Target market
Eligibility requirements	Target marketing
Employee census	Warm lead
Nominator	prospecting

▶▶ REVIEW QUESTIONS

1. How would you distinguish between target marketing and a ''shotgun'' approach to prospecting?

2. How do successful salespeople obtain referrals?

3. What guidelines are helpful in qualifying prospects obtained through personal observation?

4. You are planning to approach a prospect by means of an approach letter. What guidelines should you follow in your mailing?

5. What concerns typically faced by employers can be addressed by group DI insurance?

6. What are some of the key points a salesperson should focus on in educating an employer about the need for group DI insurance?

7. Compare and contrast the case design process for group and individual DI insurance.

8. What steps are usually part of a successful presentation?

9. What can a salesperson do when working with a client who is facing a rate increase at renewal time?

>> ANSWERS TO FOCUS QUESTIONS

Focus Question #1—A target market has the following characteristics:

- *Definition.* The prospects in the target market can be described by reference to their business, location, or what they call themselves.
- *Common characteristics.* The prospects in the target market share similarities of interests, hobbies, and/or occupations.
- *Common needs.* Because the prospects in the target market share common characteristics, they have common needs that can be met by the agent or broker's products.
- *Communication.* Because of the commonalities they share, prospects in a target market communicate among themselves. This sharing of information works in the salesperson's favor and can lead to the best advertising there is—word-of-mouth advertising among prospects and clients.

Focus Question #2—Whether the salesperson takes a shotgun approach or a target marketing approach, there are several tried and true prospecting techniques including the following:

- combing existing client files for qualified prospects,

- using lists and directories,
- seeking referrals from existing clients and centers of influence, and
- observing qualified prospects in day-to-day activities.

Focus Question #3—The primary goal of the approach is to schedule a face-to-face appointment with the employer to discuss employee benefits. In most instances, the salesperson will not focus specifically on group DI insurance, because she is unlikely to know the prospect's specific needs. Instead, the idea at this stage is to obtain an appointment for a sales interview to address a wide range of employer needs and possible solutions.

Focus Question #4—The objectives of the sales interview include the following:

- exploring the prospect's needs and concerns,
- educating the prospect about the features and benefits of group DI insurance, and
- gathering the data necessary to prepare a proposal tailored to the prospect's needs.

Focus Question #5—Although there are differences among insurers, the proposal is likely to contain the following:

- a description of the coverage, including the amount and duration of benefits and the elimination period;
- the tentative premium rates;
- a description of eligible participants;
- a description of the claim process; and
- general information about the insurer.

▸▸ ANSWERS TO REVIEW QUESTIONS

1. With the shotgun approach, the salesperson calls on a wide variety of individuals and businesses, seeking appointments with nearly anyone who will agree to meet. With target marketing, the salesperson focuses on segments of the marketplace made up of prospects that have certain things in common.

2. One proven way to obtain referrals is to approach business owners and centers of influence with a list already prepared from a review of client files and/or through the use of directories. The salesperson asks whether the client is familiar with any of the names on the list. If so, the agent of broker asks whether the nominator would be willing to provide an introduction.

3. The following guidelines are helpful in qualifying prospects obtained through personal observation:

   - financial stability,
   - relatively well-paid workers,
   - a full-time staff with low turnover,
   - no dangerous activities, and
   - accessibility.

4. The following guidelines apply to the use of approach letters:

   - Letters should be addressed to the business owner or decision-maker by name.
   - Letters should be mailed first class in time to be received mid-week. (Studies show that letters received at this time get the most attention.)
   - Letters should be followed up with a phone call to make an appointment. Phone calls should occur within three to five days of the prospect's receipt of the letter.

   Furthermore, an approach letter is more likely to be favorably received if it:

   - contains a referral from another client in the salesperson's target market or from a center of influence (a professional adviser such as an attorney or accountant);
   - indicates that the salesperson is familiar with the nature of the employer's business and has a general knowledge of the employee benefit needs of employers;
   - includes an enclosure discussing a common business problem and solutions (for example, the importance of returning disabled employees to work and the way group DI insurance facilitates meeting this objective); and
   - states that the salesperson will follow up with a phone call within three to five days.

5. Group DI insurance addresses the following employer concerns:
   - If the prospect already has a group DI plan, there may be an interest in shopping for better pricing or better service.
   - For those prospects without an existing group DI plan, a major concern is that their employee benefit package be competitive.
   - Another important factor is the sense of social responsibility many employers feel toward their employees.

6. The education process begins with an explanation of why other employer-sponsored benefit plans, government programs, and personal savings are likely to be inadequate when compared to group DI insurance. The process continues with an explanation of the features and benefits of the group DI product. The salesperson may also want to describe the claims process and how an employee can expect to be treated during the benefit period. Many group DI insurance contracts contain provisions designed to encourage employees to return to work.

7. With individual insurance, the agent or broker typically creates a computer-generated proposal that reflects a selected benefit level, elimination period, and benefit period, among other policy features. Only after the proposal is presented to the prospect is a formal application taken and submitted. In contrast, the group insurance proposal constitutes the insurer's offer to insure, and if that offer is accepted by the prospect, the group contract becomes effective. However, the insurer's offer is usually conditional, so the insurer has a certain amount of "wiggle room."

8. Regardless of the size of the case, a successful presentation usually contains four distinct steps:
   - reviewing objectives,
   - observing discrepancies,
   - matching objectives to the proposal, and
   - obtaining a signed application and collecting the check.

9. The salesperson should review the employer's experience to date and thoroughly explain the reasons for the rate increase. If the employer is considering a change of insurers because of the rate increase or dissatisfaction with service, the salesperson should remind the employer that a change may lead to additional administrative fees or loss of benefits for some employees. It should also be pointed out that changing insurers is no guarantee of lower premiums.

⟫ 5
Eligible Groups

⟫ OVERVIEW

State laws and regulations govern many aspects of group disability income insurance, including contract language, benefit limits, income taxation, and the types of groups eligible for coverage. The legislative concern underlying the laws and regulations that define the groups eligible for group insurance is consumer protection. State laws define eligible groups in a way meant to ensure adequate risk-sharing among members of the group. Group insurance is issued with little or no financial or medical underwriting, and unless the group is large enough and adequately representative of the population as a whole, there is the potential for **adverse selection**. Adverse selection occurs when the members of a group bear a greater risk of disability than the general population.

One way that state laws protect against adverse selection is by requiring a minimum group size. In most cases, a minimum of 10 participants is required; if there are fewer than 10 participants, some medical and/or financial underwriting may be required. Another way to minimize the risk of adverse selection is to require a certain level of participation among group members eligible for coverage. Most states generally require a minimum of 75 percent participation.

Although employee groups are the most common type, there are other groups eligible for DI insurance, including those associated with multiple employer arrangements, associations, franchises, and creditors.

Objectives

After reading this chapter and completing the accompanying exercises, you will be able to:

- identify the various types of groups eligible for group DI insurance, and
- discuss key characteristics of each type of group.

➤➤ EMPLOYERS

Employees of a single employer are the most common eligible group. The employer may be any type of business entity, including a corporation, partnership, limited liability company, or sole proprietorship. The definition of an eligible employee may go beyond what is normally considered a **common law employee.** For example, under the statute of one state, the term "employee" includes:

> "employees of a single employer; the officers, managers, and employees of the employer and of subsidiary or affiliated corporations of a corporation employer; and the individual proprietors, partners, and employees of individuals and firms of which the business is controlled by the insured employer through stock ownership, contract or otherwise."[1]

For group DI insurance, the definition of employee may be limited to a full-time employee (a person who works on a non-seasonal, full-time basis, with a normal work week of 30 or more hours). Part-time or temporary help may be excluded from the definition.

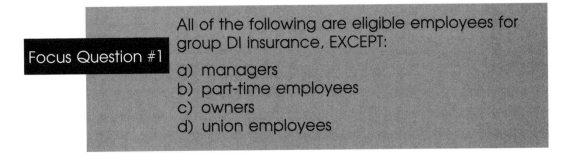

Focus Question #1

All of the following are eligible employees for group DI insurance, EXCEPT:

a) managers
b) part-time employees
c) owners
d) union employees

➤➤ MULTIPLE EMPLOYER ARRANGEMENTS

In addition to group insurance for single employers, there are two arrangements that provide group DI insurance and other group coverages to multiple employers.

Taft-Hartley Trusts

Taft-Hartley trusts are arrangements that came into play to ensure compliance with the **Taft-Hartley Act**, one of the key laws regulating employee relations. Under the Taft-Hartley Act, labor unions are guaranteed the right to negotiate benefits on behalf of their members. It is common for a single labor union to represent employees of multiple employers in a single industry (examples are the Teamsters and the United Auto Workers). To ensure that monies contributed by multiple employers are devoted solely to the benefit of participating employees, a trust must be established. The trustees, made up of an equal number of union and employer representatives, collect contributions, acquire proper insurance, make prudent investments, and administer benefits.

Under a Taft-Hartley trust, employee eligibility for benefits during a current period is typically based on a minimum number of hours worked during a previous period. Employer contributions, however, are based on the number of hours worked by employees covered under the **collective bargaining agreement**, regardless of whether these employees are eligible for benefits or not. This poses a challenge for the insurer, because employees may be eligible for benefits in a given period even though they are laid off or otherwise unemployed. To ensure that there is an adequate reserve for the payment of insurance premiums under an insured plan, employer contributions to the trust must be sufficient to cover premiums even during an economic downturn.

Focus Question #2

What legislation made it clear that unions can negotiate for benefits on behalf of their members?

a) Sherman Act
b) National Labor Relations Act
c) Taft-Hartley Act
d) Mann Act

Multiple Employer Welfare Arrangements (MEWAs)

Small employers (those with fewer than 25 employees) often wish to provide group insurance, including DI insurance, to their employees at a cost comparable to that paid by larger employers with larger employee groups. A **multiple employer welfare arrangement (MEWA)** is a vehicle for achieving this objective. Basically, an employer becomes a member of a MEWA by signing a **joinder agreement**. The joinder agreement sets forth the obligations of the employer and the coverages available to participating employees.

Benefits provided through a MEWA may be either self-funded or insured. With the fully insured **multiple employer trust (MET)**, benefits are provided solely through insurance, and an insurance company is the plan administrator acting on behalf of all employers and employees. State law prohibitions against providing group insurance to groups of fewer than 10 are avoided, because the trust is the owner of the master contract on behalf of all employee-participants. Furthermore, the small business members and their employees are able to obtain group insurance at rates comparable to those paid by large employers.

From the insurer's perspective, there are higher administrative costs and a greater adverse selection risk associated with these small employers. For example, small employers are more likely than large employers to acquire group insurance in order to make sure that an unhealthy or otherwise uninsurable owner-employee is covered. Furthermore, small employers are often subject to greater volatility in cash flow, sometimes leading to cutbacks in benefits or insolvency. And small employers often have greater employee turnover than large employers.

To deal with the greater risk of adverse selection and the greater administrative costs associated with small employers while keeping rates comparable to those charged large employers, insurers typically impose additional requirements on METs. These may include some or all of the following:

- higher participation requirements, including 100 percent for employers with fewer than five employees;
- a requirement that life insurance be among the group benefits provided;
- short-term (for example, six months) premium guarantees;

- extended probationary employment periods for new employees;
- broader preexisting conditions provisions; and
- lower monthly benefit caps for DI insurance.

Some MEWAs are administered by a third-party administrator rather than an insurance company. These arrangements may be fully insured, partly insured and partly self-funded, or entirely self-funded. A major difference between insured and self-funded plans is that, if an insured plan fails, the insurer remains liable to employers and employees. By contrast, with a self-insured plan the trust itself is liable, and if the trust assets are inadequate to meet claims, the member employers and participating employees suffer the loss.

Unfortunately, the reputation of MEWAs has been clouded by a few instances of mismanagement and outright fraud. In some cases, the insurer failed to price or underwrite the plan properly, leading to losses to the insurer and customer dissatisfaction. In some cases involving partly or fully self-funded plans, the administrator failed to require large enough contributions, charged exorbitant administration fees, or otherwise mismanaged the plan, leaving employers and employees in the lurch. In 1982, Congress enacted legislation that ceded most aspects of the regulation of MEWAs to the states, and many states have responded with tighter requirements for administrators and legislation allowing the state to fine or shut down MEWAs that are mismanaged.

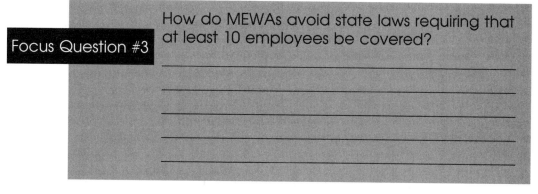

Focus Question #3

How do MEWAs avoid state laws requiring that at least 10 employees be covered?

▶▶ ASSOCIATIONS

Another allowable group for group DI coverage is an association. Examples include alumni associations, professional associations, and business associations. What binds the individual members together is a common background, profession, or interest.

As with employer groups, with associations there is a concern about adverse selection. In fact, the concern is even greater because associations by their very nature are more loosely knit than employer groups. Consequently, some state statutes define an association for purposes of group insurance in terms of the size of its membership. State law may also require an association to have been in existence for a specified number of years to ensure that it is a bona fide association and not formed solely for the purpose obtaining insurance. For example, the statute of one state provides: "The association . . . shall have at the outset a minimum of 500 persons and shall have been organized and maintained in good faith for purposes other than that of obtaining insurance; shall have been in active existence for at least five years."[2]

From the insurer's perspective, association groups are more challenging to price and underwrite, because the motivation for members to participate is generally lower. Unlike employer groups, where employees are often in one location and are available for presentations and in-person enrollment by the salesperson, association members may be geographically dispersed and solicitations may have to be by direct mail. Even so, the insurer is likely to make coverage and rates contingent on a minimal level of participation—75 percent or higher.

Like employer-sponsored group insurance, association coverage offers participants the opportunity to obtain a base level of disability income protection at a premium rate discount from individual DI insurance.

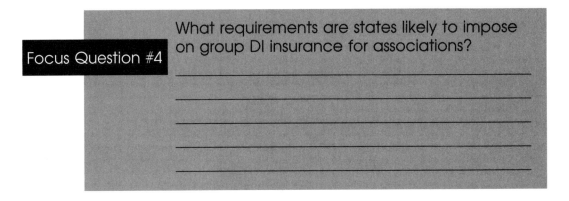

Focus Question #4

What requirements are states likely to impose on group DI insurance for associations?

►► FRANCHISES

Franchisers interested in selling franchise opportunities attempt to make their franchises more attractive through the uniqueness of their product offerings, their training programs, and their ongoing support. In addition, franchisers are increasingly willing to provide group insurance, including disability coverage, to their individual **franchisees**.

Franchise insurance raises issues similar to those of association insurance. The participating franchisees must be involved in a bona fide business venture and not merely seeking insurance. Furthermore, the state is likely to require a minimum number participants, and the insurer will make coverage and/or rates contingent on a minimum level of participation—75 percent or higher.

►► CREDITORS

Another type of group eligible for group DI insurance is creditors, including banks, credit unions, finance companies, and retailers. The concept is that the borrowers under personal, auto, home, credit card, and other loans are insured so that in the event of disability and a loss of income, the creditor is repaid from the insurance benefits. In keeping with the concept, the creditor, rather than the insured, is the beneficiary of the disability benefits, and the benefit amount may not exceed the amount of the debt. Premiums may be paid in full by either party to the loan or shared by creditor and debtor.

State law imposes additional requirements on the issuance of group DI creditor insurance. The requirements include the following:

- When the debtor pays some or all of the premium, the duration of the coverage is limited.
- When the creditor pays the entire premium, 100 percent participation is required; when the debtor contributes to the premium, 75 percent participation is required.
- A minimum number of new insureds must be signed up for the plan each year.

In addition, creditor insurance is governed by state and federal laws intended to protect consumers. In particular, creditors must clearly disclose the premium charged for insurance and inform the debtor that insurance may be obtained from sources other than the lender.

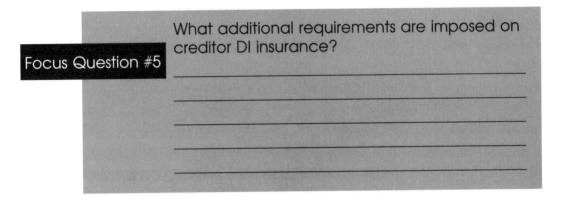

Focus Question #5

What additional requirements are imposed on creditor DI insurance?

▶▶ SUMMARY

When we think of group insurance, we typically think of a single employer and its employees. But there are several other eligible groups. Taft-Hartley trusts provide collectively bargained benefits to employees who work for multiple employers but are represented by a single union. MEWAs allow small employers that would not otherwise have employee groups large enough to qualify for group insurance to band together for a common benefit. Associations and franchisers are also buyers of group DI insurance for their members. And creditors are interested in providing group DI insurance to borrowers.

Key Terms 🔑

Adverse selection
Collective bargaining
  agreement
Common law
  employee
Franchisee
Franchiser
Joinder agreement

Multiple employer
  trust (MET)
Multiple employer
  welfare
  arrangement
  (MEWA)
Taft-Hartley Act
Taft-Hartley trust

⪢ REVIEW QUESTIONS

1. What additional requirements are likely to be imposed on METs because of the increased risk of adverse selection and higher administrative costs?

2. What problems experienced by MEWAs led to legislation that allows states to fine or shut them down for mismanagement?

⪢ ANSWERS TO FOCUS QUESTIONS

Focus Question #1—b

Focus Question #2—c

Focus Question #3—State law prohibitions against providing group insurance to groups of fewer than 10 are avoided because the trust is the owner of the master contract on behalf of all employee-participants.

Focus Question #4—With associations there is a concern about adverse selection, so some state statutes define an association for purposes of group insurance in terms of the size of its membership. State law may also require an association to have been in existence for a specified number of years to ensure that it is a bona fide association and not formed solely for the purpose obtaining insurance.

Focus Question #5—The requirements include the following:

- When the debtor pays some or all of the premium, the duration of the coverage is limited.

- When the creditor pays the entire premium, 100 percent participation is required; when the debtor contributes to the premium, 75 percent participation is required.

- A minimum number of new insureds must be signed up for the plan each year.

▶▶ ANSWERS TO REVIEW QUESTIONS

1. These may include some or all of the following:
   - higher participation requirements, including 100 percent for employers with fewer than five employees;
   - a requirement that life insurance be among the group benefits provided;
   - short-term (for example, six months) premium guarantees;
   - extended probationary employment periods for new employees;
   - broader preexisting conditions provisions; and
   - lower monthly benefit caps for disability income insurance.

2. In some cases the insurer failed to price or underwrite the plan properly, leading to losses to the insurer and customer dissatisfaction. In some cases involving partly or fully self-funded plans, the administrator failed to require large enough contributions, charged exorbitant administration fees, or otherwise mismanaged the plan, leaving employers and employees in the lurch.

NOTES

1 N.C. G.S. §58-51-80.

2 Ibid.

6
Pricing the Group

▶▶ OVERVIEW

Pricing refers to the process of determining adequate premiums for an insurer's group DI insurance coverage. In general, the premiums charged by the insurer should create assets that are adequate to meet its long-term obligations for group DI insurance under reasonably anticipated scenarios for economic trends, interest rates, claims experience, and benefit payments. In fact, the laws of each state require the company's actuary to file an opinion that, using acceptable actuarial practices, the company maintains adequate reserves for the payment of current and anticipated claims under group DI contracts.

There are many factors to consider in pricing group DI insurance, including the nature of the industry, the size of the group, the duration of the benefit, the elimination period, the percentage of participation, and, with larger groups, the actual claims experience of the group. What makes pricing especially challenging is that a premium must be charged today for experience that won't occur until the future. The actuary must proceed largely on the basis of assumptions and probabilities.

Insurers continue to use two basic approaches to group disability income pricing:

- manual rating and
- experience rating.

Manual rating is generally used for smaller groups as well as for larger groups for which no previous claims history is available. Manual rating applies to all insureds within a particular class, for example, all employers with 100 or more employees. **Experience rating** takes into account the actual experience of the insured and is generally used with larger groups. For some groups, experience rating results in modification of the manual rate that would otherwise apply to the group. For the largest groups, the premium is based solely on the group's experience.

Objectives

After reading this chapter and completing the accompanying exercises, you will be able to:

- discuss considerations in manual pricing and identify when manual pricing is appropriate, and
- discuss considerations in experience rating and identify when experience rating is appropriate.

▸▸ MANUAL RATING

Manual rating is used to determine the premium for small groups. It is also used to determine the initial premium for large groups for which there is no past experience, or when a large group's past experience is unavailable to the new insurer. (In such cases, the renewal premium may be based on experience rating.)

Although manual ratemaking requires the services of a trained and skilled actuary, the process itself and the considerations involved are relatively straightforward. Essentially, the premium charged to the customer is the **premium rate** multiplied by the number of **benefit units**.

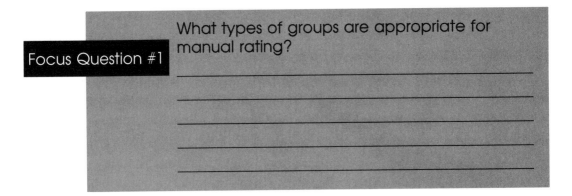

Focus Question #1

What types of groups are appropriate for manual rating?

Benefit Unit

For group DI insurance, the benefit unit is expressed in terms of the amount of income provided to a disabled employee. For short-term DI insurance plans, each $10 of weekly benefit is considered a benefit unit. For long-term plans, $100 of monthly income is a common benefit unit.

Focus Question #2

How is the benefit unit for STD expressed? For LTD?

_____

_____

_____

_____

Premium Rate

Basically, the premium rate is the **net premium rate**, as determined by the insurer's actuary, adjusted for expenses, a **risk charge**, and a contribution to **surplus**.

The net premium rate is the amount required by the insured to support expected claims. Expected claims are a function of the probability of a claim and the amount of the claim. The probability of an employee of a certain age and sex becoming disabled is referred to as **morbidity risk**. Insurers in the group DI insurance business are able to predict morbidity risk with reasonable certainty based on their past experience. In addition, past experience guides the actuary in predicting the duration and the amount of expected claims.

A net premium rate is determined for all issue ages and for both sexes. In general, females have higher morbidity rates than males. Consequently, net premium rates that reflect differences in morbidity between the sexes are higher for females than for males. Many companies offer **unisex rates** for group DI insurance. Unisex rates do not altogether disregard differences in morbidity between the sexes, but instead reflect assumptions about the ratio of males to females in a group. Unisex rates are generally higher for males than sex-distinct rates, and lower for females.

Focus Question #3

Morbidity risk is defined as:

_____

_____

_____

_____

_____

In addition to accounting for age and sex in the manual rates, group DI insurers make assumptions about the elimination period, the benefit period, geographical location, group size, and the nature of the industry. Also, for LTD the calculation of manual rates takes into account that disability benefits are reduced for Social Security, workers' compensation, and any state temporary disability income benefits to which employees are entitled.

Especially for smaller groups, insurers often offer a package plan that provides the employer with little flexibility in terms of plan design. For example, for an STD plan the insurer's rates may assume weekly benefits for 26 weeks following a waiting period of seven days for sickness and no waiting period for injuries. For these plans, a single rate table suffices.

For larger groups, multiple plan options may be available, particularly with LTD plans. These plan options provide the employer with significantly greater flexibility in plan design. Multiple rate tables are often created to reflect the manual rates associated with different choices. Also, adjustments may be made to the final premium, as discussed below, to reflect plan customization. For example, shorter elimination periods, longer benefit periods, and higher benefit caps than those assumed in the insurer's standard tables might require higher rates (and/or additional underwriting).

For the calculation of the premium rate, see Table 6.1. The net premium rate is increased by the insurer's anticipated expenses, including commissions, administration, premium taxes, and other taxes. The net premium rate is also increased by the risk charge, an amount necessary to fund a contingency reserve against unforeseeable and catastrophic events (such as a terrorist attack or a natural disaster). Finally, the net premium rate is increased by the amount the company wishes to earn on its investment. For stock insurance companies, this amount is referred to as profit; for mutual insurance companies, it is referred to as a contribution to surplus.

Table 6.1

Calculating the Premium Rate

Begin with	Net premium rate (based on expected morbidity of group)
Add	Expenses (commissions, administration, taxes)
Add	Risk charge
Add	Contribution to surplus
Equals	Premium rate

Unlike group life insurance claims, group DI claims vary significantly with economic conditions. In general, a sluggish economy with many layoffs tends to result in more and longer claims. If employees face the possibility of layoffs, they may be motivated to go on disability if they can or to stay on disability longer than they otherwise would have. Consequently, group DI insurers review rates regularly to reflect changes in the economy. Also, insurers limit rate guarantees to only one to three years, depending on the industry.

Calculation of the Final Premium Rate

The premium rate calculated in Table 6.1 is actually the starting point for determining the premium rate applicable to a particular group—the **final premium rate**. There are four steps in determining the final premium rate:

- First, the manual premium rate (the net premium rate adjusted for expenses, risk, and contribution to surplus) for each employee listed in the employee census is multiplied by the number of benefit units available to that employee. The premium for each employee is summed to determine the **unadjusted cost** for the group.

- Second, the insurer may offer an adjustment, or discount, to the unadjusted cost to reflect the savings associated with large groups. Discounts of up to 20 percent may be available for unadjusted monthly premiums of $80,000 or more. Many STD and LTD insurers also offer **pool discounts**. The pool discount is made available to a pool of employers within a geographic region or industry. Field sales representatives or managers are usually required to manage the pool to retain a certain relationship with the overall manual rate level for the business written in their office. Finally, the unadjusted cost may be adjusted upward to reflect additional risk to the insurer associated with certain industries or occupations.

■ Third, the adjusted monthly premium is divided by the total volume of coverage per benefit unit in order to arrive at a rate per benefit unit. For example, a long-term DI insurance rate for an employee group might be expressed as $2.50 per $100 of monthly benefit.

■ Finally, the adjusted monthly premium rate per $100 benefit (in the case of LTD) is multiplied by the amount of insurance in force each month to determine the monthly premium charged to the customer. Keep in mind that the amount of coverage in force is subject to variation each month because of changes in the employee population.

Table 6.2

Calculating the Final Premium Rate

Begin with	Unadjusted cost for the group (sum of the unadjusted cost for each employee—that is, the premium rate for the employee's age and sex times the number of benefit units available to the employee)
Subtract	Adjustment (discount) for larger groups, if applicable
Divide	Adjusted cost by the total amount of coverage per benefit unit ($100 for LTD)
Multiply	Rate per benefit unit by amount of total coverage
Equals	Final premium rate

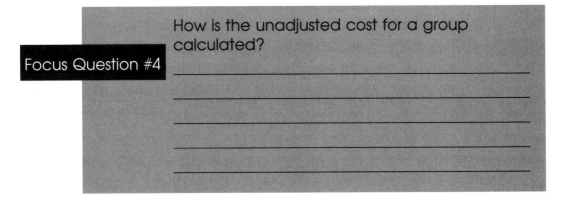

How is the unadjusted cost for a group calculated?

Focus Question #4

_____

_____

_____

_____

_____

≫EXPERIENCE RATING

While manual rating reflects the claims experience of an entire class of insureds, experience rating takes into account the experience of a particular group. Experience rating is appropriate where the size of the group is large enough to produce statistically reliable results. Arguably, experience rating is the most equitable way to determine group premiums because, unlike manual rating, it takes into account factors affecting experience that are specific to the selected group—factors such as working conditions, participant lifestyle, and motivation. Furthermore, the marketplace demands experience rating—a large employer that incurs fewer claims than other policyholders is likely to take its business elsewhere if the insurer does not grant it a price break based on that favorable experience.

Experience rating is used to determine the renewal premium for future years, as well as an insured's initial premium when the case is being transferred from one insurer to another and prior claims experience data are available. In the first case, the insured's experience with the current insurer is taken into account in calculating the renewal premium. In the latter case, the insured's experience with the previous carrier is requested and relied on. In those relatively few instances where the group LTD policy is participating, experience rating is also used to determine the policy dividend.

To determine the renewal premium or the initial premium in a transferred case, the insurer typically considers the insured's experience over the previous three to five years—the **experience period**. Essentially, cumulative claims are evaluated along with other costs associated with the coverage. Past claims and charges are brought up to date to reflect current levels, and future trends are factored in. In addition, the insurer is likely to add an amount to cover expected dividends. This amount serves as a reserve against the potential for worse than expected experience. (If the insured enjoys better than expected experience, this amount is returned to the insured at the end of the premium period.)

The process for calculating an experience-rated **dividend** is similar to the process for calculating a renewal premium. In general, an insurance dividend is a return of the policyowner's premium. The dividend, which is not guaranteed, represents lower expenses, better investment performance, or better morbidity than the insurer initially anticipated. Essentially, the premium paid for the policy year is netted against claims and other insurer expenses. If the premium paid for the year exceeds claims and other expenses, a policy dividend is earned. If there are deficits resulting from poorer than expected claims experience in prior years, the current year's dividend is used to make up the deficit. If there is no deficit from prior years, or if the current year's dividend exceeds the deficit, a dividend is credited to the policyowner.

In calculating both renewal premiums and dividends, the term **incurred claims** is used to refer to claims for the experience period (typically, one year for the dividend calculation, three to five years for the renewal premium calculation). Incurred claims are claims paid during the experience period, minus claims paid for the period that are attributable to experience in a prior period, plus estimated future claims attributable to current experience. (See Table 6.3.)

Table 6.3
Calculating Incurred Claims

Begin with	Total claims paid for the experience period
Subtract	Claims paid for the experience period attributable to claims incurred during a previous period
Add	Estimated claims incurred during the current period that will be paid in the future
Equals	Incurred claims

The concept of incurred claims is necessary because it would be inadequate to simply base renewal premiums and dividends on claims actually paid during the experience period. Inevitably some of those claims arose during a previous period, and just as inevitably some of the disabilities experienced during the experience period in question will not result in claim payments until a future period. By subtracting amounts paid for claims arising during a previous experience period and adding estimated claims for the current period to be paid in the future, a clearer picture of the group's actual claim experience emerges.

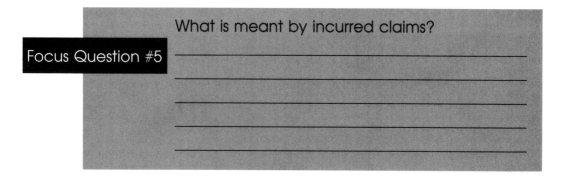

In addition, the insurer's actuary is likely to fine-tune both incurred and expected future claims by assigning a **credibility factor** to each. The credibility factor is the actuary's estimate of the accuracy of incurred and expected future claims as a predictor of future claims experience. Typically, the larger the size of the group, the higher the credibility factor. For groups of fewer than 100 participants, little or no credibility is attached to prior experience—the number of lives is simply too small to serve as a statistically reliable predictor of future performance. On the other hand, the credibility of the claims experience of groups of 1,000 or more approaches 100 percent.

By multiplying the credibility factor by incurred claims, the actuary obtains a more accurate predictor of future claims experience for purposes of calculating dividends and renewal premiums. For example, if a group of 800 employees experienced $1 million in incurred claims, the actuary might multiply this amount by a credibility factor of 0.9 to determine the amount of claims for purposes of computing future premiums and dividends.

A credibility factor is also attached to expected future claims. The credibility factor assigned to future claims is expressed as one minus the credibility factor for incurred claims. In the above example, where a credibility factor of 0.9 was assigned to incurred claims, a credibility factor of 0.1 would be assigned to expected future claims. This result reflects the commonsense notion that for a group of 800 or more employees, past experience is the best predictor of future experience.

The insurer's other costs associated with the case are also considered in the calculation of dividends and renewal premiums. These other costs include commissions, premium taxes, administrative expenses, a contribution to surplus, a risk charge to develop a contingency reserve, and a charge for interest credited to reserves. In the aggregate, such costs are referred to as the **retention charge**.

Table 6.4 illustrates in very simplified terms the steps involved in the calculation of the dividend for a year. A similar calculation would be made to arrive at the renewal premium.

Table 6.4
Calculating the Dividend

Begin with	Premiums paid
Subtract	Incurred claims (multiplied by the credibility factor)
Subtract	Expected claims (multiplied by one minus the credibility factor)
Subtract	Retention charge (the sum of commissions, premium taxes, administrative expenses, contribution to contingency reserves, surplus contribution, and interest credited to reserves)
Subtract	An amount necessary to reduce or eliminate a reserve deficit from prior periods
Equals	The net result (the dividend) is returned to the policyowner or applied to the reduction of renewal premiums.

►► SUMMARY

Pricing group DI insurance is a complex task, requiring the services of a skilled actuary. One approach is to develop and apply manual rates. Manual rates are used for small groups, for initial premium calculations for large groups for which no previous claims experience is available, and for renewal premium calculations on transferred groups for which no experience data are available. Another approach to pricing is experience rating. Experience rating bases renewal premium rates largely on the group's prior claims experience.

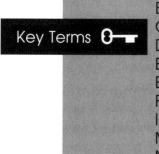

Benefit units	Net premium rate
Credibility factor	Pool discount
Dividend	Premium rate
Experience period	Pricing
Experience rating	Retention charge
Final premium rate	Risk charge
Incurred claims	Surplus
Manual rating	Unadjusted cost
Morbidity risk	Unisex rates

▶▶ REVIEW QUESTIONS

1. In general, what factors are considered in group DI insurance pricing?

2. In manual pricing, how is the premium rate calculated?

3. What is the difference between sex-distinct and unisex premium rates?

4. How do economic conditions affect DI insurance claims? What steps do insurers take to protect against changing economic conditions?

5. Why might an insurer offer a premium discount? What might cause an insurer to increase the unadjusted cost for a case?

6. In a nutshell, how is the renewal premium or the initial premium on a transferred case calculated using experience rating?

7. Why is the concept of incurred claims necessary in experience rating?

8. Employer A's group DI insurance plan insures 527 employees. Employer B's plan insures 334 employees. To which group is the actuary likely to attach a higher credibility factor? Why?

9. What factors make up the retention charge?

➤➤ ANSWERS TO FOCUS QUESTIONS

Focus Question #1— Manual rating is used to determine the premium for small groups. It is also used to determine the initial premium for large groups for which there is no past experience, or when a large group's past experience is unavailable to the new insurer. (In such cases, the renewal premium may be based on experience rating.)

Focus Question #2—The benefit unit for STD is typically expressed in cost per $10 of weekly benefit. For LTD, the benefit unit is expressed as cost for $100 of monthly benefit.

Focus Question #3— The probability of an employee of a certain age and sex becoming disabled.

Focus Question #4— First, the manual premium rate (the net premium rate adjusted for expenses, risk, and contribution to surplus) for each employee listed in the employee census is multiplied by the number of benefit units available to that employee. The premium for each employee is summed to determine the unadjusted cost for the group.

Focus Question #5—Incurred claims are claims paid during the experience period, minus claims paid for the period that are attributable to experience in a prior period, plus estimated future claims attributable to current experience.

▶▶ ANSWERS TO REVIEW QUESTIONS

1. The nature of the industry, the size of the group, the duration of the benefit, the elimination period, the percentage of participation, and, with larger groups, the actual claims experience of the group.

2. Basically, the premium rate is the net premium rate, as determined by the insurer's actuary, adjusted for expenses, a risk charge, and a contribution to surplus.

3. Sex-distinct rates reflect the differing morbidity experience of each gender. In general, females have higher morbidity rates than males, so net premium rates that reflect differences in morbidity between the sexes are higher for females than for males. Unisex rates do not altogether disregard differences in morbidity between the sexes, but instead reflect assumptions about the ratio of males to females in a group. Unisex rates are generally higher for males than sex-distinct rates, and lower for females.

4. Unlike group life insurance claims, group DI claims vary significantly with economic conditions. In general, a sluggish economy with many layoffs tends to result in more and longer claims. If employees face the possibility of layoffs, they may be motivated to go on disability if they can or to stay on disability longer than they otherwise would have. Consequently, group DI insurers review rates regularly to reflect changes in the economy. Also, insurers limit rate guarantees to only one to three years, depending on the industry.

5. The insurer may offer an adjustment, or discount, to the unadjusted cost to reflect the savings associated with large groups. Discounts of up to 20 percent may be available for unadjusted monthly premiums of $80,000 or more. The unadjusted cost may be adjusted upward to reflect additional risk to the insurer associated with certain industries or occupations.

6. Essentially, cumulative claims are evaluated along with other costs associated with the coverage. Past claims and charges are brought up to date to reflect current levels, and future trends are factored in. In addition, the insurer is likely to add an amount to cover expected dividends. This amount serves as a reserve against the potential for worse than expected experience. (If the insured enjoys better than expected experience, this amount is returned to the insured at the end of the premium period.)

7. The concept of incurred claims is necessary because it would be inadequate to simply base renewal premiums and dividends on claims actually paid during the experience period. Inevitably some of those claims arose during a previous period, and just as inevitably some of the disabilities experienced during the experience period in question will not result in claim payments until a future period. By subtracting amounts paid for claims arising during a previous experience period and adding estimated claims for the current period to be paid in the future, a clearer picture of the group's actual claim experience emerges.

8. A higher credibility factor is likely to be attached to the claims experience of Employer A. Typically, the larger the size of the group, the higher the credibility factor.

9. The insurer's other costs associated with the case, including commissions, premium taxes, administrative expenses, a contribution to surplus, a risk charge to develop a contingency reserve, and a charge for interest credited to reserves.

≫7
Underwriting The Group

≫≫OVERVIEW

Through the vehicle of insurance, an individual or group seeks to shift the risk of a designated occurrence to an insurance company. Before an insurance company agrees to accept that risk, the risk must be evaluated. **Underwriting** refers to the process of risk evaluation. Underwriting for group insurance differs from underwriting for individuals in two important respects.

First, for group DI insurance, risk is evaluated by assessing characteristics of the group. By contrast, underwriting of individual DI insurance is characterized by the assessment of the individual applicant's gender, medical history, current health, and personal financial situation.

Second, in individual DI insurance, the salesperson prepares a computer-generated proposal based on an initial fact-finding interview with the prospect. If the prospect likes the proposal, the agent or broker completes an application that includes detailed medical and financial information. Based on the information in the application, the home office underwriter makes a decision. The policy features and benefits offered by the insurer might differ from those applied for, based on the insurer's assessment of the risk. For example, the insurer might determine that the applicant is in a higher risk class than applied for, or that her income does not warrant the amount of benefit applied for.

In contrast, the group insurance proposal constitutes the insurer's offer to insure, and if that offer is accepted by the prospect, the group contract becomes effective. The insurer's offer/proposal is based on the field representative's assessment of the group, subject to approval by the home office. Consequently, the insurer's offer/proposal is usually conditional on verification of the data provided.

Based on these characteristics, group DI coverage is said to be underwritten on a **guaranteed issue** basis. This term implies that coverage is guaranteed, no questions asked, but as the foregoing discussion implies, this is hardly the case. Although individual participants are usually not required to provide health or financial information to the insurer, the group as a whole is evaluated. Furthermore, as will be discussed in this chapter, there are limitations and conditions to coverage that protect the insurer. For example, it is typically required that employees work for a specified period of time prior to qualifying for coverage.

Objectives

After reading this chapter and completing the accompanying exercises, you will be able to:

- discuss considerations in evaluating the insurer's risk, and
- describe the roles of the home office underwriter, pricing actuary, and salesperson in the underwriting process.

▶▶ EVALUATION OF THE RISK

It is important to keep in mind that underwriting of group DI insurance takes place both at the time of the initial application and at renewal. Initially, the underwriter's task is to determine if the group qualifies for the insurer's standard rates, or, if the case involves a transfer, whether there are sufficient and reliable claims data available for experience rating. At renewal, the underwriter must decide whether the current rates are adequate or whether a rate increase is appropriate. In both situations, the underwriter and the pricing actuary must act in concert. In fact, underwriting and pricing should be viewed as co-dependent processes. The underwriter's assessment of the risk affects the pricing, and the pricing and policy design help determine the factors that should be considered in risk assessment.

A major consideration in the underwriting process is to prevent adverse selection against the insurer. Adverse selection occurs when the members of the group bear a greater risk of disability than the general population. Another consideration is to protect the insurer against excessive administrative costs associated with the nature of a group.

Initial Underwriting

The initial underwriting of a case requires the underwriter to consider a variety of factors, all of which bear on the nature of the risk assumed. These factors include:

- industry,
- occupation distribution,
- number and percentage of participants,
- age distribution,
- eligibility requirements,
- elimination period,
- benefit period,
- replacement ratio,
- geographical location, and
- prior claims experience.

Industry

It should be apparent that some industries present greater than average disability risks to the insurer. For example, on balance, the risk of occupational disability of bankers is probably less than that of farmers.

Furthermore, some industries are known to have less financial stability than the norm, leading to lower than average **persistency** for their group insurance. Poor persistency—failure of the business to remain on the books—results in unrecovered insurer administrative expenses. For example, it usually takes an insurer several years to recover front-end commissions paid to sales representatives. If a case goes off the books too soon because the employer is in an unstable industry, the insurance company suffers a loss. To reflect the inherently greater risk of poor persistency associated with some industries as compared to others, insurers typically make adjustments in their standard rates and/or limit coverage.

Occupation

Insurers also recognize that even within a given industry, a particular group's occupation distribution affects the risk assumed. Depending on the occupations of the individuals that make up the group, coverage may be limited or denied altogether, or rates may be increased.

Historically, insurers have relied on occupational schedules to guide them in assessing the disability risk associated with occupations. Traditional occupational schedules divided all jobs into four categories:

- *Class One (highest)*—professionals and executive-level employees;
- *Class Two*—most clerical and middle-management jobs;
- *Class Three*—skilled trades such as plumbers, electricians, and carpenters, and manufacturing jobs not involving special hazards; and
- *Class Four (lowest)*—those involved in hazardous activities, such as construction, farm work, and waste management.

As the economy has changed, these traditional occupational classes are being challenged. For example, as the claims experience of some professionals such as accountants has proven especially poor, these professionals are being reshuffled to lower occupational classifications. Also, some insurers have begun to rethink occupational classifications altogether in light of findings that show a greater correlation between income and morbidity than between occupation and morbidity.

An interesting wrinkle on the impact of occupation on morbidity risk involves individuals who work at home. Traditionally, a group that included significant numbers of individuals who worked at home was not likely to qualify for coverage. However, recent changes in workplace technology and the economy have made telecommuting increasingly acceptable. Consequently, several insurers have begun to experiment with group insurance that covers employees who work at home.

Focus Question #1

Why is traditional thinking about occupational classes being challenged?

_____

_____

_____

_____

_____

Number, Percentage, and Age of Participants

Manual rates are based on the experience of a large number of individuals. Such rates may not be adequate if the group being underwritten is too small. In recognition of this fact, most state laws require a minimum of 10 participants for group DI insurance. If there are fewer than 10 participants, some medical and/or financial underwriting is required.

Manual rates assume a significant level of participation by the eligible group, and insurers typically deny coverage in the absence of at least 75 percent participation. Traditionally, both long-term and short-term DI insurance plans have been paid for by the employer, with little or no premium contribution by the employee. Payment of most or all the premium by the employer encourages employee participation. Recently, however, there has been greater emphasis on contributory plans, also referred to as voluntary worksite plans, which require the employee to bear a significant part of the premium burden. Again, unless participation is 75 percent or higher, the insurer may deny coverage or require some medical and/or financial underwriting. (Voluntary worksite plans are discussed in greater detail in Chapter 12.)

The employee census will reveal, among other things, the age distribution of the employee group. Inasmuch as standard manual rates assume a normal age distribution, an insurer may restrict benefits or require higher rates for a group that has a disproportionately large number of older employees.

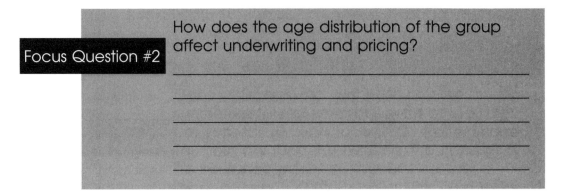

Focus Question #2

How does the age distribution of the group affect underwriting and pricing?

Eligibility Requirements

A distinction is often made between **eligibility for benefits** and **eligibility for coverage**. Eligibility for benefits is discussed in the following section. Eligibility for coverage relates to the conditions that must be met before an employee is covered under the plan.

Typically, both STD and LTD plans require the employee to serve a **probationary period** prior to the onset of coverage. For STD plans, a probationary period of three months is common; for LTD plans, three months to a year is typical.

Without such a requirement the insurer is exposed to the potential for adverse selection. For example, in the absence of such a provision there is nothing to prevent an individual with a known medical problem from joining a firm primarily to obtain benefits.

Most group DI plans limit coverage to full-time employees who are **actively at work**—that is, the employee is in fact working, usually 30 or more hours per week. Part-time, seasonal, and temporary workers are excluded from coverage because of their high turnover rate and the risk that they will seek employment solely for benefits. A higher than expected turnover rate among the employee population leads to unexpectedly high administrative expenses on the insurer's part.

Focus Question #3

Why are part-time, seasonal, and temporary workers usually excluded from group DI insurance coverage?

_____

_____

_____

_____

_____

Elimination Period, Benefit Period, and Replacement Ratio

Eligibility for benefits relates to the conditions that must be met before benefits are paid to an insured. As will be explained in greater detail in Chapter 8, group DI insurance plans typically require disability, as defined in the policy, to continue for a designated period of time (the elimination period) prior to the onset of benefits. For STD plans, elimination periods of seven or ten days are common. LTD plans often require disability to continue for as long as six months before the insured becomes eligible for benefits. Such a provision acts as a kind of co-pay or deductible, reducing the insurer's risk and, ultimately, the amount of the group insurance premium.

The duration of benefits for STD is usually limited to 26 weeks. LTD benefits were traditionally paid until age 65, but most LTD plans today extend the maximum benefit duration to the Social Security normal retirement age (SSNRA), which in many cases is 67.

Benefits are generally expressed as a percentage. The percentage of pre-disability income replaced is referred to as the **replacement ratio**. It is common for STD plans to replace between 50 and 100 percent of pre-disability income. LTD plans ordinarily replace 60 percent of salary. Unless benefits are the same across the board or determined by a formula that precludes individual selection, the insurer is at risk of adverse selection. For example, an individual who is known to be in poor health or accident-prone could be selected by the employer for additional insurance.

In addition, LTD benefits are usually capped at dollar amounts ranging between $3,000 and $6,000 per month. Once dollar limits exceed this amount, it is thought that the risk of malingering to collect benefits, rather than returning to work, is too great. In some cases an employer may wish to offer more generous benefits to a sub-group of highly compensated executives. So long as the benefit formula and cap for the sub-group is the same across the board, the risk of adverse selection is reduced. However, for exceptionally large benefit amounts (for example, $25,000 per month), it would not be unusual for the insurer to require the executives to provide some medical and financial information and/or charge higher rates for the executive coverage.

An insurer's manual rates make assumptions about the duration of the elimination and benefit periods and the replacement ratio.

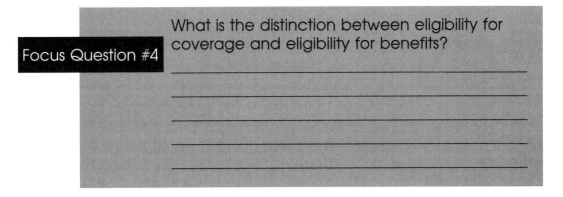

Focus Question #4

What is the distinction between eligibility for coverage and eligibility for benefits?

Geographical Location

Underwriters may also look at the geographical location of the group. Recent claims experience reveals significantly higher claims rates in some regions or localities.

Prior Claims Experience

Where the case involves a transfer, the insurer will likely evaluate the group's previous claims history as part of the underwriting process. As discussed in Chapter 6, a key consideration involves the credibility of the claims data. Working together, the underwriter and the pricing actuary must determine whether the size of the group and the duration of the previous experience period are sufficient to yield statistically reliable information.

Renewal Underwriting

In most cases, experience rating is used with renewal underwriting. Just as with the initial underwriting of a transferred case, previous claims experience is the best indicator of the risk the group poses to the insurer. Again, the underwriter and the actuary must evaluate the credibility of the claims data. Also, it cannot be overlooked that renewal underwriting and pricing usually take place in a competitive environment. Consequently, the underwriter and actuary must offer a product at a rate that meets or beats the competition without jeopardizing the insurer's profitability.

> **Focus Question #5**
>
> What concern is raised by a plan that provides a DI benefit based on a uniform percentage of salary to all employees except the owner? The owner is slated to receive a fixed dollar amount that is considerably more than she would receive using the benefit formula.
>
> _____
>
> _____
>
> _____
>
> _____
>
> _____

▶▶ PARTICIPANTS IN THE UNDERWRITING PROCESS

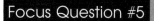

Both the sales representative and the home office underwriter play an important role in group DI underwriting.

The Sales Representative

Early on in the sales process, the agent or broker makes a decision about whether the employer, association, or other group is a qualified prospect. Based on her experience, the salesperson is in a position to determine whether the employee group is of an acceptable size, whether the employer is in an acceptable industry, and whether the employer's business is run in such a way that it is a good candidate for group DI insurance.

As the sales process continues, the sales representative gathers additional data about the employer, including financial information and the employee census, all of which are indicators of whether the employer fits the mold. An employer with a high turnover rate and/or inconsistent cash flow may not be a good risk. Furthermore, the sales representative's personal relationship with the employer (or the employer's benefits specialist) places her in a unique position to assess the potential for adverse selection. For example, the salesperson might be able to determine whether all employees are bona fide, or whether some are merely family members of the owner who hold nominal positions so that they can obtain disability income coverage.

Even after the case is submitted to the home office, the agent or broker can play a role by following up on the underwriter's questions and verifying information.

All in all, solid field underwriting can save everyone headaches and ensure that the process moves along smoothly.

The Home Office Underwriter

If the sales representative has done a good job of qualifying the employer and packaging the case for submission, the home office underwriter's job is made that much easier. However, the underwriter must verify that the occupational and age distribution is within standard pricing, that eligibility criteria protect against adverse selection, and that the geographical location of some or all the employees does not raise a concern.

To the extent that the parameters of a case vary from the standard pricing assumptions, the home office underwriter must work closely with the pricing actuary. For example, if the employer wants a shorter probationary period and significantly greater benefits for the executive class than normally made available, the underwriter and the actuary must work together to determine what combination of higher rates and/or additional underwriting is necessary to place the case. Many times, this work is done under competitive pressures, the case being open to bid or up for renewal. The underwriter and the actuary must balance the need to protect the company and generate surplus against the need to come up with a solution that will win the day.

Typically, even after the group data are evaluated and a proposal (an offer to insure) is made, the underwriter will require that a significant percentage of employees participate. Also, to further protect the company, the proposal remains subject to change, based on the employee census at the time the insurance actually goes in force (rather than when the application was made).

▶▶ SUMMARY

Unlike the underwriting process for individual DI insurance, which evaluates the medical and financial risk posed by the individual applicant, the underwriting process for group insurance evaluates the risk posed by the group. Although group insurance is said to be guaranteed issue, guaranteed issue at standard rates is contingent on the group meeting the insurer's underwriting requirements.

In particular, the insurance company's underwriting requirements are designed to protect against adverse selection. Thus, the nature of the industry, occupation and age distribution within the employee group, the length of the probation period, the size of the group, and the percentage of employees participating all come into play in evaluating risk.

Key Terms	
Actively at work	Persistency
Eligibility for benefits	Probationary period
Eligibility for coverage	Replacement ratio
Guaranteed issue	Underwriting

►► REVIEW QUESTIONS

1. How does individual underwriting differ from group underwriting?

2. What is the role of a probationary period?

3. In setting benefit levels, what steps can be taken against adverse selection?

4. Why might an employer choose to pay most or all of the premium for group DI insurance?

➤➤ ANSWERS TO FOCUS QUESTIONS

Focus Question #1—As the economy has changed, these traditional occupational classes are being challenged. For example, as the claims experience of some professionals such as accountants has proven especially poor, these professionals are being reshuffled to lower occupational classifications. Also, some insurers have begun to rethink occupational classifications altogether in light of findings that show a greater correlation between income and morbidity than between occupation and morbidity.

Focus Question #2—Inasmuch as standard manual rates assume a normal age distribution, an insurer may restrict benefits or require higher rates for a group that has a disproportionately large number of older employees.

Focus Question #3—Part-time, seasonal, and temporary workers are excluded from coverage because of their high turnover rate and the risk that they will seek employment solely for benefits. A higher than expected turnover rate among the employee population leads to unexpectedly high administrative expenses on the insurer's part.

Focus Question #4—Eligibility for coverage relates to the conditions that must be met before an employee is covered under the plan. Eligibility for benefits relates to the conditions that must be met before benefits are paid to a covered employee.

Focus Question #5—The concern relates to adverse selection. Because the president's benefit amount is individually selected, standard group insurance rates are likely to be inadequate to pay for the insurer's risk. To avoid the potential for adverse selection, the president should be individually underwritten for some or all of the coverage.

➤➤ ANSWERS TO REVIEW QUESTIONS

1. First, for group DI insurance, risk is evaluated by assessing characteristics of the group. By contrast, underwriting of individual DI insurance is characterized by the assessment of the individual applicant's gender, medical history, current health, and personal financial situation.

Second, in individual DI insurance, the salesperson prepares a computer-generated proposal based on an initial fact-finding interview with the prospect. If the prospect likes the proposal, the agent or broker completes an application that includes detailed medical and financial information. Based on the information in the application, the home office underwriter makes a decision. The policy features and benefits offered by the insurer might differ from those applied for, based on the insurer's assessment of the risk.

In contrast, the group insurance proposal constitutes the insurer's offer to insure, and if that offer is accepted by the prospect, the group contract becomes effective. The insurer's offer/proposal is based on the field representative's assessment of the group, subject to approval by the home office. Consequently, the insurer's offer/proposal is usually conditional on verification of the data provided.

2. Without such a requirement the insurer is exposed to the potential for adverse selection. For example, in the absence of such a provision there is nothing to prevent an individual with a known medical problem from joining a firm primarily to obtain benefits.

3. The amount of benefits should be the same across the board or determined by a formula that precludes individual selection (for example, a percentage of salary or wages).

4. Aside from the usual reason of wanting to provide an attractive benefits package that draws and keeps employees, payment of some or all of the premium for a group DI insurance plan encourages a higher percentage of employee participation.

8
Product Features

▶▶ OVERVIEW

Eligibility for coverage and benefits, onset of benefits, duration of benefits, and amount of benefits—these all depend on carefully defined terms in the group disability income insurance contract. Merely being employed does not necessarily guarantee coverage—instead, an individual must satisfy eligibility requirements set forth in the plan. Similarly, being unable to work does not necessarily constitute a disability that entitles one to benefits—benefits are payable only if the employee meets the definition of disability included in the policy. Furthermore, some contracts require a claimant not only to demonstrate disability, but also to show a loss of earnings of a certain percentage of pre-disability income. And the amount of an individual's benefit may not be simply a flat percentage of salary—plan benefits are usually coordinated with benefits received from other sources.

In addition, group plans may offer features that go beyond merely replacing a disabled employee's income. For example, a policy may offer a survivor benefit in the event an employee dies, or it may guarantee continued retirement plan contributions for a disabled employee. The conditions for payment of the survivor benefit are spelled out in the policy, as are the requirements for retirement plan contributions.

There is more flexibility with some features than with others. For example, while all DI policies provide some guarantees of continued coverage and premium rates, there is relatively little flexibility in negotiating the terms of these guarantees with an insurer (except in cases involving large employers), because pricing tends to reflect fixed assumptions about the durations of rate guarantees and conditions for cancellation. On the other hand, there are many LTD plan designs with choices of elimination periods, benefit periods, and benefit amounts.

Furthermore, it should be apparent that policy features and benefits directly influence pricing and underwriting. For example, a plan that limits the duration of benefits to two years is likely to be considerably less expensive than one that continues benefits until age 65 or beyond. Also, a plan that offers survivor benefits and provides for continuance of retirement plan contributions will cost more than a plan that lacks these features.

Finally, it is worth mentioning that over the last few years, the contractual differences between group and individual DI insurance have narrowed. For example, it can no longer be said without qualification that the definition of disability is more restrictive in group insurance than in individual policies. In addition, it is increasingly common for group plans to contain provisions relating to partial disability and rehabilitation that parallel those found in individual contracts.

However, the distinction between the group and individual products remains. With individual DI insurance, the contract is between the insured individual and the insurance company. With group DI insurance, the **master contract** is between the sponsor of the coverage (for purposes of this chapter, it is assumed that the sponsor is an employer) and the insurer. Each employee receives a **certificate of coverage** proving participation in the employer's plan.

Objectives

After reading this chapter and completing the accompanying exercises, you will be able to:

- discuss the considerations related to premium and coverage guarantees,
- explain eligibility for coverage provisions,

- distinguish among the various definitions of disability,
- explain the benefit period and the elimination period,
- explain how the benefit amount is determined,
- describe rehabilitation benefits, and
- discuss provisions relating to coordination of benefits and exclusion of certain claims.

▶▶ PREMIUM GUARANTEES

In any insurance policy, one consideration is the nature and length of the premium guarantee. There is a distinction between **non-cancelable** (non-can) and **guaranteed renewable** DI insurance policies.

Non-cancelable

Non-cancelable coverage offers the greatest protection to the insured and places the insurer at the greatest risk. With a non-can policy, the insurer promises that, for a specified period or until the insured reaches a specified age, the policy cannot be cancelled, the premium rate at issue cannot be increased for any reason, and the other policy provisions (relating, for example, to definitions of disability, the benefit amount, and the benefit period) cannot be changed.

While some insurers continue to offer non-cancelable individual DI policies, group DI coverage is universally guaranteed renewable.

Guaranteed Renewable

Under the guaranteed renewable approach, for a specified period or until the insured reaches a specified age, the insurer guarantees that the policy cannot be cancelled (except for non-payment of premium) and that policy provisions (relating, for example, to definitions of disability, the benefit amount, and the benefit period) cannot be changed by the insurer. However, unlike with a non-cancelable policy, the insurer reserves the right to increase premiums to reflect increases in risk or actual losses following the initial premium guarantee period.

State insurance laws require that increases in manual premium rates apply across the board. That is, the insurer cannot increase manual rates for individually selected employers; instead, manual rate increases must apply to the entire class of insureds. For larger employers, group rates are usually based on the group's experience, and the employer's rate is guaranteed by contract between the parties for a specified period, usually one to three years.

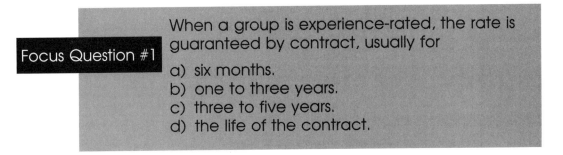

Focus Question #1

When a group is experience-rated, the rate is guaranteed by contract, usually for

a) six months.
b) one to three years.
c) three to five years.
d) the life of the contract.

▸▸ ELIGIBILITY FOR COVERAGE

In Chapter 7 you learned that one of the ways insurers protect themselves against adverse selection with group DI insurance is imposing requirements for eligibility for coverage. The concept is that a required probation period, for instance, prevents individuals from seeking employment solely or primarily for the purpose of obtaining disability benefits.

Requirements for eligibility for coverage tend to differ depending on whether the plan is a short-term or long-term plan.

Short-Term Disability (STD) Plans

Employers are usually quite generous in providing STD coverage. If there is a probationary period, it is likely to be short, usually three months or less. Furthermore, it is common for the plan to be available to all full-time employees who are actively at work on the date the probationary period is satisfied. Part-time, seasonal, and temporary workers are usually excluded because of the high turnover and adverse claims experience associated with these employees. High turnover and adverse claims experience translates into higher administrative expenses and claims costs for the insurer, which are ultimately passed on the employer in the form of higher premiums.

Long-Term Disability (LTD) Plans

Eligibility requirements for LTD plans are often more restrictive. These plans can be costly, and employers want to make sure they get the greatest possible benefit from their outlay.

- An employer may limit coverage only to salaried employees or to employees above a certain salary level. Plans that cover hourly wage employees are more expensive for the employer because of the higher frequency of claims and longer duration of claims among these employees. In addition, the exclusion of hourly wage and lower-salaried employees can be justified on the grounds that Social Security benefits will replace an adequate amount of these employees' income.

- The probationary period for LTD plans is likely to range from three months to a year. As discussed in Chapter 7, a longer probationary period reduces the risk of adverse selection occurring when individuals join an employer solely or primarily to obtain disability coverage.

- The actively-at-work requirement of LTD plans may be more stringent than that of STD plans. For example, a plan may require not only that an employee be actively at work on the day he becomes otherwise eligible for coverage, but that he be on the job without illness or injury for as long as 30 days prior to the onset of coverage.

▶▶ THE DEFINITION OF DISABILITY

The contractual definition of disability lies at the heart of the DI insurance policy. Only if the employee meets the terms of the precise policy language will a claim for benefits be paid. One distinction often made in defining disability is between "**own occupation** (own occ)" and "**any occupation** (any occ)." Another key distinction is between **total disability** and **partial disability**. These definitions focus on a loss of duties, but another definition of disability focuses on **loss of earnings**. Concepts of **residual** and **presumptive disability** also come into play with group DI insurance.

Like eligibility for coverage, eligibility for benefits as determined by the definition of disability is likely to differ between short-term and long-term plans.

Own Occupation

From the insured's perspective, the most desirable definition of disability is the own occupation definition. Although the specific language may differ from policy to policy, the basic undertaking of the insurer is to pay the promised benefits if the insured is unable to perform the substantial and material duties of her regular occupation because of illness or injury. It does not matter whether the insured could theoretically work in another occupation, or even if she found other work—the benefit is payable when the insured cannot perform the duties of her regular occupation.

Example 8.1

Mike, a PhD and a nuclear engineer with Piedmont Energy, suffered an injury to his neck and back that prevented him from stooping and bending to check gauges and adjust valves. Mike filed a claim and qualified for disability benefits under the company's group DI insurance plan. The plan provides benefits when an employee is unable to perform the "material duties of his or her regular occupation." After several months, Mike was able to find part-time work as an instructor at a local college. But Mike's disability benefits under the group plan's own occ definition continue even though he is able to find work elsewhere.

This definition of disability places the insurer at considerable risk, because the insured's motivation to recover and return to work in his own occupation is minimized. For this reason, own occ definitions of disability are used sparingly in group DI insurance contracts. When an own occ definition of disability is used, it is often limited in duration or combined with a loss of earnings or residual disability income benefit.

Any Occupation

The any occupation definition of disability is considerably more restrictive than the own occupation definition. The any occ definition requires that the insured be unable to perform the duties of any gainful occupation for which he is suited because of education, training, or experience. For instance, in Example 8.1 Mike's new job as an instructor is certainly different from his old job, but it is a job for which he is suited because of his education, training, or experience. Under a straight any occ definition of disability, Mike would not be entitled to benefits.

Although the any occ definition is more restrictive than the own occ definition, it is not nearly as restrictive as the Social Security definition of disability. As you recall from Chapter 2, to qualify for benefits under Social Security, the individual's disability must be so severe that it prevents her from working at any gainful activity and must be expected to last for 12 consecutive months or result in death.

Loss of Earnings

As explained above, own occ and any occ definitions of disability focus on the claimant's inability to perform certain work-related duties. In contrast, a loss of earnings contract focuses on earnings lost because of disability.

Under a loss of earnings contract, when a claimant returns to work in any occupation (under an any occ definition) or his own occupation (under an own occ definition) and suffers a loss of earnings greater than a certain level (usually 20 percent, but sometimes 25 percent), the policy pays a proportionate benefit. The loss of earnings contract places an additional burden on the claimant. Not only must he prove the amount of the financial loss for each month he claims benefits, he must also provide a physician's report that verifies that the earnings loss was caused by disability (and not, for instance, by an economic downturn or layoff).

In Example 8.1 above, if Mike's LTD plan had an own occ definition of disability with a loss of earnings requirement, Mike would qualify for benefits when he returned to work as an instructor only as long as he remained unable to work as an engineer and his earnings as an instructor were less than 80 percent of his pre-disability income.

Partial Disability

The term partial disability is often used by group insurers to refer to any situation in which the insured is able to return to work in a partial capacity. However, under a true partial disability approach, it is defined as the insured's inability to perform some or all of the duties of his own occupation, or his inability to perform the duties of his own occupation on a full-time basis. In general, the concept is that an insured who is able to perform some but not all of the duties of his own occupation, or is able to work part-time, may qualify for some benefits.

Typically, income loss is not a factor with a true partial disability provision. Instead, the contract typically provides for a benefit equal to a flat percentage (commonly 50 percent) of the total disability benefit. Theoretically, under such a provision an insured could return to work part-time at her own occupation and earn 100 percent of her pre-disability income, while at the same time receive partial disability benefits (although in practice this rarely occurs).

To protect the insurer from the risk of loss associated with over-insurance and the lack of motivation to return to work, partial disability provisions are typically coupled with a requirement of total disability for a stated period (which usually coincides with the elimination period) and a benefit period of limited duration (usually three to 12 months).

Residual Disability

Residual disability is another approach that encourages individuals to return to work, at least part-time, following a disability. In general, a residual disability is a disability that results in the inability of the insured to perform some of the duties of his own occupation full-time, leading to a loss of income.

Basically, pre-disability income is compared to post-disability income to determine the **earnings percentage loss**. The earnings percentage loss is then multiplied by the benefit the insured would receive if he were totally disabled. The result is the residual disability benefit.

It is typical to require that the insured's earnings be reduced by a minimum amount (usually 20 percent) for residual benefits to become available. It is also typical to provide that if the loss is significant enough, the insured will be considered economically disabled and qualify for the total disability benefit. The level at which the earnings loss is significant enough to trigger

| Example 8.2 | Jake has suffered a back injury in an automobile accident. His pre-disability net earnings were $2,400 per month. Following the disability, he is able to work only two days a week, and his earnings have fallen to $1,000 per month. In the event of total disability, Jake's LTD policy pays a monthly benefit of 60 percent of pre-disability salary ($1,440 per month).

The policy also provides for a residual disability benefit in the event Jake returns to work but suffers a loss of income. Jake has suffered a 58 percent loss in earnings because of his disability. This percentage is multiplied by the $1,440 total disability benefit to arrive at a residual disability benefit of $835. |

total disability benefits differs from policy to policy, but it is typically in the 75 to 80 percent range.

Another provision common to policies providing residual benefits is a minimum residual benefit of at least 50 percent of the total disability benefit. In many instances, the minimum benefit may be limited to the first six months of residual disability. Following this six-month period, the residual benefit is based on the actual percentage of loss of earnings.

Not surprisingly, whether an own occupation with residual benefit policy or a loss of earnings policy is better from the consumer's perspective is a matter of some debate in the industry. On the one hand, own occupation with residual benefit policies are considerably more expensive, but they offer the insured the opportunity to earn income from another occupation without reducing disability benefits. Loss of earnings policies are less expensive, but they offer reduced benefits, even when the insured is unable to return to her own occupation.

The significance of the concepts of partial and residual disability and their implications for claims management and return-to-work programs associated with modern-day group LTD plans are discussed further in Chapter 11.

Focus Question #2

With residual disability, how is the amount of the benefit determined?

_____

_____

_____

_____

_____

Presumptive Disability

Another way an employee can qualify for benefits under a group DI insurance plan is by becoming presumptively disabled. Under a presumptive disability provision, an insured is presumed disabled in the event she suffers certain specified injuries or illnesses. Examples of presumptive disability include:

- loss of the power of speech,
- loss of sight in both eyes,
- loss of hearing in both ears, and
- loss of the use of or severance of both hands, both feet, or one hand and one foot.

As with other total disabilities, benefits cease if the insured recovers. For example, an individual might lose his sight because of a stroke and qualify as presumptively disabled. If the individual gradually recovers sight, the presumptive disability benefits would end.

On the other hand, an individual continues to receive presumptive disability benefits for as long as the disability continues, even if he is able to return to work in his own occupation full-time. For example, an individual who loses both legs in an automobile accident qualifies for benefits for the duration of the benefit, even if he is able to return to work at his old job in a wheelchair.

STD Plans Versus LTD Plans

As mentioned earlier, there are often differences between the definitions of disability in STD contracts and LTD contracts. STD plans typically contain a version of the own occupation definition of disability. For example, disability might be defined as ''the total and continuous inability of the employee to perform each and every duty of his or her regular occupation.''

Although partial disability benefits are not common in short-term plans, some of the more recent plans include a partial disability benefit.

Long-term plans are likely to combine own occupation and any occupation definitions of disability. For example, during the first 24 to 36 months of disability, an insured would be eligible for benefits when she is unable to perform the duties of her own occupation. Following this period, the definition shifts to any occupation—benefits are payable only in the event the employee suffers from ''the total and continuous inability to engage in any and every gainful occupation for which she is qualified or shall reasonably become qualified by reason of training, education, or experience.''

Although the specifics of provisions relating to partial disability, residual benefits, and loss of earnings benefits vary from insurer to insurer and plan to plan, their overriding goal is to encourage employees to return to work. The distinction between partial and residual disability is sometimes blurred with group insurance, but a key difference is that policies providing partial disability benefits usually require a period of total disability, while those providing residual benefits do not.

➤➤ THE ELIMINATION PERIOD

Both short-term and long-term DI insurance plans typically require an **elimination period** (also known as a waiting period) prior to the onset of benefit payments. A common elimination period for short-term plans is seven days, particularly in the case of illness. Short-term plans often require no elimination period for injury. Waiting periods for plans covering illness tend to range from one to seven consecutive days. If insured employees are covered by a sick-pay plan, the elimination period for the STD plan is often coordinated with the sick-pay plan so that short-term benefits begin when sick-pay benefits cease.

Similarly, LTD plans often impose an elimination period that is coordinated with benefits under a short-term plan. Consequently, elimination periods, during which the insured must be disabled prior to receiving long-term benefits, often stretch for as long as three to six months.

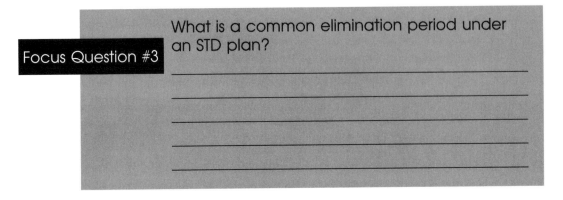

Focus Question #3

What is a common elimination period under an STD plan?

►►BENEFIT AMOUNTS

There is no set amount of benefits provided under a group DI insurance plan. The amount of the benefit often varies from employer to employer and among classes of employees of the same employer. In general, however, it is common to provide benefits based on a uniform percentage of salary, capped at a flat dollar amount.

As with individual DI insurance, insurers are reluctant to offer benefits that replace over 70 percent of pre-disability earnings, or provide a dollar benefit that is overly large. The concern is that a disabled employee who receives too high a percentage of his pre-disability income has little incentive to recover and return to work. Furthermore, dollar benefits that are larger than granted in the policy may subject group insurers to adverse selection risk, unless these larger amounts are individually underwritten.

A significant issue is what types of income to consider in determining the amount of pre-disability earnings. A common approach is to include only regular wages and salary, excluding overtime, bonuses, and deferred compensation. While such an approach works well with hourly wage earners, it tends to work less well with salaried employees, whose earnings increasingly tend to be based in part on performance. In an effort to respond to a compensation trend that provides more and more employees with a base salary and incentive compensation in the form of bonuses that may be taken currently or deferred in whole or in part, some plans define compensation more broadly than just salary or wages. Bonuses, other incentive compensation, and deferred compensation may be taken into account in determining the amount of the disability benefit.

STD Plans

It is common for STD plans to replace between 50 and 100 percent of pre-disability salary or wages. One approach is to replace 100 percent of salary or wages for four weeks and then reduce the benefit to 70 percent.

LTD Plans

LTD plans typically replace 50 to 70 percent of pre-disability salary or wages, subject to a maximum dollar amount cap. The most common percentages of salary or wages replaced are 60 and $66^2/_3$ percent. Dollar amount caps of $3,000 to $6,000 per month are common, but some group carriers pay up to $10,000 or even (rarely) $25,000 per month. These larger dollar amount caps are often used to ensure that highly paid executives are receiving adequate protection under group plans.

For example, a plan that provides a 60 percent benefit with a cap of $5,000 per month works well for an employee earning $60,000—the $3,000 monthly benefit is well below the $5,000 monthly dollar limitation. On the other hand, the plan is less attractive to an executive earning $200,000. Here the $5,000 monthly benefit cap represents only half of what the executive would be entitled to under the 60 percent limitation. Raising the monthly dollar limit to $10,000 for a class that includes highly compensated executives is one approach to addressing this problem. Another solution is to add individual DI policies to the executives' insurance portfolios.

►► THE BENEFIT PERIOD

The **benefit period** is the length of time for which benefits are payable under the policy. As with the elimination period, group plans often offer employers choices.

STD Plans

Benefit periods of 13 and 26 weeks are common under STD plans. However, some plans extend benefits for as long as two years. One package plan, the **1-8-26 plan**, provides a 26-week benefit period beginning on the first day of a disability resulting from an accident and the eighth day of a disability caused by illness.

LTD Plans

Benefits under LTD plans may extend for as little as two years or for as long as the life of the insured. The **Age Discrimination in Employment Act (ADEA)** prohibits limiting benefits to age 65. Most common today is a benefit that extends to age 65 for disabilities occurring before a certain age (for example, age 55). Employees incurring disabilities after the specified age receive benefits for a scheduled period of time. For example, an employee who is disabled at age 53 receives benefits until age 65, while an employee who becomes disabled at age 63 might receive benefits for five years.

Table 8.1

Benefit Period Schedule

Age at Disability	Benefit Period
59 and younger	To age 65
60-64	5 years
65-69	To age 70
70-74	1 year
75 and older	6 months

Benefit periods for LTD are not necessarily the same for all classes of employees. As will be discussed further in Chapter 9, it is not uncommon for an employer to provide one benefit period to hourly wage employees and another to salaried employees. For example, an employer might provide an STD benefit of 26 weeks to all employees, a two-year LTD benefit for hourly wage earners, and a benefit to age 65 for salaried employees who suffer a disability before age 60.

Recurring Disability

An issue that relates to the duration of disability benefits is **recurring disability**. Unlike life insurance policies, for which there is only one death claim, DI insurance plans may pay several claims to the same insured. Most group plans provide that when an employee's disability recurs within a certain period of time of the previous disability (usually three to six months of continuous, full-time employment), the disabilities are treated as one disability. Consequently, the benefit period does not restart, and in most cases neither does the elimination period.

Example 8.3

David, a 62-year-old full-time employee with Acme, Inc., became disabled with a knee injury on July 1, 2003. After satisfying the 26-week waiting period under the company's LTD plan, David qualified for benefits on January 1, 2004. At David's age, benefits under the plan are payable for five years.

David received benefits under the LTD plan for 18 months before returning to work on July 1, 2005. A month later, David's bad knee flared up again, and he filed a claim for disability. Under the LTD plan, a disability recurring within three months of an earlier claim is treated as a continuation of the earlier disability. Consequently, David is entitled to only 42 additional months of disability benefits, because he has already used up 18 months of his benefit for what is considered the same disability as the current one.

An exception typically applies when the following two criteria are met:

- the subsequent disability arises from an unrelated cause, and
- the subsequent disability begins after the employee returns to work.

In the example of David, the exception does not come into play, because David' second disability resulted from the original knee injury. If, however, David's second disability had been caused by a new back injury, a new elimination period and a new benefit period would begin. Thus, if the benefit period for insureds age 64 (David's age at the time of the second disability) were five years, David would be entitled to 60 (not 42) months of benefits for the disability caused by the back injury.

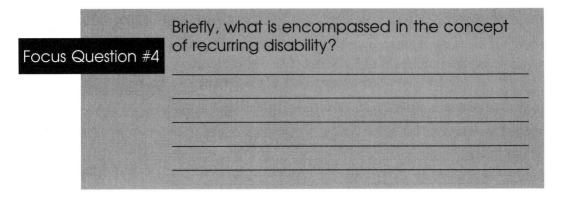

Focus Question #4

Briefly, what is encompassed in the concept of recurring disability?

_____

_____

_____

_____

_____

▶▶ REHABILITATION BENEFITS

Payment of **rehabilitation benefits** for disabled insureds has become an increasingly important feature of both individual and group DI insurance policies. In most instances, the contractual language concerning rehabilitation benefits is broad enough to allow for a wide range of solutions. Furthermore, in an effort to reduce claims, insurers have become increasingly open to structuring rehabilitation benefits to meet an insured's personal needs.

From the employee's perspective, the insurer's payment of rehabilitation costs can open the door to a productive life. Through physical therapy, job training, or adaptive aids, an individual may be able to return to work, at least on a part-time basis.

From the insurer's perspective, a relatively small upfront outlay for rehabilitation benefits can potentially eliminate or lessen benefit payments considerably. An insured who receives rehabilitation benefits may be able to return to work after a few months, reducing the disability benefit payable.

Mandatory rehabilitation provisions (MRPs) are becoming key components in a number of managed disability products. Like other managed disability provisions, MRPs aim to control claim costs and provide competitive prices. However, unlike some managed disability approaches that focus on excluding or limiting claim payments, MRPs, when properly administered, may provide a positive outcome for claimants, employers, and insurers. MRPs typically have the following requirements:

- There must be a plan of rehabilitation that claimants can reasonably be expected to participate in and complete.

- There must be a realistic expectation that the plan will enable the claimant to be employed in a job providing 60 to 80 percent of pre-disability income.

- The insurer must prepare the plan, taking into account the nature and severity of the claimant's medical condition and work potential, based on accepted vocational assessment techniques.

MRPs are, as the name states, mandatory. Thus, insurers can reduce or stop benefit payments if claimants refuse to cooperate or stop cooperating in the rehab plan *without good cause*. One creative MRP uses interim and permanent outplacement as a part of the rehab plan.

Even where the group LTD contract does not include a rehabilitation provision, many insurers will pay for rehabilitation anyway in an effort to shorten the duration of disability and reduce the insurer's overall outlays. As discussed in Chapter 11, return-to-work incentives have become an increasingly important aspect of DI insurance claims management and a major factor in the profitability of DI insurance.

▶▶ EXCLUSIONS

Group DI insurance plans typically contain certain exclusions from payment of benefits, even where the employee is otherwise eligible for coverage and benefits. In general, the exclusions protect the insurer from payment of benefits in those situations where the employee bears some legal or moral culpability.

Exclusions in STD plans normally include any disability:

- during which the insured is not under the regular care and attendance of a licensed physician or other medical practitioner,

- that is intentionally self-inflicted, or
- that began while the employee was not covered under the policy.

Although it was once common for STD plans to exclude pregnancies, federal law now requires that employers with 15 or more employees provide benefits during pregnancy. Short-term plans have removed this exclusion to provide coverage consistent with the requirements of the law.

Like short-term plans, LTD plans also have a number of exclusions. Common exclusions are any disability:

- during which the insured is not under the regular care and attendance of a licensed physician or other medical practitioner;
- that is intentionally self-inflicted;
- that began while the employee was not covered under the policy;
- that results from war, declared or undeclared;
- that results from participation in an assault or felony; or
- that results from a **preexisting condition**.

In addition, limits are typically imposed on disabilities resulting from mental illness, alcoholism, or drug addiction. The usual approach is to limit benefits to 24 months. Coverage is usually provided beyond two years if the disabled insured is a patient confined to an appropriate hospital.

Although policy language differs from company to company, a common approach to preexisting conditions is to state that a disability results from a preexisting condition when the disability begins within the first 12 months of the employee's coverage, and when the employee received treatment or medical advice for the disabling condition:

- prior to the date the employee became eligible under the LTD plan, and
- within 90 days of the effective date of the coverage.

The rationale underlying the exclusion for preexisting conditions is reducing the risk of adverse selection. As a practical matter, it is rare to see preexisting condition exclusions in group cases with more than 100 employees. The spread of risk in these larger cases, as well as the likelihood that the purchase decision is not being made to benefit a single individual, reduce the risk of adverse selection sufficiently to enable the insurer to drop the exclusion.

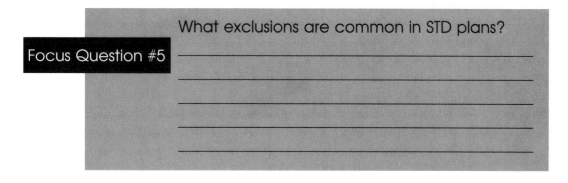

What exclusions are common in STD plans?

Focus Question #5 _____

_____

_____

_____

_____

▸▸ COORDINATION OF BENEFITS

A concern of insurers is **over-insurance**. An individual is over-insured for disability if she can receive more income through being disabled than by working. Insurers fear that the lack of an incentive to continue working or return to work following a disability increases the number and duration of claims. With experience-rated plans, this only translates into higher premiums for employers.

To discourage malingering and encourage employees to return to work, benefits from group plans are typically coordinated with other benefits an employee may receive because of a disability. The group plan is intended to integrate with these other plans, not provide a benefit in addition to what these other plans provide. In fact, group rates take this coordination into account.

STD Plans

STD plans that are not limited to non-occupational disability are usually integrated with workers' compensation, so that amounts received from workers' compensation reduce the STD benefit that would otherwise have been payable. Similarly, if a state offers temporary disability income benefits, these benefits also reduce STD benefits. Finally, STD benefits are usually integrated with Social Security; however, Social Security integration is only necessary if the benefit period under the STD plan runs longer than the five-month waiting period for Social Security.

LTD Plans

It is common for LTD benefits to be integrated with the following:

- workers' compensation;
- temporary disability benefits under state law;
- Social Security benefits, if applicable;
- sick-pay and other employer-sponsored disability benefit plans; and
- earnings from any other employment.

As a general rule, group LTD benefits are not integrated with individual DI benefits. However, the amount of individual DI insurance an insurer will issue is limited to reflect coverage from other sources, including group insurance.

▶▶ SUMMARY

Although contractual language varies from plan to plan, there are several features that are common to group DI insurance plans. These plans offer limited premium guarantees, require employees to work for a probationary period prior to becoming eligible for coverage, increasingly define disability to include partial disability in an effort to promote an employee's return to work, require elimination periods prior to payment of benefits, limit benefits to durations shorter than the lifetime of the insured, and base the amount of benefits on a uniform percentage of compensation subject to a dollar cap. It is also common for these plans to exclude disabilities with certain causes and to coordinate income from other sources.

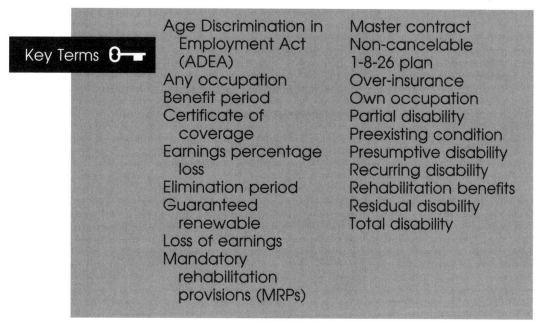

Key Terms

Age Discrimination in Employment Act (ADEA)	Master contract
	Non-cancelable
	1-8-26 plan
Any occupation	Over-insurance
Benefit period	Own occupation
Certificate of coverage	Partial disability
	Preexisting condition
Earnings percentage loss	Presumptive disability
	Recurring disability
Elimination period	Rehabilitation benefits
Guaranteed renewable	Residual disability
	Total disability
Loss of earnings	
Mandatory rehabilitation provisions (MRPs)	

►► REVIEW QUESTIONS

1. In what ways are eligibility for coverage requirements likely to be more restrictive in LTD plans than in STD plans?

2. What is a common approach to defining disability in an LTD contract?

3. Myra suffered internal injuries in an automobile accident. Her pre-disability net earnings were $3,000 per month. Following the disability, she is able to work only two days per week, and her earnings have

slipped to $1,200 per month. Her LTD policy pays a monthly benefit of 60 percent of pre-disability earnings ($1,800) in the event of total disability. The policy also provides for a residual disability benefit in the event Myra returns to work but suffers a loss of income. How much is Myra's residual disability benefit?

4. Discuss the considerations involved in determining compensation for purposes of calculating the disability benefit.

5. Why do insurers benefit by providing rehabilitation benefits to disabled employees?

6. What is a common approach to preexisting conditions, and why are preexisting conditions often excluded from coverage?

⟫ ANSWERS TO FOCUS QUESTIONS

Focus Question #1—b

Focus Question #2—Basically, pre-disability income is compared to post-disability income to determine the earnings percentage loss. The earnings percentage loss is then multiplied by the benefit the insured would receive if he were totally disabled. The result is the residual disability benefit.

Focus Question #3—A common elimination period for short-term plans is seven days, particularly in the case of illness. Short-term plans often require no elimination period for injury. Waiting periods for plans covering illness tend to range from one to seven consecutive days. If insured employees are covered by a sick-pay plan, the elimination period for the STD plan is often coordinated with the sick-pay plan so that short-term benefits begin when sick-pay benefits cease.

Focus Question #4—Most group plans provide that when an employee's disability recurs within a certain period of time of the previous disability (usually three to six months of continuous, full-time employment), the disabilities are treated as one disability. Consequently, the benefit period does not restart, and in most cases neither does the elimination period.

Focus Question #5—Exclusions in STD plans normally include any disability:

- during which the insured is not under the regular care and attendance of a licensed physician or other medical practitioner,
- that is intentionally self-inflicted, or
- that began while the employee was not covered under the policy.

⟫ ANSWERS TO REVIEW QUESTIONS

1. First, an employer may limit coverage only to salaried employees or to employees above a certain salary level. Second, the probationary period for LTD plans is likely to range from three months to a year. Third, the actively-at-work requirement of LTD plans may be more

stringent than that of STD plans. For example, a plan may require not only that an employee be actively at work on the day he becomes otherwise eligible for coverage, but that he be on the job without illness or injury for as long as 30 days prior to the onset of coverage.

2. Long-term plans are likely to combine own occupation and any occupation definitions of disability. For example, during the first 24 to 36 months of disability, an insured would be eligible for benefits when she is unable to perform the duties of her own occupation. Following this period, the definition shifts to any occupation—benefits are payable only in the event the employee suffers from ''the total and continuous inability to engage in any and every gainful occupation for which she is qualified or shall reasonably become qualified by reason of training, education, or experience.''

3. Myra has suffered a 60 percent loss in earnings because of her disability. This percentage is multiplied by the $1,800 total disability benefit to arrive at a residual disability benefit of $1,080.

4. A common approach is to include only regular wages and salary, excluding overtime, bonuses, and deferred compensation. While such an approach works well with hourly wage earners, it tends to work less well with salaried employees, whose earnings increasingly tend to be based in part on performance. In an effort to respond to a compensation trend that provides more and more employees with a base salary and incentive compensation in the form of bonuses that may be taken currently or deferred in whole or in part, some plans define compensation more broadly than just salary or wages. Bonuses, other incentive compensation, and deferred compensation may be taken into account in determining the amount of the disability benefit.

5. A relatively small upfront outlay for rehabilitation benefits can potentially eliminate or lessen benefit payments considerably. An insured who receives rehabilitation benefits may be able to return to work after a few months, reducing the disability benefit payable.

6. Although policy language differs from company to company, a common approach to preexisting conditions is to state that a disability results from a preexisting condition when the disability begins within the first 12 months of the employee's coverage, and when the employee received treatment or medical advice for the disabling condition prior to the

date the employee became eligible under the LTD plan and within 90 days of the effective date of the coverage.

The rationale underlying the exclusion for preexisting conditions is reducing the risk of adverse selection. As a practical matter, it is rare to see preexisting condition exclusions in group cases with more than 100 employees. The spread of risk in these larger cases, as well as the likelihood that the purchase decision is not being made to benefit a single individual, reduce the risk of adverse selection sufficiently to enable the insurer to drop the exclusion.

9

Special Features and Plan Design

▶▶ OVERVIEW

Although there are variations from plan to plan, virtually all group disability income insurance plans contain the basic features discussed in Chapter 8. They all require that employees meet eligibility requirements, contain definitions of disability similar to those discussed in Chapter 8, impose waiting periods, provide a level of benefits based on a uniform percentage of compensation (subject to a dollar cap), and limit the duration of benefits.

While short-term plans remain fairly standard from insurer to insurer, a variety of special product features are available to help the salesperson tailor an LTD plan to meet a customer's unique needs and objectives and differentiate the plan from competing proposals. In fact, as much as anything, it is the salesperson's skill in **plan design** that is likely to be the determining factor in a sale.

This chapter discusses some of the more common special features in the market today. These special features can take the form of either product enhancements or options, and options can enhance benefits either across the board or for only a select group of executives. Special features can also include benefit limitations aimed at reducing the cost of a plan.

Some insurers choose to add new features directly to their standard contracts. Others prefer to provide a basic offering and allow policyowners to
select the additional features they find desirable. These additions are usually
handled in the form of a **policy rider**—a document that fully describes
the features of the plan adjustments and becomes part of the contract.

Objectives

After reading this chapter and completing the accompanying exercises, you
will be able to:

- describe popular reduced cost options;
- explain how COLA provisions work;
- discuss annuity, pension, and medical benefit supplements;
- describe survivor income and critical illness benefits;
- describe supplemental DI plans for executives; and
- discuss considerations related to conversions.

▶▶ REDUCED COST OPTIONS

Increasingly common among group LTD carriers are products designed to
reduce employer costs. These products are the industry's attempt to balance
the insured's need for comprehensive coverage in the event of disability
with the objective of cost containment. These relatively new products often
limit benefits for certain disabilities, modify the definition of disability so
that benefits are payable in fewer situations, and offer benefits to facilitate
or require a disabled employee's return to work. Three of the most popular
of these cost-cutting options are discussed below.

Special Conditions Limitation Rider

As mentioned in Chapter 8, it is common for LTD policies to limit the
benefit period for disabilities caused by mental illness, alcoholism, and
drug abuse to 12 to 24 months. The rationale for such limitations is that
these are **subjective disabilities**, meaning that they are more difficult to
verify than physical disabilities that can be confirmed by readily observable
documentation such as X-rays and lab results. Another consideration is the
cost associated with these disabilities—treatments can be expensive, and the

effectiveness of certain treatments remains in doubt. A third consideration is that motivation plays a significant role in the healing process with these types of disabilities, and a lengthy benefit period removes much of the motivation to overcome the illness, to the detriment of the employer, the employee, and the insurer.

The cost-containment policies offered by some insurers go beyond the usual limitations and offer riders that limit other **special conditions** to the same 12- to 24-month period. These special conditions might include the following:

- mental illnesses, except those with organic causes, schizophrenia, dementia, delirium, and amnesia syndrome;
- musculoskeletal and connective tissue disorders of the neck and back, with a fairly long list of exceptions for neck and back disorders for which standard medical tests produce objective data substantiating the presence of a condition that could cause disability;
- carpal tunnel syndrome;
- chronic fatigue syndrome;
- environmental allergic illness;
- fibromyalgia;
- myofascial pain syndrome; and
- alcohol, drug, or chemical abuse, dependency, or addiction and resulting mental illness.

In some contracts, the LTD carriers might combine these conditions, using a broader description such as **self-reported injuries**. As the name suggests, this category includes a range of conditions in which the diagnosis is based solely on the input of the covered employee. Without objective supporting documentation from an attending physician, benefits for most of these conditions will be terminated following the first 12 to 24 months of claim payments.

Many insurers are offering premium discounts in the 3 to 7 percent range for limitations on self-reported injuries.

An approach that limits benefits for certain types of disabilities is certain to give rise to controversy, and special condition and self-reported injury riders are no exception. Those arguing against them contend that it is unfair to discriminate against insureds based on the nature of their disability. Those in favor of such riders advance the following arguments:

- First, and most importantly, these riders help curb the recent abuses by unscrupulous claimants that have contributed to poor profitability of LTD insurers in the past several years.

- Second, they help expand coverage for currently uninsured workers by providing meaningful coverage to employers and their employees in otherwise uninsurable industries.

- Finally, with these riders employers can afford to provide employees with excellent benefits for serious disabilities, create a return-to-work incentive for the less seriously disabled, and help prevent the cost arising from potential abuses of the product.

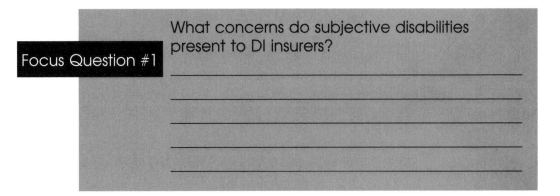

Focus Question #1

What concerns do subjective disabilities present to DI insurers?

_____

_____

_____

_____

Catastrophic Benefits Riders and Activities of Daily Living Riders

Another cost-cutting technique involves borrowing a page from the long-term care playbook. Specifically, some LTD policies contain definitions for disability that include references to **activities of daily living (ADLs)**. The six basic functions of everyday living include bathing, dressing, transferring (moving on your own from one spot to another), toileting, continence, and eating. The insured's inability to perform certain ADLs is a common benefit trigger in long-term care contracts.

One approach, sometimes referred to as a **catastrophic benefits rider**, couples an own occupation definition of disability with a definition of disability that refers to the insured's inability to perform certain ADLs. For example, for the first 24 months following injury or illness, disability might be defined as the inability to perform the duties of one's own occupation. After this initial 24-month period, disability is defined as the inability to perform one or more ADLs. A disability that requires the loss of two of six ADLs requires a rather severe condition, thus limiting the number of expected claims. While this is a more stringent definition, the benefit percentage may also increase after the initial period, in part because of the increased expenses claimants with severe disabilities are likely to experience. These riders are typically marketed to blue-collar workers and provide a reasonable rate for good long-term disability coverage.

Other LTD plans offer separate ADL benefits. Under an **activities of daily living rider**, if an employee becomes disabled and is unable to perform one or more ADLs without standby help, has a cognitive impairment, or suffers from a terminal illness, she will be eligible to receive an additional benefit. The additional benefit is based on a percentage of earnings, not to exceed a predetermined dollar amount. For example, the additional benefit could equal 10 percent of the insured's pre-disability earnings, not to exceed $3,000 per month. This type of rider appeals to white-collar workers and offers increased security but not necessarily a lower premium.

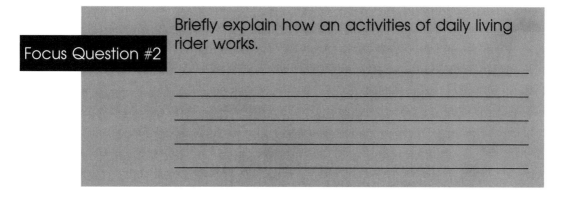

Focus Question #2

Briefly explain how an activities of daily living rider works.

Worksite Modification Rider

A disabled employee may be able to remain at work or return to work if some adjustments are made to his worksite. The **worksite modification**

rider reimburses the employer for a percentage of the expenses incurred for accommodations that allow an employee currently receiving a disability benefit to remain at work or return to work.

The sooner an employee is able to return to work, the better it is for everyone. The employee's morale is boosted, the employer's premium costs are reduced, and the insurer's operating expenses are kept in check.

⟫ COST OF LIVING OPTIONS

In Chapter 8, you learned that the initial amount of benefits is typically based on a uniform percentage of salary or wages, subject to a dollar amount cap. As compensation increases, because of merit increases or to keep pace with inflation, an employee's benefit automatically increases (at least up to the dollar amount cap). Consequently, the initial benefit an employee receives under a group DI insurance plan should reflect increases in the cost of living during the period the coverage has been in effect *prior to the onset of disability.*

But what about increases in the cost of living *during disability*? The purchasing power of the initial benefit may be eroded significantly by inflation, as illustrated in Table 9.1.

In the example in the table, where inflation was assumed to be a modest 2 percent over a 15-year period, an initial monthly benefit of $3,000 was reduced in purchasing power to only $2,261—a loss of $739 each month. That represents about a 25 percent decline in purchasing power. How many of us could afford that?

To address this concern, most insurers offer a **cost of living adjustment (COLA) rider** that is intended to keep disability benefits even with inflation. Because the increases are available without additional underwriting, the insurer typically charges an additional premium for the option itself. In fact, a controversial aspect of this option is its cost, which is typically significantly higher than the base premium. This apparently high price

Table 9.1

The Impact of Inflation on Disability Benefits

Year	Cost of Inflation at 2 Percent	Purchasing Power of Initial Benefit of $3,000
1		$3,000.00
2	$60.00	$2,940.00
3	$118.80	$2,881.20
4	$176.42	$2,823.58
5	$232.90	$2,767.10
6	$288.24	$2,711.76
7	$342.47	$2,657.53
8	$395.62	$2,604.38
9	$447.71	$2,552.29
10	$498.76	$2,501.24
11	$548.78	$2,451.22
12	$597.81	$2,402.19
13	$645.85	$2,354.15
14	$692.93	$2,307.07
15	$739.07	$2,260.93

reflects the fact that even modest rates of inflation can result in significant benefit increases. For example, a benefit of $2,000 per month could potentially increase to $3,025 in 14 years with only 3 percent inflation. That's slightly more than a 50 percent increase.

The amount of the annual benefit increase may be a fixed percentage, or it can be tied to an index, such as the Consumer Price Index (CPI), that roughly tracks inflation. The percentage increase may be based on either compound or simple interest, with simple interest being considerably less expensive. In either case, the annual percentage increase is typically capped at a maximum of 3 to 8 percent. The greater the amount of the cap, the higher the premium charged for the option.

►► ANNUITY, PENSION, AND MEDICAL BENEFIT SUPPLEMENTS

Not only does an individual's ability to meet current expenses diminish when disability strikes, but the ability to save for the future and to continue to participate in employer-sponsored benefit plans is also jeopardized. In recognition of this harsh reality, several companies have introduced riders that continue savings and contributions to employer-sponsored plans in the event of disability.

Annuity Benefit

Non-qualified annuities have taken on an increasingly important role in personal financial planning in recent years. In recognition of this fact, at least one group LTD insurer offers a **retirement plan supplement option** with its group LTD products. The option helps employees build retirement savings by:

- paying a contribution to a non-qualified annuity during periods of disability,
- continuing these payments until the employee retires or is no longer disabled, and
- paying this contribution in addition to the normal disability benefit.

The goal is to help bridge the gap created when employees are unable to contribute to their 401(k), IRA, or other retirement savings plans because of disability. The option is offered outside of the qualified retirement plan arena and is available to all employees, regardless of their participation in a retirement plan. The annuity contributions are not reduced by other income sources.

Focus Question #3

What does a retirement plan supplement option do?

a) It continues contributions to an employee pension plan.
b) It pays disability benefits through pension plans.
c) It pays contributions to a non-qualified annuity.
d) It continues employee contributions to a 401(k) plan.

Pension and Medical Supplements

As discussed in Chapter 2, many employers continue to contribute to a disabled employee's tax-qualified pension plan during a disability. Such ongoing contributions by the employer ensure that once an employee's disability benefit ceases, there are adequate benefits in the pension plan to fund retirement income needs. In recognition of the employer's ongoing cost of funding these pension contributions, some insurers offer **pension benefit riders** or separate contracts under which the disability benefit is increased by the amount of the employer's contribution, thus reimbursing the employer for its outlay.

Similarly, some insurers offer riders that continue medical insurance premiums for a disabled insured. Without the continuance of medical insurance, a disabled employee is not only subject to a loss of income but can also experience the burden of having to pay out of pocket additional medical costs associated with the disability. Typically, the **medical supplement rider** pays a pre-set dollar amount of the premium for major medical coverage.

➤➤ SURVIVOR INCOME AND CRITICAL ILLNESS BENEFITS

A disabling disease or injury may accelerate death. Although an LTD benefit provides an employee with a source of income while she remains alive, benefits cease at death. As a supplement to LTD monthly benefits and for an additional premium, some contracts provide continuing benefits to a deceased employee's survivors.

Typically, under a **survivor income benefit**, LTD benefits are reduced following death and are likely to continue for no longer than 24 months. Such benefits clearly are not intended to replace an individual's need for adequate life insurance, but rather to help survivors (including a spouse and children under the age of 21) through what may be a trying adjustment period following a breadwinner's death.

⊙━ A **critical illness benefit** provides benefits, usually in the form of a lump-sum cash payment, to employees who suffer from certain critical illnesses such as life-threatening cancer, heart attack, kidney failure, stroke, and major organ transplants. The amount of the payment is often a multiple of the monthly LTD benefit (commonly 12 times the monthly benefit), subject to a dollar amount cap. Typically, there is no restriction on the manner in which disabled employees may spend the cash payment.

Under most contracts, the critical illness benefit is payable when an insured can show that he is disabled (under the policy definition) because of one of the critical illnesses listed in the policy, and that he has satisfied the elimination period. However, at least one company makes the benefit available without the insured being disabled and satisfying an LTD elimination period, provided the employee has been diagnosed with one of the listed illnesses.

Focus Question #4	How are benefits typically paid under critical illness benefit riders? a) In a monthly benefit. b) As reimbursement for medical expenses. c) As a survivor benefit. d) In a lump-sum cash payment.

▶▶ SUPPLEMENTAL EXECUTIVE BENEFITS

In group DI insurance, different benefits are often provided to different classes of employees. Employers are often especially interested in providing supplemental DI insurance benefits to those executives whose talents and hard work are most responsible for the company's success. Several common approaches to addressing these employers' objectives are discussed below.

Traditional Combination Plans

An issue that often arises with group LTD coverage is that the dollar benefit cap, while adequate for rank-and-file employees, inappropriately limits highly paid executives' benefits. For example, an LTD plan that provides a monthly benefit of 60 percent of salary or wages up to a maximum of $5,000 per month works well for employees earning under $100,000, but is less than adequate for executives earning over that amount, especially those highly compensated executives earning $150,000 or more. A traditional **combination plan** (also known as a carve-out or wrap-around plan) combines group LTD with individual DI coverage for executives. The result can be a win-win for all involved.

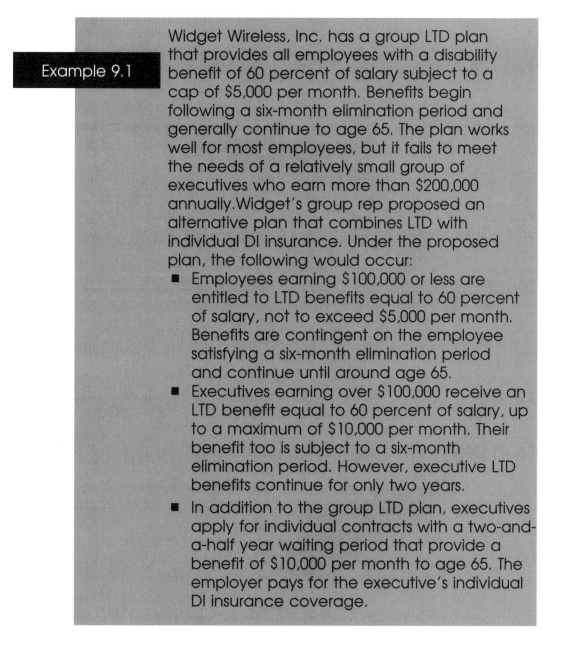

Example 9.1

Widget Wireless, Inc. has a group LTD plan that provides all employees with a disability benefit of 60 percent of salary subject to a cap of $5,000 per month. Benefits begin following a six-month elimination period and generally continue to age 65. The plan works well for most employees, but it fails to meet the needs of a relatively small group of executives who earn more than $200,000 annually. Widget's group rep proposed an alternative plan that combines LTD with individual DI insurance. Under the proposed plan, the following would occur:

- Employees earning $100,000 or less are entitled to LTD benefits equal to 60 percent of salary, not to exceed $5,000 per month. Benefits are contingent on the employee satisfying a six-month elimination period and continue until around age 65.

- Executives earning over $100,000 receive an LTD benefit equal to 60 percent of salary, up to a maximum of $10,000 per month. Their benefit too is subject to a six-month elimination period. However, executive LTD benefits continue for only two years.

- In addition to the group LTD plan, executives apply for individual contracts with a two-and-a-half year waiting period that provide a benefit of $10,000 per month to age 65. The employer pays for the executive's individual DI insurance coverage.

A plan like that in the example maximizes benefits while controlling costs. A group LTD plan that provides a maximum $10,000 benefit for only two years for the executives is relatively inexpensive. Because the individual contracts have a two-and-a-half year elimination period, premiums for these policies are also relatively inexpensive. At the same time, the executives receive a much more valuable dollar benefit under the combination plan than under the straight group plan. Furthermore, the definition of disability under an executive's individual policy may be more generous than that of the group LTD plan, and unlike the group coverage, the individual policy is fully portable. If the executive is downsized or quits, she can take the policy along to the next job or to self-employment without any further medical or financial underwriting.

Focus Question #5

What are the circumstances under which a traditional combination plan would make sense?

_____

_____

_____

_____

_____

Buy-Ups

A **buy-up** refers to a plan where employees are given the opportunity to acquire individual DI coverage in addition to the employer's group LTD coverage. By sponsoring the additional individual coverage, agreeing to deduct the premiums for it from employees' payroll, and offering it to most or all employees, the employer should be able to receive a premium discount and/or underwriting concessions from the insurer. These discounts and concessions get passed along to the employees.

As an example, consider a case where a company provides a group LTD plan that pays a benefit equal to 60 percent of salary up to a maximum of $7,500 per month to age 65 or thereabouts. While the plan meets the needs of rank-and-file employees, it falls short for highly compensated executives.

An alternative is to give each employee the option to purchase as much individual coverage as he qualifies for through payroll deduction. Under this alternative, there is little or no hard-dollar cost to the company, just the soft-dollar cost of allowing insurance company representatives to meet with employees on company time. The benefit to the employees, of course, is that they are able to acquire individual coverage at a discount.

Executive DI

Group LTD does a great job of providing a layer of income protection to all employees at reasonable rates, and for many employees paid on an hourly or salaried basis, this level of protection is enough to enable them to weather a disabling condition. However, for those employees who earn more than the LTD plan's covered earnings or derive income from bonuses or incentive compensation, group LTD alone may not provide adequate coverage.

As discussed above, individual disability insurance has been a good solution for under-insurance, but it is not always affordable, and applicants must complete an exhaustive underwriting process that may ultimately result in a decline. A recent development in disability insurance is **executive disability income insurance (executive DI)**, which works with group LTD. Offered on a multi-life basis—usually 10 or more employees—executive DI is like individual DI insurance in that it provides flexible individual disability coverage. But it also offers affordable rates, streamlined underwriting, and guaranteed issue—characteristics normally associated with group coverage.

The starting point for an executive DI plan is determining if employees in a certain category need more than the maximum monthly benefit provided by the group DI plan. Earnings, title, or other criteria may define this class of employees. Once the need for additional disability income replacement is established and an executive DI plan is chosen as the right approach, the insurer crafts coverage to meet the specific needs of an employer group.

Executive DI plan designs include all the features of an individual disability contract, but they typically use standard provisions and unisex rates for all participants. Plan provisions such as elimination periods, maximum benefit periods, and limitations dovetail with the LTD plan to produce consistent results at claim time.

Even if premiums are paid by the employer, executive DI policies are generally issued to and owned by the covered employee, making them fully portable. Multi-life discounts are generally portable too, although this practice varies by carrier.

Service is an important consideration with these plans. Many executive DI plans are offered as an employee benefit and administered through the benefits manager. Carriers that provide a coordinated executive DI and group LTD plan can reduce the burden to the employer through streamlined underwriting and administration. Employees should also benefit from consistent claims decisions and avoid duplicate information requests when the same claim analyst adjudicates both claims.

▸▸ CONVERSIONS

An often cited concern with group LTD is its purported lack of portability. As a general rule, the coverage ceases when employment terminates. **Conversion** coverage provides employees who leave a plan, particularly those who are changing jobs, with LTD coverage after their departure. Demand for this feature has risen, as the workforce has become more transient and individual DI coverage more difficult to obtain.

Although conversions of group LTD coverage to individual DI insurance are becoming more common, this has not always been the case. Many carriers have struggled with the administrative functions associated with conversions and are uncomfortable with the risk management aspects of converted policies. After all, if an employee's income is lost because of a layoff or voluntary termination on the employee's part, there is nothing to insure.

Recently, however, some insurers have introduced long-term disability conversion products that provide full turn-key administrative services and reinsurance capacity for disability conversion policies. Administrative services often include application and eligibility review, policy billing, financial management, medical underwriting, claim management, and toll-free telephone support for employees who have converted their LTD coverage.

⟫SUMMARY

A variety of special riders and contractual features are available to help group salespeople and marketers custom-design group LTD plans to meet their clients' needs. Cost-cutting options include limitations on benefits for special conditions, riders that define disability as the inability to perform certain ADLs, and benefits for changes to an employee's worksite that hasten a return to work. A COLA rider allows a claimant's disability benefits to keep pace with inflation. Other special riders provide for contributions to non-qualified annuities, health insurance plans, and pension plans, even while an employee is disabled. Survivor and critical illness benefits make cash payments to survivors or claimants in the event of death or critical illness. Where traditional group LTD plans fall short of meeting the needs of highly compensated executives, plans that combine LTD with individual DI insurance and relatively new executive DI plans are available. Finally, where portability of the group LTD plan is a concern, recent designs facilitate conversion and the administration of converted contracts.

Key Terms 🔑

Activities of daily living (ADLs)
Activities of daily living rider
Buy-up
Catastrophic benefits rider
Combination plan
Conversion
Cost of living adjustment (COLA) rider
Critical illness benefit
Executive disability income insurance (executive DI)
Medical supplement rider
Pension benefit rider
Plan design
Policy rider
Retirement plan supplement option
Self-reported injury
Special conditions
Subjective disability
Survivor income benefit
Worksite modification rider

▶▶ REVIEW QUESTIONS

1. When an employer is seeking to cover most disabilities but also contain costs as much as possible, what feature(s) might you recommend?

2. What are the arguments for and against riders and contractual provisions that limit benefits for subjective and other disabilities?

3. LiteBrite Corporation offers a pension benefit to employees as well as a group disability benefit. LiteBrite wants to continue pension contributions for disabled employees, so that they have a retirement benefit when disability benefits run out. However, LiteBrite's benefits manager believes the cost of doing so would be prohibitive. What solution could you offer?

4. The president of Hickory Furniture, Inc. recently saw his wife, who did not work at the company, suffer through a difficult bout of cancer before finally succumbing to the disease. He's asked you what the company could do to help employees who suffer from cancer and other terrible diseases. What can you suggest? How would it work?

5. BigTime, Inc.'s group LTD plan provides all employees with a disability benefit of 60 percent of salary, subject to a cap of $5,000 per month. The plan works well for most employees, but it fails to meet the needs of a relatively small group of executives who earn more than $200,000 annually. Briefly describe the approaches available for addressing the executives' needs.

▶▶ ANSWERS TO FOCUS QUESTIONS

Focus Question #1—These disabilities are more difficult to verify than physical disabilities that can be confirmed by readily observable documentation such as X-rays and lab results. Another consideration is the cost associated with these disabilities—treatments can be expensive, and the effectiveness of certain treatments remains in doubt. A third consideration is that motivation plays a significant role in the healing process with these types of disabilities, and a lengthy benefit period removes much of the motivation to overcome the illness, to the detriment of the employer, the employee, and the insurer.

Focus Question #2—Under an activities of daily living rider, if an employee becomes disabled and is unable to perform one or more ADLs without standby help, has a cognitive impairment, or suffers from a terminal illness, she will be eligible to receive an additional benefit. The additional benefit is based on a percentage of earnings, not to exceed a predetermined dollar amount. For example, the additional benefit could equal 10 percent of the insured's pre-disability earnings, not to exceed $3,000 per month.

Focus Question #3—c

Focus Question #4—d

Focus Question #5—An issue that often arises with group LTD coverage is that the dollar benefit cap, while adequate for rank-and-file employees, inappropriately limits highly paid executives' benefits. For example, an LTD plan that provides a monthly benefit of 60 percent of salary or wages up to a maximum of $5,000 per month works well for employees earning under $100,000, but is less than adequate for executives earning over that amount, especially those highly compensated executives earning $150,000 or more. A traditional combination plan (also known as a carve-out or wrap-around plan) combines group LTD with individual DI coverage for executives. The result can be a win-win for all involved.

►► ANSWERS TO REVIEW QUESTIONS

1. The employer should consider adding a special conditions rider to limit benefits for certain conditions that are especially hard to verify and/or treat. An activities of daily living rider and/or a catastrophic benefits rider can also reduce costs, by using a definition of disability that is made restrictive because of its reliance on the insured's inability to perform certain ADLs. A worksite modification rider facilitates an employee's return to work, thus increasing employee productivity, improving employer profitability, and stabilizing premiums.

2. An approach that limits benefits for certain types of disabilities is certain to give rise to controversy, and special condition and self-reported injury riders are no exception. Those arguing against them contend that it is unfair to discriminate against insureds based on the

nature of their disability. Those in favor of such riders advance the following arguments:

- First, and most importantly, these riders help curb the recent abuses by unscrupulous claimants that have contributed to poor profitability of LTD insurers in the past several years.

- Second, they help expand coverage for currently uninsured workers by providing meaningful coverage to employers and their employees in otherwise uninsurable industries.

- Finally, with these riders employers can afford to provide employees with excellent benefits for serious disabilities, create a return-to-work incentive for the less seriously disabled, and help prevent the cost arising from potential abuses of the product.

3. A pension benefit rider could be just the ticket. Under this rider, the disability benefit is increased by the amount of the employer's contribution to the pension plan, thus reimbursing the employer for its outlay.

4. A critical illness benefit provides benefits, usually in the form of a lump-sum cash payment, to employees who suffer from certain critical illnesses such as life-threatening cancer, heart attack, kidney failure, stroke, and major organ transplants. The amount of the payment is often a multiple of the monthly LTD benefit (commonly 12 times the monthly benefit), subject to a dollar amount cap. Typically, there is no restriction on the manner in which disabled employees may spend the cash payment.

   Under most contracts, the critical illness benefit is payable when an insured can show that he is disabled (under the policy definition) because of one of the critical illnesses listed in the policy, and that he has satisfied the elimination period. However, at least one company makes the benefit available without the insured being disabled and satisfying an LTD elimination period, provided the employee has been diagnosed with one of the listed illnesses.

5. A traditional combination plan combines group LTD for all employees with individual DI insurance for executives. The individual insurance allows executives to receive coverage that is in excess of the group benefit, or that is in lieu of the group benefit where an executive's

group benefit period has expired. A buy-up allows executives who wish larger amounts of coverage to simply buy as much individual DI insurance as they qualify for and can afford. Executive DI, like individual DI insurance, provides flexible individual disability coverage, but it also offers affordable rates, streamlined underwriting, and guaranteed issue.

10
Claims Administration— Adjudicating The Claim

>> OVERVIEW

The insurer's promise to pay benefits under both STD and LTD plans is conditioned on the participant submitting a claim for benefits based on the procedures described in the policy and meeting the policy's precise definition of disability. From the insurer's perspective, making appropriate claims decisions and managing the claim process is at least as important as pricing and underwriting. After all, poor underwriting and pricing merely create a *risk* of higher than expected claims or lower than expected profits. On the other hand, poor claims administration results in the *actual payment* of claims that for any number of reasons may not be valid. This translates into actual lost profits and a strain on surplus.

Several factors have placed an even greater emphasis on claims administration. First, economic conditions have led to layoffs, which tend to lead to an increase in DI claims. Second, disability advocacy campaigns and legislation such as the Americans with Disabilities Act have sensitized employers and employees alike to disability issues and made them more tolerant of disability claims. Third, less skepticism about mental disabilities, including clinical depression and **post-traumatic stress disability (PTSD)**, has led to a larger number of subjective claims, which tend to be more difficult to adjudicate and are likely to have a longer duration than other claims.

Claims administration includes:

- **claim adjudication**, the process of deciding the validity of a claim;
- paying valid claims;
- denying invalid ones; and
- **case management**—managing the disability case clinically or vocationally, pursuing other sources of income for the claimant, etc.

Case management has taken on increasing importance in recent years and has become more prevalent in the group DI insurance field. This important topic is considered in Chapter 11.

In the area of claims administration, the insurer is guided by several considerations, including the company's claims strategy, state laws and regulations, and industry guidelines. The claims strategy is usually determined by senior management and seeks to balance insurer financial considerations with the interest of claimants. Model statutes, developed by the **National Association of Insurance Commissioners (NAIC)** and adopted in a number of states, the Unfair Claims Settlement Practices Act, and the Unfair Trade Practices Model Act set forth guidelines for the prompt and fair settlement of insurance claims.

For a variety of reasons, including in relatively rare instances claimant fraud, claims are sometime denied. In these cases, the claimant may seek relief through an administrative process or in the courts. In some cases, the claimant's appeal or litigation will result in payment of the claim or settlement of the lawsuit.

For claimants, the claim process can be intimidating. Often the claimant lacks an understanding of the terms of her policy and the claim adjudication process. A claimant who is no longer working or drawing a paycheck can find herself having to deal with strangers in what seems to be a large, impersonal insurance company. Claimants are often confused about their coverage, their rights, and the claim process. All of this makes communication with the claimant critical throughout the claim adjudication process. It is important for the claims professional to educate the claimant about the policy and the process of adjudication, to notify her of the current status of adjudication efforts, and to facilitate information gathering.

The broker or agent who sold the plan also has a stake in the claim process. The salesperson is identified with the insurer, so if the insurer is viewed as mistreating an employee or acting improperly, the salesperson may be blamed for the problem. This can cost the agent or broker not only the particular coverage in question, but also any other business he may have with that employer.

Objectives

After reading this chapter and completing the accompanying exercises, you will be able to:

- explain the steps in the DI claim adjudication process,
- describe the handling of fraudulent disability claims, and
- discuss considerations involved in claim litigation and settlement.

Chapter 11 focuses on the process of ongoing case management following approval of a claim and the current emphasis on rehabilitation and return to work.

➤➤ THE CLAIM ADJUDICATION PROCESS

The steps in the claim adjudication process are straightforward. They include:

- filing the claim,
- evaluating the claim, and
- making the claim decision.

Each of these is discussed below.

Filing the Claim

The claim process begins when an employee suffers what is believed to be a disabling injury or illness and submits an initial claim for benefits. The form that is used is referred to as the **claim form**, and it is usually available from the employer's human resources or personnel department.

Although claim forms differ from insurer to insurer, the typical form contains one section for the insured to complete, another section for the attending physician, and another for the employer. The claim form requests information concerning the dates of disability, the nature of the disability, physicians and hospitals providing treatment, and the expected length of disability. With group insurance, information concerning hire and termination dates, salary or wages, occupation, job duties, possible return to work, and other sources of income is requested from the employer.

There is usually a contractual requirement that the claim form be filed shortly following the onset of the disability, but insurance company practices tend to offer flexibility in recognizing claims filed after the time period specified in the policy has expired. The requirement that claims be filed promptly stems from several concerns:

- A late claim may make it more difficult for the insurer to find proof of the disability, yet make it hard to be reasonably certain that proof of disability is not available.

- The claimant's condition may have worsened (or improved) during the time elapsed since the claimed onset of disability, making it hard to assess how disabled the claimant might have been earlier.

- A late filing may make it more difficult for the insurer to help the claimant mitigate the loss, thus increasing the insurer's liability from what it would or could have been had the claimant filed on a timely basis.

The claim form may be submitted on paper via traditional mail delivery or, in today's electronic world, via fax or online. Some insurers may accept claims for short-term disabilities over the phone. Following receipt of the claim form by the insurer, a claim file is established and a **claims examiner** takes responsibility for resolving the claim.

In many cases, it will be unclear to the insured and/or the agent whether the disability will last beyond the elimination period. Even so, most sales professionals believe that the claim form should be filed promptly. Evaluation of the claim can take some time, and the sooner the claim is filed, the sooner the evaluation can begin. Also, filing the claim is likely to provide the insured with peace of mind at a troubling time. He can rest assured that if the disability does last beyond the elimination period, there will be little or no further delay in receiving benefits.

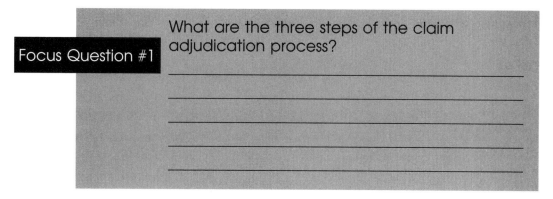

Focus Question #1

What are the three steps of the claim adjudication process?

_____

_____

_____

_____

_____

Evaluating the Claim

The claim process continues with claim evaluation. Although the steps are discussed here in sequential order, the process is often more iterative than it might seem from this discussion. Keep in mind that with disability insurance, the insured may file more than one claim under the contract. Consequently, the evaluation of a claim involves a consideration not just of the current claim, but of the entire claims record. Furthermore, as will be discussed more fully in Chapter 11, claim evaluation is really an ongoing process with modern disability income insurance, given the emphasis on residual benefits, rehabilitation, and return to work.

Confirming Eligibility for Coverage

A first step is for the claims examiner to confirm eligibility for coverage. It must be verified that the disability occurred following expiration of the probationary period and before any termination of coverage resulting from termination of employment. An employee whose disability arose before the probationary period was completed will not be entitled to benefits. As you recall from Chapter 8, this period can be as long as six months or a year for LTD. Also, if the disabling event occurs even one day after the employee's employment has ended, coverage will not be in effect.

Verifying Compliance with the Elimination Period

A second step is for the claims examiner to verify that the claimant has satisfied the elimination period. Again, as you recall from Chapter 8, it is common for both STD and LTD plans to require that the disability continue for some minimum period before eligibility for benefits can be established.

Determining Eligibility for Benefits

A third step in the process is for the claims examiner to determine whether the insured's health status meets the definition of disability in the contract. As discussed in Chapter 8, for STD an own occupation definition of total disability is most common (although STD policies containing provisions for partial disability are not uncommon these days). Long-term plans are likely to combine own occupation and any occupation definitions of disability. For example, during the first 24 to 36 months of disability, an employee may be eligible for benefits when he is unable to perform the substantial and material duties of his own occupation. Following this period, the definition shifts to an any occupation definition. Under a contract such as this, the claims examiner must evaluate the nature of the disability both at the time of the initial claim and at the time when the definition shifts. In a few cases, presumptive disability may be applicable.

In addition, if the contract contains a loss of earnings provision, the claims examiner must request financial information from the claimant sufficient to support the claim that the disability has caused the requisite loss of earnings. The claimant may be required to produce pay stubs, bank statements, and/or tax forms such as W-2s and 1099s.

An **attending physician's statement (APS)** is a document used to help the claims examiner make a determination concerning whether the claimant's condition warrants payment of benefits. For better or worse, the attending physician's statement is only occasionally adequate **proof of claim**. Attending physicians usually have little awareness of the occupational requirements of the claimant. Also, attending physicians may not be skilled at assessing limitations to the claimant's activity and may accept the claimant's comments at face value.

In addition to the APS, the claims examiner may request medical records. The most common reasons for requesting medical records are to obtain adequate proof of claim and to evaluate the quality of care received by the claimant for the purpose of assessing whether anything can be done to improve the claimant's probability of recovery or sufficient improvement to return to work. The claims examiner may also seek medical records to ascertain whether disability results from an injury or illness. This may be important where, for example, the STD contract requires no waiting period for a disability resulting from an injury, but requires a seven-day wait for disabilities caused by sickness.

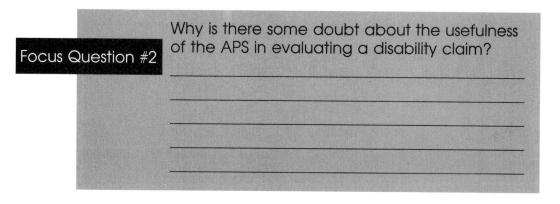

Focus Question #2

Why is there some doubt about the usefulness of the APS in evaluating a disability claim?

In many cases, a **claim investigation** may be required. An investigation may be initiated when a **red flag** triggers the claims examiner's suspicion. Red flags include the following:

- self-reported symptoms without objective physical findings,
- complaints of pain in excess of objective physical findings,
- restrictions and limitations on activity not consistent with the diagnosis,
- failure to seek regular care of a physician when appropriate,
- the disability certified is outside of the attending physician's expertise or specialty,
- non-compliance with medical recommendations,
- multiple missed medical appointments,
- significant discrepancies among treating physicians, and
- physician shopping.[1]

The claims investigator may engage in any or all of the following activities:

- Reviewing the existing medical records for evidence of falsification. One of the ways claimants and/or their physicians commit fraud is to falsify medical records in an effort to show that a condition is more serious than it actually is, or that its impact on the claimant's ability to work is more severe than it is.

- Reviewing financial records, perhaps with the assistance of a CPA. Determining the amount of a claimant's applicable earnings both pre- and post-disability comes into play with residual disability benefits. The determination of earnings is usually straightforward for blue-collar wage earners and employees receiving straight salary compensation, but it can be more challenging for senior managers when at least a portion of a claimant's earnings are incentive-based or deferred.

- Ordering an **independent medical examination (IME)** by a physician other than the claimant's attending physician at the insurer's expense. This is especially appropriate where the disability is likely to be long-term and/or the claimed disability stems from a subjective condition such as depression.

- Ordering inspection reports to verify occupation, income, and other insurance coverages.

- Making telephone calls directly to the insured.

- Making telephone calls to the employer, usually to verify eligibility for coverage and income and to obtain information concerning the claimant's ability to engage in a transitional return-to-work program.

- Conducting **personal interviews** with the claimant and other involved parties, such as the insured's physician.

- Conducting surveillance of the claimant, including video surveillance, especially where there is suspicion of fraud.

In addition to the above activities, the insurer may seek to require the claimant to undergo a **functional capacity evaluation (FCE)**. An FCE is usually conducted by a physical or occupational therapist with a view to determining whether the claimant can perform certain activities. One concern with these evaluations is that the claimant (or her legal representative) may contend that they are not examinations, but rather tests. Chances are the disability contract requires the insured to submit to examinations but does not require her to undergo more invasive procedures such as tests.

A legal issue raised by the review of medical records, interviews with third parties (such as employers and physicians), and surveillance is invasion of the claimant's privacy. Both state and federal laws protect the claimant's privacy rights and give rise to a cause of action against the insurer when those rights are violated.

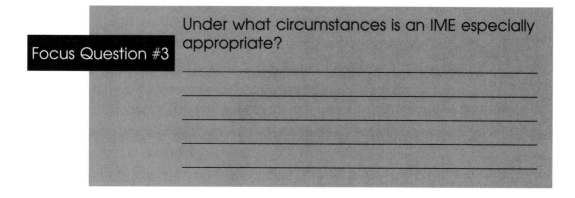

Focus Question #3 — Under what circumstances is an IME especially appropriate?

Interestingly, some have observed that while both group and individual DI insurers take a similar approach to verifying disability, there are significant differences between group and individual disability claims-handling operations.[2] In general, group and especially group LTD operations tend to put greater emphasis on person-to-person contact with both claimant and attending physician than do their individual counterparts. Such person-to-person contact:

- sets appropriate expectations about what is possible in terms of the claimant's return to work,

- keeps the claimant focused on recovery, and

- allows the insurer to gather *real-time* claim status information. In essence, these contacts are viewed as communication strategy *and* assessment strategy.

Another significant area of difference involves examinations. With individual DI insurance, independent examinations and surveillance tend to be the tools of last resort. Individual DI claims examiners generally do not call for independent exams early in the claim process, and they tend not to use the exams at all unless they are suspicious about a claim. By contrast, in group and especially group LTD operations, claimants are often told up front that they may be asked to undergo an independent medical exam as a second opinion that will help more accurately assess the potential for recovery. If an FCE is used, however, it is not sprung on claimants with little or no notice. Group examiners point out that the information gathered from medical records and directly from person-to-person contact with the claimant before the exam can be compared with the results of the exam to obtain a better overall claim assessment.

Ruling Out Exclusions

Another task is to ascertain that no exclusions apply that would prevent payment of benefits. As you recall from Chapter 8, both STD and LTD plans contain a variety of exclusions, including disabilities caused by self-inflicted injuries and those for which the claimant is not under the care of a physician. In addition, LTD plans often contain exclusions for preexisting conditions.

A typical definition of a preexisting condition is one for which the claimant was treated in the three months prior to policy issue, provided that the disability begins within 12 months after policy issue. For the claim to be denied, the disability must generally be caused by the preexisting condition (or in some policies, by that condition or any related condition). Often, there is also a **treatment-free provision** stating that a condition that otherwise would be considered preexisting will not be deemed preexisting if the claimant goes at least three months without treatment for it.

Making the Claim Decision

After all the facts are in, the claims examiner makes a decision to pay or deny the claim. In some instances, this decision is straightforward. For example, if the disability is caused by a preexisting condition or the insured failed to satisfy the elimination period, the claim will be denied. On the other hand, if the disability is one clearly covered under the contract, the claim will be approved and benefit payments will begin, usually 30 days following expiration of the elimination period.

If a decision is made to pay benefits, the insurer will require the filing of an updated supplemental claim form, physician's statement, and/or a

continuance of disability form as the disability continues. The nature of this form and the frequency with which updated certification of disability is required depends on the expectations about the possible recovery of the claimant, as well as on the necessity of checking to ensure that appropriate medical care is being received. For long-term claims with no recovery date in sight, every three or six months is a common frequency, and every 12 months is not uncommon. Of course, if the claimant's physician projects a quick recovery, or if the insurer's expectation given the claimant's condition, age, etc. is for a fairly rapid recovery, then an updated proof of claim would be requested with greater frequency.

As discussed in Chapter 11, the increased emphasis on return-to-work programs has made ongoing evaluation of a claimant's situation integral to the claims process. As rehabilitation is administered and as the claimant begins to transition back to work, monitoring both physical health and earnings is at the heart of claims management.

As will also be discussed in Chapter 11, another aspect of ongoing claims management is coordination of the benefits payable with the receipt of other benefits. Typically, group disability insurance benefits are reduced by Social Security, workers' compensation, state temporary disability income benefits, and other employer-sponsored disability benefits. Monitoring the receipt of these benefits by a claimant and coordinating their payment with DI insurance benefits presents another challenge to the claims professional.

▶▶ FRAUDULENT CLAIMS

The large majority of claims submitted by insureds are bona fide. In most instances, the insured honestly represents his medical history and condition and his financial situation. In most cases, the insured has suffered an injury or illness resulting in an inability to work and genuinely believes he is entitled to policy benefits.

On the other hand, there are a few situations where the insured engages in behavior that is anything but honest and genuine. In these situations, the insured is out to defraud the insurer into providing coverage and/or paying benefits that would not have been provided or paid had the insurance company been accurately informed.

What Is Fraud?

Fraud is a **tort**, a civil wrong that may give rise to a claim for recovery of damages or serve as an insurer defense against a claim for benefits. Fraud may also be the basis for criminal penalties, depending on the nature of the fraud, the dollar amount involved, and the applicable state and federal laws.

In general, fraud has several elements:

- a material statement of fact is made;
- the statement is false;
- the individual making the false statement intends to deceive or mislead the insurer to which the statement is made with the expectation of receiving something of value—in this case disability income insurance coverage or benefits; and
- the insurer to which the false statement is made relies on the statement to its detriment.

The key element that distinguishes fraud from mere negligence or reckless-ness is the *intent* to deceive. It is one thing to sincerely forget or misunder-stand, or to be unaware of facts one should perhaps know. It is an entirely different matter to mean to deceive someone with the expectation of gaining something in return.

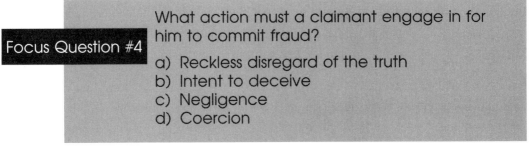

Focus Question #4

What action must a claimant engage in for him to commit fraud?
a) Reckless disregard of the truth
b) Intent to deceive
c) Negligence
d) Coercion

Disability income insurance fraud typically takes the form of **application fraud** or **claim fraud**.

Application Fraud

In group DI insurance, the employer is the applicant and typically there is little or no individual underwriting (financial or medical) performed on the employees. However, there still remains the potential for fraud. In applications for group disability insurance, the critical considerations include:

■ the nature of the employer's industry,

■ the nature of the employer's business,

■ the employer's geographical location,

■ the length of time the employer has been in business,

■ the employer's financial status, and

■ the information contained in the employee census (including compensation, age and occupation distribution, and employment dates).

A misrepresentation about any of these matters may be considered a **material misrepresentation** and may amount to fraud.

Claim Fraud

The key issues in disability claim fraud are whether the claimant has made a misrepresentation to the insurer concerning a disability claim and whether that misrepresentation is material to the insurer's claim decision.

Misrepresentations in the claim process fall into two categories:

■ medical misrepresentations, and

■ financial, income, or occupation misrepresentations.

The most common kind of disability claim fraud involves misrepresentations about the claimant's disability, medical condition, and/or **restrictions** and **limitations** on her activities. Limitations relate to those activities that the claimant is not physically or mentally capable of doing because of the disabling condition. Restrictions relate to those activities that the claimant should not do because they would aggravate or worsen the condition.

Exaggerations or completely false information about the claimant's condition and purported symptoms are particularly troubling with **subjective**

disabilities. These are disabilities for which there is no medical test or objective medical protocol available to substantiate the existence (or non-existence) of the condition or its symptoms. In claims based on subjective conditions, the treating physician relies largely on histories and symptom statements provided by the claimant. This leads to one of the most challenging aspects of this kind of fraudulent claim—determining whether the claimant's physician is also a perpetrator of fraud, or merely a strong advocate for the patient.

In other claim fraud cases, the claimant misrepresents pre-disability and post-disability occupation, income, and finances. Because group insurance benefits are typically a percentage of pre-disability income, and because post-disability earnings come into play in determining a claimant's residual benefits, misrepresentations about such matters are considered material.

▶▶ THE REGULATORY AND LEGAL ENVIRONMENT

Claims handling does not take place in a vacuum. There are state laws that apply to insurers in their handling of claims and to the situations where insurers and claimants have genuine disagreements about whether benefits should be paid and/or the amount and duration of benefits.

State Regulation

Both the Unfair Claims Settlement Practices Act and the Unfair Trade Practices Model Act, developed by the National Association of Insurance Commissioners and adopted by most states, set forth guidelines for the prompt and fair settlement of insurance claims.

These laws require that a claim file and accompanying records be maintained for the calendar year in which the claim is closed and for three years thereafter. The claim file must be maintained so that it shows the inception, handling, and disposition of each claim. Also, the claim file must be sufficiently clear and specific that pertinent events and the dates of these events can be reconstructed. One purpose of these requirements is that if the claimant decides to sue, his attorney will be able to discover the insurer's file for purposes of the lawsuit.

For disability income insurance, a claim file must include the notice of claim, claim forms, medical records, proofs of loss, correspondence to and from claimants or their representatives, claim investigation documentation, and claim handling logs. It also must include any written communication, document, or recorded telephone communication related to the handling of the claim and any other documentation necessary to support claims-handling activity.

Insurers are also required to maintain procedures for complaint handling and complaint records. The complaint records must include a **complaint log** or register in addition to the actual written complaints. The complaint log or register is required to show the total number of complaints for the current year and the three years immediately preceding; the classification of each complaint by line of insurance and by complainant (such as insured, state insurance department, third party, etc.); the nature of each complaint; the insurer's disposition of each complaint; and the complaint number assigned by the state insurance department, if applicable.

As a general rule, the insurer is required to have a procedure for handling each complaint, including an appeals procedure.

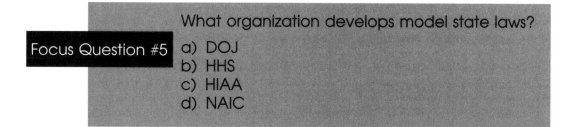

Focus Question #5

What organization develops model state laws?

a) DOJ
b) HHS
c) HIAA
d) NAIC

Litigation and Settlement

Recent years have seen an increase in litigation on the part of claimants. Part of what is driving this growth in lawsuits is the ever-increasing complexity of contractual rights and obligations created by policy features. As the definition of disability becomes more sophisticated and as concepts such as partial and residual disability come into play, disagreements are inevitable. Other contributing factors, alluded to earlier, are changing attitudes toward disability and the increasing number of subjective claims, which are difficult to verify.

The reality is that litigation is expensive and time-consuming. Consequently, it is often in the interest of both insurers and claimants to agree to an **out-of-court settlement**. The settlement may take the form of a cash benefit, or it may be a **structured settlement** that includes not only cash benefits but also job retraining, workplace modification, and coordination with other benefits.

It is important to keep in mind that the courts tend to construe contractual language against the insurer and in favor of the insured. The reason for this is that insurance contracts are classified as **contracts of adhesion**. Under a contract of adhesion, one party determines the contractual language and the other party has little or no negotiating power.

If the insurer denies a claim, a settlement is not reached, and a court eventually finds in favor of the claimant, the insurer will be required to pay **compensatory damages**. Compensatory damages indemnify the insured for the amount of the loss suffered and are likely to be roughly equal to the amount of benefits that would have been paid to the insured had the claim not been denied.

In some states and in some cases, **punitive damages** may be assessed. Punitive damages are awarded when the claimant is able to show that the insurer demonstrated bad faith in denying the claim. Bad faith arises in several contexts. The insurer may show a pattern of denying a certain type of claim without regard to the underlying facts. Or the insurer may refuse to pay where the validity of the claim is clear. Or the insurer may simply drag its feet, refusing to pay but refusing to deny the claim outright. Punitive damage awards can be several times the amount of the compensatory damages and are intended to be large enough to deter the insurer from engaging in bad faith behavior in the future.

➤➤ SUMMARY

Claim adjudication and management are key to the success of an insurer's group DI line of business. The claim adjudication process involves filing the claim in a timely manner, evaluating the claim, and making a claim decision. Although most claims are bona fide, claim fraud is a growing concern for insurers. To demonstrate fraud, an insurer must show that the claimant acted with intent to deceive for the purpose of obtaining coverage or benefits to which she was not entitled. State laws require insurers to maintain claim files and implement procedures for complaints and appeals. In those instances where claim decisions cannot be resolved amicably, litigation may result. Insurers have been held liable for both compensatory and punitive damages and in many cases may choose to settle out of court rather than litigate.

Key Terms 🔑

Application fraud
Attending physician's
    statement (APS)
Case management
Claim adjudication
Claim form
Claim fraud
Claim investigation
Claims examiner
Compensatory
    damages
Complaint log
Continuance of
    disability form
Contract of adhesion
Functional capacity
    evaluation (FCE)
Independent medical
    examination (IME)
Limitation

Material
    misrepresentation
National Association
    of Insurance
    Commissioners
    (NAIC)
Out-of-court
    settlement
Personal interview
Post-traumatic stress
    disability (PTSD)
Proof of claim
Punitive damages
Red flag
Restriction
Structured settlement
Subjective disability
Tort
Treatment-free
    provision

▸▸ REVIEW QUESTIONS

1. Why should insurers be concerned about late claims?

2. What red flags indicate the need for a claim investigation?

3. In what ways does the claim adjudication process for individual DI insurance differ from that for group insurance?

4. As a general rule, an insurer is required to have procedures for handling complaints. Describe these procedures.

5. Describe compensatory and punitive damages.

>> ANSWERS TO FOCUS QUESTIONS

Focus Question #1—Filing the claim, evaluating the claim, and making the claim decision.

Focus Question #2—Attending physicians usually have little awareness of the occupational requirements of the claimant. Also, attending physicians may not be skilled at assessing limitations to the claimant's activity and may accept the claimant's comments at face value.

Focus Question #3—An IME is especially appropriate where the disability is likely to be long-term and/or the claimed disability stems from a subjective condition such as depression.

Focus Question #4—b

Focus Question #5—d

>> ANSWERS TO REVIEW QUESTIONS

1. ■ A late claim may make it more difficult for the insurer to find proof of the disability, yet make it hard to be reasonably certain that proof of disability is not available.

   ■ The claimant's condition may have worsened (or improved) during the time elapsed since the claimed onset of disability, making it hard to assess how disabled the claimant might have been earlier.

   ■ A late filing may make it more difficult for the insurer to help the claimant mitigate the loss, thus increasing the insurer's liability from what it would or could have been had the claimant filed on a timely basis.

2. ■ Self-reported symptoms without objective physical findings,
   ■ complaints of pain in excess of objective physical findings,
   ■ restrictions and limitations on activity not consistent with the diagnosis,
   ■ failure to seek regular care of a physician when appropriate,
   ■ the disability certified is outside of the attending physician's expertise or specialty,
   ■ non-compliance with medical recommendations,
   ■ multiple missed medical appointments,
   ■ significant discrepancies among treating physicians, and
   ■ physician shopping.

3. In general, group and especially group LTD operations tend to put greater emphasis on person-to-person contact with both claimant and attending physician than do their individual counterparts.

   Another significant area of difference involves examinations. With individual DI insurance, independent examinations and surveillance tend to be the tools of last resort. Individual DI claims examiners generally do not call for independent exams early in the claim process, and they tend not to use the exams at all unless they are suspicious about a claim. By contrast, in group and especially group LTD operations, claimants are often told up front that they may be asked to undergo an independent medical exam as a second opinion that will help to more accurately assess the potential for recovery.

4. The complaint records must include a complaint log or register in addition to the actual written complaints. The complaint log or register is required to show the total number of complaints for the current year and the three years immediately preceding; the classification of each complaint by line of insurance and by complainant (such as insured, state insurance department, third party, etc.); the nature of each complaint; the insurer's disposition of each complaint; and the complaint number assigned by the state insurance department, if applicable.

5. If the insurer denies a claim, a settlement is not reached, and a court eventually finds in favor of the claimant, the insurer will be required to pay compensatory damages. Compensatory damages indemnify the insured for the amount of the loss suffered and are likely to be roughly

equal to the amount of benefits that would have been paid to the insured had the claim not been denied.

In some states and in some cases, punitive damages may be assessed. Punitive damages are awarded when the claimant is able to show that the insurer demonstrated bad faith in denying the claim. Bad faith arises in several contexts. The insurer may show a pattern of denying a certain type of claim without regard to the underlying facts. Or the insurer may refuse to pay where the validity of the claim is clear. Or the insurer may simply drag its feet, refusing to pay but refusing to deny the claim outright. Punitive damage awards can be several times the amount of the compensatory damages and are intended to be large enough to deter the insurer from engaging in bad faith behavior in the future.

NOTES

1 Katz, Gerald. "Disability Insurance Claims: An Inside View—Part Three." *Broker World,* p. 22, March 2003.

2 Ameigh, Mark, and Fleitman, Arthur. "Apply Group DI Claim Practices to Individual DI." *National Underwriter*, March 1, 1999.

11
Claims Management

⟫ OVERVIEW

Chapter 10 discussed the traditional approach to claim adjudication. Claims personnel continue to adjudicate disability claims and make difficult decisions about whether to pay benefits or not. However, in the last 20 years, the incidence of disability has increased dramatically, partly as the result of an aging population, new medical conditions and medical technology, a breakdown in traditional employer-employee relationships, and major restructuring in large sectors of our economy. In response to these momentous changes, disability insurers have made significant changes in contractual language and in their approach to disability income claims handling.

While LTD contracts continue to use a dual definition of total disability—some variant of an own occupation definition for an initial period, followed by an any occupation definition that continues until retirement—in recent years there has been an increased emphasis on partial and residual disability and a greater focus on lost earnings rather than the ability to perform occupational duties.

These changes in contractual language and the economic shifts that have brought them about have had implications for claims administration. While a claim must still be adjudicated, the emphasis has shifted to keeping the employee at work or transitioning her back to work as quickly as possible through early intervention, rehabilitation, flexible working arrangements, and payment of benefits that are based on loss of earnings.

This greater emphasis on keeping employees at work or transitioning them to back to work has led to changes in the make-up of claims departments. Whether the expertise is maintained entirely in-house or acquired through outsourcing, teams that include nurses, occupational and physical therapists, psychological counselors, and even financial advisers frequently handle today's claims.

In addition, in an effort to improve employee productivity and lower employer benefit costs, there has been an increased emphasis on integrated disability management, which includes coordination or integration of non-occupational short-term and long-term disability, workers' compensation claims, and medical case management. Some programs have even gone to the next step, total absence management.

This chapter considers these important changes and their implications.

Objectives

After reading this chapter and completing the accompanying exercises, you will be able to:

- discuss issues related to return-to-work programs, and
- explain approaches to integrated disability management.

≫ RETURN-TO-WORK PROGRAMS

The rationale for **return-to-work (RTW) programs** is that they benefit employees, lower employer costs, and increase insurer profitability.

The Benefits of RTW Programs

Benefits to Employees

Employees who return to work are believed to benefit from increased self-esteem and the opportunity to generate earnings comparable to or in some cases greater than what they would have received had they not returned to work. Furthermore, it is generally believed that employees who return to work are likely to enjoy better post-disability health. Finally, most employees want a return to normality as soon as possible following a disabling illness or injury, and RTW programs are effective in facilitating resolution of disability-related lifestyle interruptions.

A recent study provides interesting insights into the psychological character-istics of employees who return to work quickly compared to those that get caught in a **disability rut**. The study, a joint effort by Fortis Benefits Insurance Company, the Gallup Organization, and a unit of the Menninger Clinic, quantifies the impact of age, sex, marital status, and other characteris-tics of claimants who return to work. Among the results are the following:

- Claimants who are less resilient in dealing with their problem are less likely to return to work quickly. About 76 percent of quick returners said they refused to feel victimized by their condition, compared to 43 percent of slow returners.

- Conscientious people return to work more quickly. The study showed that 52 percent of quick returners read books or articles about their medical treatment or therapy, while only 41 percent of slow return-ers did.

- Quick returners demonstrate will power. In the study, 47 percent of quick returners said they felt they could bounce back from their situation, compared with 30 percent of slow returners who felt that way.

- Proactive workers return to work quickly. Of quick returners, 87 percent focus on what the future may hold for them, compared with 77 percent of slow returners.

- Younger workers return to work more often than older employees; females are more likely to return than males; and workers who have never been married are more likely to return to work than married, widowed, or divorced people.

- The research shows that six out of ten workers whose disability is not work-related returned to work. By comparison, 46 percent of workers with work-related disability returned.

- Individuals are more likely to return to work after an accident (68 percent) than after an illness (56 percent).

Many of these findings agree with common sense, but in combination they have been used to create a set of psychological and demographic tools to help predict how particular claimants will respond to particular claims management initiatives.[1]

Focus Question #1

The rationale for return-to-work programs includes all of the following EXCEPT:

a) They ensure compliance with state laws.
b) They benefit employees.
c) They lower employer costs.
d) They increase insurer profitability.

Benefits to Employers

Employers benefit from RTW programs through lower costs caused by increased claims management efficiencies and through the quicker return to work of valued employees. Employers also benefit when DI policies are translated into human resource management policies that address claimant motivation. These policies can include combinations of incentives for engaging in rehabilitative efforts and disincentives for falling into the disability rut.

As an example of the way return-to-work programs benefit employers, a recent study by researchers at Watson Wyatt Worldwide found that 18 percent of employers with return-to-work programs said they had reduced the percentage of their payroll consumed by short-term disability costs, and 25 percent were able to cut the percentage of payroll consumed by long-term disability costs. On the other hand, when Watson looked at employers without return-to-work programs for workers out on disability leave, it found that none had managed to cut either short-term or long-term disability costs. All of the employers that did not take RTW action experienced cost increases. (The survey's results are based on responses from 178 large employers. Participating employers had an average of 13,500 employees and spent an average of $30 million a year on disability-related costs.)[2]

Benefits to Insurers

RTW programs benefit insurers through increased effectiveness of claims personnel, who can more quickly tailor their interaction with claimants and more accurately prescribe successful claim approaches. This translates into shorter claim durations, an overall reduction in costs for insurers, and an increased **return on investment (ROI)** in the DI product line.

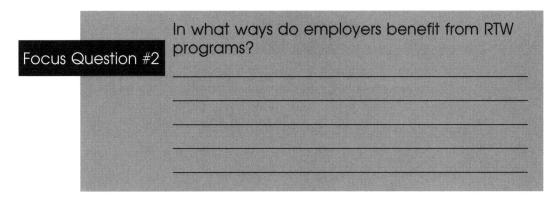

Focus Question #2

In what ways do employers benefit from RTW programs?

Characteristics of RTW Programs

Virtually all of the major LTD carriers now have some sort of RTW plan in operation. Most have at least the basic services described below.

Case Management

Home office claims personnel acting as case managers provide an important link between the disabled worker, the employer, and the physician. They coordinate care, ensure that treatment is appropriate and that health care providers understand available RTW options, and help keep the lines of communication open between employers and disabled employees.

A key component of the case management approach is early intervention. A formal early intervention program routinely screens STD claims for rehabilitation potential according to predetermined guidelines. Such a program also has a dedicated staff, the main goal of which is to identify and work with rehabilitation candidates. In a study conducted by Sun Life, it was found that early intervention dramatically reduced the length of a disability claim and helped more claimants (47 percent more) return to work during the STD stage. In addition, the process not only reduces duration of claims, it also reduces the number of STD claims that become LTD claims.[3]

The best programs focus on the needs of individual claimants on a case-by-case basis. They use objective criteria to identify claims where the disability duration could be excessive if not properly managed, or to identify claims requiring assistance in coordinating an early or modified return to work. Case managers may include vocational rehabilitation or medical personnel, including those who have professional credentials such as the CRC (Certified Rehabilitation Counselor). Case managers should work on a case basis, making adaptations to meet individual claimant needs. To expedite recovery and return to work, they should foster communication between employer, employee, physician, and insurer.

It is recommended that even if a claim does transfer to LTD status, the original case manager should stay with the claimant for the duration of the claim. If the claim transfers to another rehabilitation specialist unfamiliar with the case, the employee's return to work may be jeopardized during the time it takes for new relationships, trust, and rapport to develop.

Employees who have access to a nurse case manager during their absence are 22 percent more likely to ask their supervisor about returning to work, according to research. Similarly, disabled employees who have regular conversations with their manager are more satisfied with their experience than those who have minimal contact, and they are back on the job in half the time.[4]

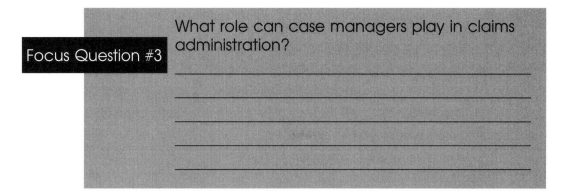

Focus Question #3

What role can case managers play in claims administration?

Job Accommodations and Transitional Duties

Job accommodations and transitional duties are ways of allowing employees to come back to work and be productive, even if they are not yet functioning as before the disability. The concept is that a relatively small expenditure up front by the employer and/or insurer to modify a job location or to allow an employee to transition to work over a period of time, doing as much as she can as time goes on, can result in greater productivity for the employer and reduced claim payments for the insurer.

Contingency planning before claims are filed provides employers with options that become immediately useful in the disability management process. These options may focus on original job functions as well as productive alternative functions. They can be given to the treating physician on the initial visit, thus introducing the question of work immediately as a natural consideration within recovery and treatment planning. This is important, because various studies indicate that prolonged time away from work makes recovery and return to work progressively less likely.

Some insurers help employees with job counseling and job searches, especially where it appears likely that the employee will not be able to return to work with the current employer. Retraining and educational benefits to facilitate a change in occupation may be available. And at least one insurer pays for moving, family care, and other expenses that may arise out of a change in occupation.

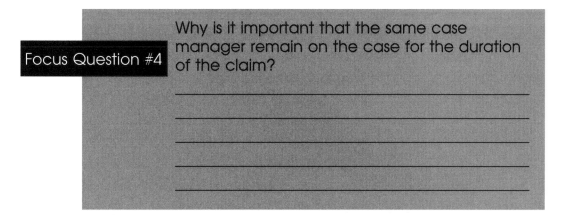

Focus Question #4

Why is it important that the same case manager remain on the case for the duration of the claim?

Other Programs

Some insurers are providing Social Security award assistance, counseling employees on how to apply for disability through Social Security. As a general rule, if the employee qualifies for Social Security, Social Security benefits will reduce the insurer's LTD benefit payments.

Wellness programs, disease management programs, ergonomic interventions, and employee assistance programs all contribute to reduced absence by keeping employees healthy, reducing the incidence and severity of work-related injuries, and raising employee satisfaction levels. These RTW interventions can be applied to any disabling injury or illness claim, regardless of whether it is work-related.

Trends

The management of disabilities is a relatively new field. Further product development and design will have to be responsive to what works, as well as to changes in rehabilitative sciences and practices. Success in this area will require the disability insurance provider to remain open to trying new ideas and to be flexible in responding to the needs of employers and employees.

Success will also depend on employers recognizing the connection between disability income insurance, RTW programs, and employee productivity. So far, it appears that the industry has much work to do in educating employers in this regard. A recent study by HIAA and JHA found that only about 9 percent of employers viewed their LTD plans as having an impact on an employee's return to work.[5]

≫ INTEGRATED DISABILITY MANAGEMENT PROGRAMS

Integrated disability management (IDM) programs have come on the scene within the last decade. However, relatively few insurers offer these programs, and their success has been difficult to quantify.

Typically, IDM refers to the management of two or more benefit programs, such as STD, LTD, workers' compensation, and **Family and Medical Leave Act (FMLA)** absences. (FMLA provides job protection for eligible employees from the very first day of qualified absences and runs concurrently with other absences, such as short-term disabilities.) But integration goes beyond simply providing a single phone number for claimants to call when an absence occurs. Rather, it refers to a means of optimizing the administrative flow of information, beginning with **day-one reporting** and tracking of all absence transactions in a single technology system.

A word sometimes used to describe such plans is seamless. From the employee's perspective, an absence is an absence, and insurer and employer intervention can be expected at the outset. The nature of the intervention and response is tailored to each employee's situation, and the employee need not be concerned about what specific benefit program is in play.

The underlying idea is that integrated absence management enhances employee productivity by shortening the duration of an employee absence (from nearly any cause) and returning the employee to work through early intervention and the coordination and integration of a combination of benefit programs. Quicker return to work coupled with effective and efficient use of benefit programs such as sick leave, workers' compensation, STD, and LTD is expected to improve employer profitability, reduce overall health care costs, and stabilize premiums.

As IDM programs have evolved, they have become more responsive to the particular needs of the market. For example, small employers often want to keep things simple—one application, one contract, and one bill. Because long-term disability is a relatively small part of total disability costs for these employers, a heavy clinical case management focus is probably not a top priority in this market.

On the other hand, employers with 1,000 to 5,000 employees have experienced rising costs of workers' compensation insurance and have compared LTD incidence trends for their companies against national standards. Although simplified administration offers some value for this mid-size market, these employers are mostly concerned with employee absence management and are likely to appreciate the productivity benefits of IDM programs.

Large employers justify the need for employee absence management programs on purely economic grounds. These employers may have a number of employees out on disability or sickness at any given time, so the need for active clinical case management on the first day is very important to them. These employers are likely to demand superior service, detailed absence tracking, timely reporting, and integration of multiple products.

Insurers in the IDM marketplace have developed bundled IDM offerings for each of the following market segments:

- *Integrated health, life, dental, vision, workers' compensation, and short-term disability products.* This IDM product focuses on simplified sale through administration with one application, one enrollment (possibly with Internet capabilities), one contract, one bill, and maybe even one claim form (for a variety of coverages including workers' compensation, STD, and LTD).

- *Integrated health, workers' compensation, STD, and possibly LTD.* This IDM product leverages the absence management expertise of the workers' compensation product. It focuses directly on early intervention, employee assistance programs, safety inspections, wellness facilities, and rehabilitation and return-to-work programs. Unlike the first package type, this approach has a strong focus on the employee absence event. Success can be measured in terms of workers' compensation cost savings or reduction of group disability incidence rates against national standards.

- *Integration of STD (to include administrative-services-only, statutory, and fully insured plans), LTD, possibly workers' compensation, and employee absence management expertise.* This integrated product leverages the combined power of each company's proprietary claims database and uses a triage of shorter-duration claims, combined with active clinical management, to improve employee productivity. Its intent is to actively manage an employee's absence from its initial occurrence through its duration. Tracking and reporting results are critical to employers and often differentiate competitors in a bid situation.

IDM programs continue to evolve as new technologies and new competencies emerge. Whether or not this approach is the wave of the future is likely to depend on whether employers will be able to obtain the expected productivity gains and whether senior management at insurance companies continues to invest in programs that represent such a significant departure from the past.

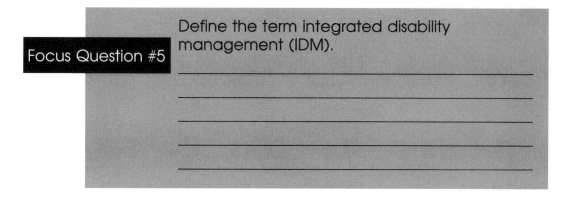

Focus Question #5

Define the term integrated disability management (IDM).

_____

_____

_____

_____

_____

▶▶ SUMMARY

In response to a variety of economic and demographic changes, disability insurers have made significant changes in contractual language and their approach to DI claims handling. As a general rule, there has been an increased emphasis on return-to-work (RTW) programs and integrated disability management (IDM) programs.

RTW programs are characterized by a focus on early intervention, rehabilitation, changes in the work environment including flexible hours and workplace accommodation, and payment of partial and residual benefits.

IDM programs coordinate employee absences with a variety of causes and coordinate the delivery of benefits under FMLA, sick pay, STD, and LTD programs. Again, the emphasis is on early intervention with the goal of returning employees to work as soon as possible in an effort to increase employer productivity.

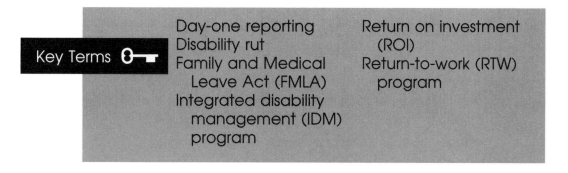

Key Terms

Day-one reporting
Disability rut
Family and Medical
    Leave Act (FMLA)
Integrated disability
    management (IDM)
    program

Return on investment
    (ROI)
Return-to-work (RTW)
    program

▶▶ REVIEW QUESTIONS

1. What factors have contributed to major changes in the way group DI insurers handle claims?

2. How do employees benefit from RTW programs?

3. How do insurers benefit from RTW programs?

4. What is the role of early intervention in case management?

5. What type of IDM product design is likely to make the most sense for a small employer?

▸▸ ANSWERS TO FOCUS QUESTIONS

Focus Question #1—a

Focus Question #2—Employers benefit from RTW programs through lower costs caused by increased claims management efficiencies and through the quicker return to work of valued employees. Employers also benefit when DI policies are translated into human resource management policies that address claimant motivation.

Focus Question #3—Home office claims personnel acting as case managers provide an important link between the disabled worker, the employer, and the physician. They coordinate care, ensure that treatment is appropriate and that health care providers understand available RTW options, and help keep the lines of communication open between employers and disabled employees.

Focus Question #4—If the claim transfers to another rehabilitation specialist unfamiliar with the case, the employee's return to work may be jeopardized during the time it takes for new relationships, trust, and rapport to develop.

Focus Question #5—Typically, IDM refers to the management of two or more benefit programs, such as STD, LTD, workers' compensation, and Family and Medical Leave Act (FMLA) absences.

▸▸ ANSWERS TO REVIEW QUESTIONS

1. First, recent years have seen an increased emphasis on partial and residual disability and a greater focus on lost earnings rather than on a person's ability to perform occupational duties. Second, while the

claim decision must still be adjudicated, the emphasis has shifted to keeping the employee at work or transitioning the employee back to work as quickly as possible through early intervention, rehabilitation, flexible working arrangements, and payment of benefits based on loss of earnings. Third, the emphasis on return-to-work has caused changes in the make-up of claims departments, whether the expertise is maintained entirely in-house or acquired through outsourcing. Teams that include nurses, occupational and physical therapists, psychological counselors, and even financial advisers frequently handle today's claims. Fourth, there has been an increased emphasis on integrated disability management, which includes coordination or integration of non-occupational short-term and long-term disability, workers' compensation claims, and medical case management.

2. Employees who return to work are believed to benefit from increased self-esteem and the opportunity to generate earnings comparable to or in some cases greater than what they would have received had they not returned to work. Furthermore, it is generally believed that employees who return to work are likely to enjoy better post-disability health. Finally, most employees want a return to normality as soon as possible following a disabling illness or injury, and RTW programs are effective in facilitating resolution of disability-related lifestyle interruptions.

3. RTW programs benefit insurers through increased effectiveness of claims personnel, who can more quickly tailor their interaction with claimants and more accurately prescribe successful claim approaches. This translates into shorter claim durations, an overall reduction in costs for insurers, and an increased return on investment (ROI) in the DI product line.

4. A formal early intervention program routinely screens STD claims for rehabilitation potential according to predetermined guidelines. Such a program also has a dedicated staff, the main goal of which is to identify and work with rehabilitation candidates. In a study conducted by Sun Life, it was found that early intervention dramatically reduced the length of a disability claim and helped more claimants return to work during the STD stage. In addition, the process not only reduces duration of claims, it also reduces the number of STD claims that become LTD claims.

5. An IDM product that focuses on a simplified sale through administration with one application, one enrollment (possibly with Internet capabilities), one contract, one bill, and maybe even one claim form for a variety of coverages (including workers' compensation, STD, and LTD) is likely to make the most sense for small employers. These businesses are primarily interested in simplicity and cost savings.

NOTES

1 Altoff, John, and Andruss, Mark. "Study Finds Attitude Does Affect Return-To-Work." *National Underwriter*, February 19, 1996.

2 Bell, Allison. "Return-To-Work Programs Cut Costs." *National Underwriter,* November 15, 1999.

3 Arrunda, Ken. "Early Intervention = Substantial Savings." *National Underwriter*, March 5, 2001.

4 Robinson, Betsy. "Return-To-Work Programs Make Sense in a Recession." *National Underwriter*, February 24, 2003.

5 Cashdollar, Winthrop, and Updike, Marcy. "Survey Probes Employer and Planner Attitudes Toward Disability Income Insurance." *National Underwriter,* February 24, 2003.

» 12
Voluntary Worksite Products

» OVERVIEW

Thus far, this text has focused on group disability income insurance products. As you have learned, group products paid for largely with employer dollars continue to make up an important and dynamic part of the employee benefit landscape. However, a recent trend among employers has been to shift more of the cost of benefits to employees. Nowhere is this more evident than in the retirement planning field, where defined benefit pension plans, fully funded by employer contributions, have been replaced or supplemented by 401(k) plans, primarily funded by employee pre-tax contributions. Significantly, this trend is not limited to retirement plans, but has spilled over into life, disability, and health insurance.

Life, disability, and health insurance products requiring substantial contributions from employees are variously known as voluntary, worksite, or payroll deduction plans, or some combination of these terms. As an indication of employer interest in these products, a 2001 MetLife study revealed that 90 percent of employers were considering offering some type of voluntary program within the next 18 months.[1]

The trend of shifting benefit costs to employees is fueled by several factors. From the employer's perspective, a soft economy and lowered earnings have forced businesses to consider alternative approaches to providing employee benefits. Although many employees do not realize it, it is widely accepted that employee benefits make up about one-third of employee compensation. Despite today's weak economy and corporate downsizing, the MetLife study referenced above reveals that three quarters of employers named employee retention as their top benefits objective. This is because of the high cost of attracting, hiring, training, and developing new employees. Following closely behind, the second most critical benefits objective is "controlling health/welfare benefits costs."[2] Employer sponsorship of voluntary products is a cost-effective way to provide employees with valuable benefits.

From the employee's perspective, uncertainties in the job market help make the case for voluntary products. More so than at any time in the recent past, mergers, acquisitions, and business failures translate into downsizing, layoffs, and forced early retirement. Voluntary insurance coverage is an affordable, convenient solution that can be readily continued in the event employment is terminated.

In many situations, voluntary worksite insurance is not offered as an alternative to group insurance, but instead as **supplemental insurance** intended to bolster the benefits provided under a group plan.

The challenges posed to home office and field personnel by voluntary products are similar to those presented by group DI insurance, but they also differ in important ways. This chapter focuses on those differences and how voluntary products can be used to create a comprehensive benefits package.

Objectives

After reading this chapter and completing the accompanying exercises, you will be able to:

- discuss the product features of voluntary worksite DI insurance products,
- describe approaches to the sale and marketing of these products, and
- explain the major considerations in the service and administration of voluntary worksite products.

⊶ VOLUNTARY WORKSITE PRODUCTS

⊶ In this text the term **voluntary worksite product** is used to refer to a disability income insurance product that is paid for entirely or mostly by employees. By contrast, most group plans are paid for largely by the employer. As you recall, group insurers (and state laws) typically require significant levels of employee participation in order to adequately spread the risk associated with guaranteed issue coverage. Employee participation is boosted when the employer pays most or all the group insurance premium.

Payroll Deduction

A characteristic of voluntary worksite products that distinguishes them from regular individual policies is that premium payment is made more convenient through payroll deduction. The employee simply signs a form authorizing the employer to withhold a portion of her wages and forward the funds to the insurer for payment of premiums. And because the employee never actually receives the amount deducted for insurance coverage, she does not consider it available for spending—like income and employment taxes, the premium comes ''right off the top.''

Underwriting and Pricing

A characteristic of voluntary worksite coverage that distinguishes it from traditional group insurance is the way it is underwritten. With group insurance, there is usually no individual medical or financial underwriting. By contrast, voluntary worksite products may be offered on a guaranteed issue, ⊶ **simplified issue**, or individually underwritten basis.

Simplified issue typically means that the employee answers a few health-related questions (for example, whether he has been diagnosed with cancer or HIV infection), but he is not required to answer detailed questions or to submit to a physical exam or testing. Guaranteed issue voluntary products are usually structured as group products, while simplified issue products may be structured as either group or individual products.

Guaranteed or simplified issue is typically conditioned on having a high enough level of employee participation. Guaranteed issue plans usually require participation levels of 75 percent or higher. Simplified issue typi-cally calls for participation levels of 25 to 40 percent of the employee population. Salespeople agree that to obtain this level of participation, the employer must contribute some portion of the premium. For example, the employer might agree to pay for 25 or 50 percent of the premium to entice a large enough percentage of employees to participate. The cost savings to the insurer associated with guaranteed or simplified underwriting, payroll deduction of premiums, and administration of consistent product definitions and other features are passed along to both employer and employee.

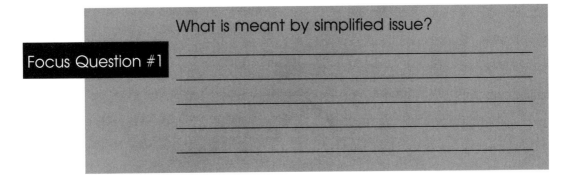

Focus Question #1

What is meant by simplified issue?

Voluntary worksite plans are typically priced using manual rates, and the pricing is designed to facilitate the understanding of employees during the enrollment process. For example, one insurer's voluntary STD plan is presented in handouts so that employees can see how much $100 of weekly benefit costs for various ages (see Table 12.1). The employee simply multiples the cost for his age of $100 of weekly benefit by the number of units he wants (subject to a limit) to get the biweekly premium. For example, a 57-year-old employee who wanted and qualified for $300 of weekly benefit would pay $18.00 biweekly.

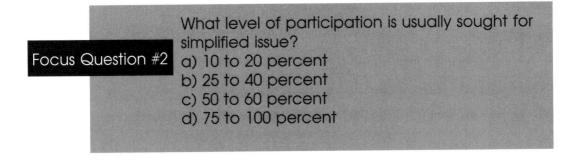

Focus Question #2

What level of participation is usually sought for simplified issue?
a) 10 to 20 percent
b) 25 to 40 percent
c) 50 to 60 percent
d) 75 to 100 percent

Table 12.1

Example: The Biweekly Premium for $100 of Weekly Benefit

Employee Age	Biweekly Premium
Under 30	$3.14
30-34	$3.14
35-39	$3.14
40-44	$3.14
45-49	$3.46
50-54	$4.30
55-59	$6.00
60-64	$7.10
65-69	$7.52
70+	$7.52

Product Features

Voluntary worksite DI products contain the same basic features as group products. For example, an insurer might offer a voluntary STD product with the following basic features:

- *Definition of disability.* Disability means that, as a result of sickness, pregnancy, or accidental illness, the insured is receiving appropriate care and treatment from a doctor on a continuing basis, and he is unable to earn more than 80 percent of his pre-disability earnings at his own occupation for an employer in his own geographical area.

- *Maximum monthly benefit.* The maximum monthly benefit is stated in $50 increments between $100 and $1,000 per month, not to exceed 60 percent of pre-disability income. The schedule in Table 12.2 is an example of how much benefit an employee might be entitled to based on her weekly salary.

- *Elimination period.* Employers may be offered a choice of elimination periods, and the periods may differ depending on whether the disability results from injury or illness. (See Table 12.3 for an example.) The price per benefit unit varies according to the choice selected. For example, employers that select an elimination period of 30 days for both accident and illness will pay a lower rate per benefit unit than employers that choose the option of zero days for accident and seven days for sickness.

Table 12.2

Example: Maximum STD Benefit

To Buy This Amount of Monthly Benefit	Employee Must Earn at Least This Amount Per Week	To Buy This Amount of Monthly Benefit	Employee Must Earn at Least This Amount Per Week
$100	$166	$600	$1,000
$150	$250	$650	$1,084
$200	$334	$700	$1,167
$250	$417	$750	$1,250
$300	$500	$800	$1,334
$350	$584	$850	$1,417
$400	$667	$900	$1,500
$450	$750	$950	$1,584
$500	$834	$1,000	$1,667
$550	$917		

Table 12.3

Example: Elimination Period Choices

	Option #1	Option #2	Option #3	Option #4	Option #5
Accident	0 Days	7 Days	0 Days	14 Days	30 Days
Sickness	7 Days	7 Days	14 Days	14 Days	30 Days

- *Benefit period.* Employers may also have a choice between benefit periods of three, six, and twelve months. The premium rates paid by employees will be higher for longer benefit periods than for shorter ones.

- *Coordination with other benefits.* Benefits under the plan may be integrated with other employer-provided benefits for non-occupational disabilities, Social Security, and any income earned from other sources. A minimum monthly benefit equal to the greater of 10 percent of the gross monthly benefit or $100 may be guaranteed.

- *Limitations.* The contract may contain a limitation on benefits for preexisting conditions using a common definition such as ''disabilities caused by an accident or illness for which the insured received treatment within three months prior to the effective date of coverage if the disability begins less than 12 months after the insured's effective date of coverage.''

- *Exclusions.* Benefits are likely to be excluded for disabilities caused by participation in a felony, intentionally self-inflicted injuries, active participation in a riot, commission of a crime for which the insured has been convicted, and participation in war.

- *Portability.* The contract may allow employees to continue current levels of coverage for up to 12 months after employment with the current employer ends. The insurer may reserve the right to individually underwrite the new coverage.

- *Rehabilitation.* The contract may include a rehabilitation benefit. As an incentive for rehabilitation, one insurer's contract increases the weekly benefit amount by 10 percent while the insured is participating in a rehabilitation program.

The typical voluntary STD contract is straightforward, with few bells and whistles, and it may or may not offer partial or residual benefits. The contract's simplicity facilitates understanding and acceptance by employees, who cannot be expected to be familiar with the nuances of disability income insurance.

Similarly, voluntary LTD contracts are also likely to be straightforward. The following are the highlights of a typical voluntary LTD offering:

- *Definition of disability.* For an initial period, disability is defined as the inability to perform the substantial and material duties of one's own occupation. Thereafter, disability is the inability to perform the duties of any occupation for which the insured is reasonably suited by experience, training, and education.

- *Maximum monthly benefit.* The maximum monthly benefit is usually stated in $100 increments between $300 and $6,000 per month, not to exceed 40 to 60 percent of pre-disability income. The insurer reserves the right to obtain evidence of medical insurability for larger amounts.

- *Elimination period.* The elimination period is coordinated with the STD plan. Employers may choose from options of 60, 90, 180, and 365 days.

- *Benefit period.* Employers are offered several options, all of which comply with the Age Discrimination in Employment Act (ADEA). Recurring disability is addressed—if the insured returns to work for less than six months and becomes disabled again because of the same or a related illness or injury, a new elimination period is waived.

- *Coordination with other benefits.* Benefits under the plan are integrated with other employer-provided benefits for non-occupational disabilities, Social Security, and any income earned from other sources. A minimum monthly benefit equal to the greater of 10 percent of the gross monthly benefit or $100 is guaranteed.

- *Limitations.* The contract contains a limitation on benefits for preexisting conditions defined as disabilities caused by an accident or illness for which the insured received treatment within three months prior to the effective date of coverage if the disability begins less than 12 months after the insured's effective date of coverage. Also, benefits for mental illness and substance abuse are limited to six months.

- *Exclusions.* Benefits are excluded for the typical reasons, including disabilities caused by participation in a felony, intentionally self-inflicted injuries, active participation in a riot, commission of a crime for which the insured has been convicted, and participation in war.

- *Portability.* The insurer's contract allows employees to continue their current level of coverage for up to 12 months after employment with the current employer ends. The insurer reserves the right to individually underwrite the new coverage.

- *Rehabilitation.* The insurer agrees to pay for specified mandatory rehabilitation as an incentive to return the employee to work.

- *Survivor benefits.* If the insured is disabled for 180 days and dies while eligible for disability benefits, his beneficiary will be paid a lump-sum benefit equal to three months of the insured's disability benefit.

Again, this is an example of a straightforward LTD plan with few special features. The contract is likely to be understood and appreciated by both employers and employees.

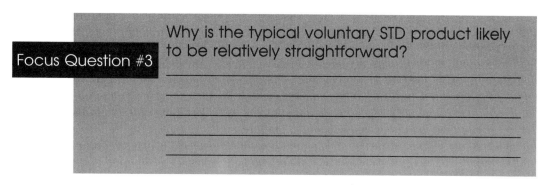

Focus Question #3

Why is the typical voluntary STD product likely to be relatively straightforward?

⟫SALES AND MARKETING

Distribution of voluntary worksite insurance is similar to that of group products, especially where the voluntary product is offered on a guaranteed issue basis as part of the group insurance line of business. Group representatives are likely to take the lead in wholesaling the product to agents and brokers, and they also serve as consultants on larger cases.

Where the offering is designed as an individual product with either full or simplified underwriting, it will more than likely be distributed through the insurer's brokerage managers and/or general agencies. Home office and agency-level specialists are available to assist with all aspects of the sales process.

One major difference in the sales process for voluntary products compared to that for group plans funded entirely by the employer is that voluntary products really involve two sales—one to the employer and another to the employee. The reason is simple—with voluntary worksite plans, the employee must be sold on the benefit of paying most or all of the premium for the coverage.

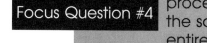

Focus Question #4

What is a major difference between the sales process for voluntary worksite DI insurance and the sales process for group DI plans funded entirely by the employer?

Selling the Employer

The employer must be convinced of the importance of sponsoring voluntary insurance, and the employer must be willing to give the salesperson time to meet with employees during working hours for the purpose of presenting the product, answering questions, and conducting an enrollment. The Met-Life study mentioned earlier provides insights into what employers generally want from employee benefit programs and worksite programs in particular. According to the study:

- Employers view employee retention (78 percent) and controlling health/welfare benefit costs (73 percent) as their most critical benefits objectives.

- In support of these objectives, 58 percent of employers rate providing employees with benefits designed to balance their work and personal lives as one of their most important benefits strategies.

- Approximately 90 percent of employers currently offer, or plan to offer in the next 18 months, at least one voluntary benefit.

- Optional term life insurance is currently the most popular voluntary benefit. More employers (12 percent) are planning to add long-term care insurance in the next 18 months than any other voluntary offering.

- Employers offering voluntary benefits tend to be more progressive in their approach to employee benefits and the use of technology.

Skilled salespeople will use these findings to guide their sales approach to employers. The following points should be central to any sales presentation for voluntary DI insurance plans:

- Voluntary insurance products are an important component of the employer's employment offer and can provide a competitive advantage in recruiting employees. Voluntary insurance can be inexpensive, easy to apply for, convenient to pay for, and may be portable if and when the employee moves on.

- Voluntary DI insurance can help with employee retention by creating incentives for return to work through rehabilitation and case management. Also, DI insurance is crucial to maintaining quality of life if an employee is unable to work because of illness or injury.

- Many employers and employees are already familiar with voluntary insurance products. Employees already appreciate the convenience and potential cost savings associated with these products. Why not make voluntary DI insurance part of the total package?

- Although voluntary life insurance and long-term care insurance are more prevalent, the need for disability insurance is more important than ever. The likelihood of a long-term disability is about three times greater than that of premature death.[3] And, while it is true that long-term care is not just for seniors, it is mostly seniors who benefit from long-term care insurance—during one's working life, the likelihood of a disability that can be recovered from through rehabilitation and a gradual transition back to work is considerably greater than the likelihood of a disability that requires long-term care at home or in a nursing home. Thus, while life insurance and long-term care needs are important, disability should be addressed first.

Because employers that provide voluntary benefits are likely to be more progressive and more technologically savvy than those that do not, salespeople should consider taking advantage of intranet and Internet marketing of voluntary products. The MetLife survey shows that, as of November 2001, more than 40 percent of employers with 1,000 or more employees and 18 percent of smaller employers offer employees **e-benefits** capabilities.[4]

The agent or broker will usually conduct one or more meetings with the employer's decision-makers. Once the go-ahead is received, the agent or broker meets with payroll personnel to set up an interface between the employer's payroll deduction system and the insurer's premium collection system. Arrangements are made for the next step in the sales process—selling the employee.

Selling the Employee

Unlike many group DI plans, where the employer pays most or all of the premium, with voluntary DI insurance the employee is being asked to pay the lion's share of the premium. But even though the employee pays the bulk of the premium, a high level of employee participation is essential to the success of the program. There are a variety of reasons for this, including the following:

- High participation confirms to the employer that the program is popular and that the required administration effort is worthwhile.

- High participation creates confidence and even higher participation among employees.

- High participation maximizes the salesperson's efforts in the initial enrollment and sets the stage for higher participation with new employees and more successful re-enrollments.

- High participation is often required to obtain underwriting and pricing concessions.

Therefore, each employee must be educated about the features and benefits of voluntary products, the ins and outs of payroll deduction, and the need for voluntary coverage in his particular case. The first step in making sales to employees is to conduct an **introductory employee meeting**, in which employees or groups of employees are introduced to the concept of voluntary insurance. It is usually in the agent or broker's interest to hold the introductory meeting on the employer's premises during working hours, so employer sponsorship is key to the success of the meeting.

The concept is presented (often with the help of visual aids supplied by the insurer), a sample needs analysis is illustrated, sample forms are made available, and employee questions are addressed. The salesperson explains the enrollment process and any underwriting requirements. Brochures and/ or other explanatory materials are usually passed out. The introductory meeting can be promoted through payroll stuffers reminding employees of the time and date of the meeting, and through the use of posters, mouse pads, computer sign-on screens, and other promotional materials.

Enrollment takes place shortly after the introductory meeting. In large cases, enrollment can be an impersonal event, often conducted by third-party enrollers, via mail, or online. The emphasis is on performing the administrative function of collecting applications and obtaining the employees' consent to the payroll deduction arrangement. There may be little time or attention devoted to relationship-building with employees.

With smaller employers, the agent or broker typically meets with each employee individually to establish the financial need for the coverage and to conduct the enrollment. The need for the coverage is typically established through a **needs analysis** that evaluates the employee's current income and her expenses both while she is working and in the event she is unable to work because of a disability. Except for the unusual case where the employee has significant unearned income, it is relatively easy to demonstrate the financial crisis that will occur if disability stops family income. In fact, expenses may even increase, because of medical bills and other costs associated with a disability. Many insurers provide employees with worksheets, software programs, or Websites that facilitate a needs analysis. (Table 12.4 is an example of an expense worksheet.)

Table 12.4
Example: Expense Worksheet

Monthly Expense Summary

Mortgage or rent	$
Food	$
Clothing	$
Loans and installment purchases	$
Utilities	$
Insurance premiums	$
Medical/dental care	$
Auto expenses	$
Personal expenses	$
Education	$
Gifts	$
Other expenses	$
Total	$

Once monthly expenses are identified, income from sources other than work is determined. This might include dividends, interest, employer-sponsored disability benefits, and rental income. The total of these income sources is subtracted from total expenses, and the net amount is the amount of the disability income insurance need.

Unless the voluntary insurance is offered as a supplement to existing group STD and/or LTD coverage, chances are that most employees will have an insurance need that exceeds the maximum amount of voluntary coverage they can purchase. (For example, in the sample products discussed earlier in this chapter, the maximum amount of voluntary coverage an employee could purchase was 60 percent of pre-disability earnings.) This leads to another aspect of the voluntary sale. Most insurers offer individual disability products that may be purchased to supplement the voluntary insurance and/or existing group coverage. The best salespeople will be able to spot the need for additional individual DI insurance and transition the sales process to that need. In most (but not all) cases, the buy-up to individual coverage is especially appropriate for highly paid executives. These individuals not only need the coverage, they can afford to buy it—or in some cases the employer will agree to pay some or all of the cost for them.

With simplified issue, it is typical that employees may be enrolled at any time convenient to the employer. With guaranteed issue, enrollment is generally restricted to one 30-day period per year.

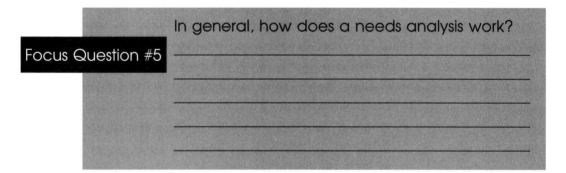

In general, how does a needs analysis work?

Focus Question #5

▶▶ POLICY ADMINISTRATION AND CUSTOMER SERVICE

From a home office perspective, the administrative aspects of voluntary worksite products are similar to those of group insurance. However, where individual DI insurance is issued in lieu of or as a supplement to group insurance, individual contracts must be issued to each individual insured. (By contrast, with group insurance a group master contract is issued to the employer, and certificates of coverage are provided to employees.)

Premium billing and collection is facilitated through payroll deduction of employee contributions.

The claim process for voluntary products is similar to that of group insurance. First, the claim must be adjudicated to determine whether or not the employee has fulfilled eligibility requirements, qualifies for coverage, and has satisfied the elimination period. The claim process continues with an ongoing evaluation of the disability, coordination of benefits, and management of rehabilitation and other return-to-work incentives.

The Importance of Policy Service

The ability of the home office to effectively and efficiently conduct pricing, underwriting, policy issue, and claims handling is a threshold requirement for entry into the voluntary worksite market. However, on an ongoing basis, it is the service delivered to the customer by the agent or broker who sells the case that is likely to be most determinative of customer satisfaction. It is the agent or broker who has the opportunity to develop a face-to-face relationship with both the employer and the employee; it is the agent or broker who is first on the scene when a problem arises concerning enrollment, billing, or claims handling; and it is the agent or broker who has the financial incentive to turn service challenges into new sales opportunities.

The importance of ongoing policy service at the agent or broker level cannot be overemphasized. Many organizations distinguish between two levels of service: the minimum required level of service and superior client service. In their book, *Delivering Knock Your Socks Off Service,* Kristin Anderson and Ron Zemke define this superior level of service in terms of five components:

- reliability—the ability to provide what was promised dependably and accurately;
- responsiveness—the willingness to help clients promptly;
- assurance—the knowledge and courtesy you show to clients and your ability to demonstrate competence and build trust;
- empathy—the degree of caring and individual attention you show clients; and
- tangibles—the physical appearance of your office and the way you dress and carry yourself.

Providing Superior Employer Service

Because the voluntary worksite sale is really two sales, beginning with a sale to the employer and continuing with a sale to the employee, it is helpful to maintain the distinction in connection with providing service. There are several opportunities for providing truly superior employer service. These include:

- establishing rapport with bookkeeper/payroll personnel,
- policy delivery,
- periodic reviews, and
- mailing of pertinent magazine or newspaper articles.

Let's consider each of these in turn.

Establishing Rapport with Bookkeeper/Payroll Personnel

After the agent or broker obtains the employer's consent to go forward with voluntary worksite coverage, the next step is often to request a meeting with the bookkeeper (or other designated person). This is the person in the company responsible for making sure payroll checks are correct in amount and delivered on time. This person is also responsible for ensuring that state and federal income tax and payroll tax withholding is accurate and that employee contributions for benefits such as health insurance and 401(k) plans are properly deducted. This is the person who needs to understand the details of how the billing and collection arrangement with the selected insurer works, when to begin deducting for employee contributions from payroll, how much to deduct and how, and when to pay the premium billings received from the insurer.

The agent or broker should take the time at the outset to explain the features and benefits of the voluntary program to the bookkeeper. The salesperson can facilitate ongoing contact between the bookkeeper and the home office service center by supplying phone numbers, names, and Website addresses for appropriate contact personnel.

Policy Delivery

Where the voluntary coverage is provided through an individual DI insurance product, policy delivery provides an opportunity for the salesperson to demonstrate superior client service to both the employer and employee. For larger employers, the agent or broker can usually choose from several methods of policy delivery:

- in person to each individual insured, securing a delivery receipt at the time of delivery;
- to the employer or appropriate company officer, who must sign a group receipt for all of the policies; or
- by mail.

For small employers and associations, the preferred method of delivery is in person. In-person delivery allows the agent or broker to reinforce the benefits of the program with each insured and set the stage for add-on or supplemental sales.

Periodic Reviews

Periodic reviews are a proactive way for the agent or broker to head off potential problems before they arise. Periodic reviews with the employer are best received if they are:

- regularly scheduled,
- brief,
- conducted with an agreed-upon agenda, and
- followed up.

Some salespeople use a standardized **six-month review** to confirm with the employer that the program is accomplishing its objectives. The six-month review also facilitates the identification of issues for resolution, ranging from employee dissatisfaction to interest in adding the program for a newly formed subsidiary. At least as important, the six-month review positions the agent or broker to seek referrals to other employers for group and voluntary worksite coverage and to bridge to add-on sales with the employer.

Mailing of Pertinent Magazine or Newspaper Articles

Another good way to keep in touch with employers and demonstrate superior service is for the agent or broker to position herself as a resource. Typically, top salespeople look for articles that keep employers abreast of developments in financial services, employee benefits, and/or developments in their industry.

Providing Superior Employee Service

Superior employee service not only ensures greater appreciation of the voluntary DI insurance program, it also opens the door to add-on sales and cross-sales. There are several opportunities for agents and brokers to provide ongoing service to employees:

- policy delivery;
- periodic reviews;
- mailing of approved greeting cards on birthdays, holidays, etc.;
- maintaining contact with terminated employees; and
- re-enrollment.

Smooth handling of policy delivery not only impresses the employer, it cements the voluntary sale with the employee. When handled in person, policy delivery is just one more chance for the salesperson to demonstrate his professionalism and build relationships with employees.

The same guidelines discussed above in connection with employer reviews also apply to employee reviews. Periodic interviews should be regularly scheduled, brief, conducted with an agreed-upon agenda, and followed up.

Sending out greeting cards on birthdays, holidays, job anniversaries, etc. is another way to keep in touch with employees. Sending insureds personal cards on special occasions shows that the agent or broker cares about them and values them as customers.

It is important to keep in mind that a client is not necessarily lost when an employee leaves an employer sponsoring a voluntary worksite program. If the voluntary coverage is an individual product, it is completely portable, and even group voluntary products may offer conversion privileges or may continue for six to twelve months after termination of employment. Agents and brokers can provide a valuable service by following up with employees who leave to remind them that although the payment method and cost may change, if there was a need for DI insurance in the past, there will be a continuing need in the future.

Finally, a major aspect of employee service is re-enrollment. Successful re-enrollment ensures that the families of those employees already in the program continue to receive quality DI insurance. Beyond this, successful re-enrollment brings new employees into the fold and allows employees currently participating to increase their contributions.

▶▶ SUMMARY

A challenging economy, in which employers are focused on cutting costs and increasing productivity, has led to an increased interest in voluntary worksite products. From the employee's perspective too, these products are viewed as convenient, valuable, and easily portable to the next job or self-employment situation. These products are characterized by payroll deduction (with most of the premium paid by the employee), straightforward policy design, simplified issue, and competitive pricing. Unlike traditional STD and LTD, where the employer pays most or all of the premium, selling voluntary products involves a sale to both the employer and employee. The employer must be convinced to sponsor the program, to allow the agent or broker to meet with employees on company time, and to deduct employee premiums from payroll. In most cases, the employer is encouraged to make at least some contribution in order to increase employee participation. The employee must be convinced of the financial need for the coverage, the ease of application, and the convenience of paying for the coverage through payroll deduction. Once the plan is in place, there are ongoing opportunities for the agent or broker to provide continuing service and look for add-on sales.

Key Terms

E-benefits	Six-month review
Introductory employee meeting	Supplemental insurance
Needs analysis	Voluntary worksite
Simplified issue	product

▶▶ REVIEW QUESTIONS

1. Why have employers shown an increased interest in voluntary worksite plans?

2. If you were selling voluntary worksite DI insurance, what are some of the key sales points you would want to make to an employer?

3. Why is high participation by employees in voluntary worksite programs key to their success?

4. Charlotte has a $1,200 monthly mortgage payment. Also, each month she spends about $400 on food, $100 on clothing, $150 on utilities, $200 on insurance, $50 on medical care, $300 on auto expenses, and $150 on personal expenses. She earns $100 per month in interest and dividends. About how much monthly disability income benefit does Charlotte need?

5. What are key components of superior service to an employer that sponsors voluntary DI insurance?

➤➤ ANSWERS TO FOCUS QUESTIONS

Focus Question #1—Simplified issue typically means that the employee answers a few health-related questions (for example, whether he has been diagnosed with cancer or HIV infection), but he is not required to answer detailed questions or to submit to a physical exam or testing.

Focus Question #2—b

Focus Question #3—The contract's simplicity facilitates understanding and acceptance by employees, who cannot be expected to be familiar with the nuances of disability income insurance.

Focus Question #4—One major difference in the sales process for voluntary products compared to that for group plans funded entirely by the employer is that voluntary products really involve two sales—one to the employer and another to the employee. The reason is simple—with voluntary worksite plans, the employee must be sold on the benefit of paying most or all of the premium for the coverage.

Focus Question #5—A needs analysis evaluates the employee's current income and her expenses both while she is working and in the event she is unable to work because of a disability. Except for the unusual case where the employee has significant unearned income, it is relatively easy to demonstrate the financial crisis that will occur if disability stops family income. In fact, expenses may even increase, because of medical bills and other costs associated with a disability. Many insurers provide employees with worksheets, software programs, or Websites that facilitate a needs analysis.

›› ANSWERS TO REVIEW QUESTIONS

1. A soft economy and lowered earnings have forced businesses to consider alternative approaches to providing employee benefits. Employer sponsorship of voluntary products is a cost-effective way to provide employees with valuable benefits.

2. ■ Voluntary insurance products are an important component of the employer's employment offer and can provide a competitive advantage in recruiting employees. Voluntary insurance can be inexpensive, easy to apply for, convenient to pay for, and may be portable if and when the employee moves on.

   ■ Voluntary DI insurance can help with employee retention by creating incentives for return to work through rehabilitation and case management. Also, DI insurance is crucial to maintaining quality of life if an employee is unable to work because of illness or injury.

   ■ Many employers and employees are already familiar with voluntary insurance products. Employees already appreciate the convenience and potential cost savings associated with these products. Why not make voluntary DI insurance part of the total package?

   ■ Although voluntary life insurance and long-term care insurance are more prevalent, the need for disability insurance is more important than ever.

3. ■ High participation confirms to the employer that the program is popular and that the required administration effort is worthwhile.

   ■ High participation creates confidence and even higher participation among employees.

   ■ High participation maximizes the salesperson's efforts in the initial enrollment and sets the stage for higher participation with new employees and more successful re-enrollments.

   ■ High participation is often required to obtain underwriting and pricing concessions.

4. Charlotte needs about $2,450 in monthly DI insurance benefits. Her monthly expenses are listed below.

Monthly Expense Summary

Mortgage or rent:	$1,200
Food:	$400
Clothing:	$100
Loans and installment purchases:	
Utilities:	$150
Insurance premiums:	$200
Medical/dental care:	$50
Auto expenses:	$300
Personal expenses:	$150
Education:	
Gifts:	
Other expenses:	
Total	$2,550

Her monthly expenses are reduced by her unearned income of $100, giving her a monthly need of $2,450.

5. ■ reliability—the ability to provide what was promised dependably and accurately;

■ responsiveness—the willingness to help clients promptly;

■ assurance—the knowledge and courtesy you show to clients and your ability to demonstrate competence and build trust;

■ empathy—the degree of caring and individual attention you show clients; and

■ tangibles—the physical appearance of your office and the way you dress and carry yourself.

NOTES

1 MetLife Insurance Company. "The MetLife Study of Employee Benefits Trends." p. 6, November 2001.

2 Ibid.

3 National Association of Insurance Commissioners Disability Table.

4 MetLife Insurance Company. "The MetLife Study of Employee Benefits Trends." p. 10, November 2001.

13
The Regulatory Environment

›› OVERVIEW

Group disability income insurance is regulated at both the state and federal levels. By virtue of the McCarran-Ferguson Act of 1945, the states have the authority to impose requirements on insurers regarding the conduct of business, allowable contractual language, and the manner in which products are marketed and sold. A major thrust of state legislation and regulation is consumer protection. State statutes relating to insurance often begin by establishing the office of the insurance commissioner and charging it with the regulation of insurance practices so that buyers are adequately protected from insurer insolvency, faulty product design or pricing, and unethical sales and marketing practices.

Although there is wide variation among state laws, there are ongoing attempts at establishing uniformity. The National Association of Insurance Commissioners (NAIC) has been influential in developing model laws. Although states are not required to adopt the NAIC's model laws, many states have enacted them, often with only minor changes.

Federal law is less concerned with the operation of insurance companies and more concerned with the regulation of employee benefit plans, which are often funded with insurance products. The thrust of these laws is the protection of employees against discrimination in the provision of benefits and the protection of employee funds from mismanagement, fraud, or embezzlement.

Objectives

After reading this chapter and completing the accompanying exercises, you will be able to:

- discuss the regulation of disability income insurance products at the state level, and

- discuss the regulation of disability income insurance products at the federal level.

►► STATE REGULATION

A detailed discussion of the laws that regulate insurance at the state level is beyond the scope of this chapter. There is simply too much variation in the insurance codes and general business laws of the 50 states to allow a complete treatment of the subject. Consequently, the effort here is to provide an overview of the key areas of state regulation, with a focus on:

- the formation and licensing of insurers,

- insurance company operations, and

- regulatory jurisdiction.

Another important area of state regulation is the taxation of group DI insurance premiums and benefits. This is discussed in Chapter 14.

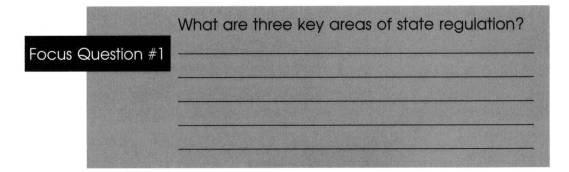

Focus Question #1

What are three key areas of state regulation?

The Formation and Licensing of Insurers

Most states set high standards for the licensing of insurance companies to conduct business. The rationale for imposing higher standards on insurance companies than on other businesses is that insurance is a complex, little understood product that the public depends on in times of need. High standards for the formation and licensing of insurance companies help to ensure that the public's trust is not misplaced.

The first step for most group insurers is to file the appropriate legal papers, usually with the secretary of state and the insurance commissioner. Most insurers are formed as corporations, and incorporation is evidenced by **articles of incorporation** and **bylaws**.

Next, the state insurance department typically reviews the insurer's financial status to determine whether it has adequate initial surplus and capital to conduct business. The standards vary from state to state and according to the lines of business the insurer intends to pursue.

In addition to reviewing the insurer's initial financial condition, the insurance commissioner may consider the company's managerial expertise and experience as part of the licensing process. Background checks on officers and directors may be conducted. Insurance commissioners typically have considerable discretion in determining whether or not to grant a license, based on their findings.

Insurance Company Operations

The licensing of group insurers is only the beginning of state regulation. To protect policyholders from unfair treatment and insolvency, many aspects of insurance operations are regulated on an ongoing basis. The following are important areas of regulation:

- the definition of groups eligible for group insurance coverage,
- contractual provisions,
- rates,
- reserves,
- assets and surplus values,
- investments,
- claims practices, and
- sales and marketing practices.

Eligible Groups

Eligible groups were discussed in detail in Chapter 5. As you recall, the types of allowable group sponsors include:

- employers,
- multiple employer arrangements,
- associations,
- franchisers, and
- creditors.

Basically, state laws define eligible groups in a way that ensures adequate risk sharing among members of the group. Group insurance is issued with little or no financial or medical underwriting, so unless the group is large enough and adequately representative of the population as a whole, there is the potential for adverse selection.

Contractual Provisions

Chapters 8 and 9 discussed the provisions found in most group DI insurance contracts. As a general rule, state laws do not specify the length of probationary periods, the language that must be used in defining disability, the duration of elimination periods, or the duration of benefit periods. Instead, it is left to market forces to determine the specifics of such features. However, state laws do regulate what provisions must be contained in contracts and often provide a range of acceptable alternatives. For example, many states require group DI insurance contracts to include the following contractual provisions:

- *Entire contract clause*—provides that the policy (including endorsements and attached papers) constitutes the whole contract between the parties. Its purpose is to protect both parties from claims that arise from oral or other ''side agreements.''
- *Grace period*—grants the employer a grace period for the payment of premiums. The number of days may differ from state to state, but 31 days for a monthly premium is common. Its purpose is to prevent the insurer from canceling coverage when the insured may have inadvertently delayed premium payment.

- *The definition of disability*—contains the definition of total disability. Typically there is considerable variability in the specific contract language that is acceptable. For example, a few states require that LTD contracts contain an own occupation provision for a minimum of one to two years, before switching to a more restrictive definition, but there are usually allowable differences in how the own occupation provision is actually drafted. In addition, provisions concerning recurring, partial, presumptive, and residual disability may be required in the contract, and they may be subject to regulation. For example, a state may regulate the types of conditions that give rise to a presumptive disability. Or a state may require the payment of at least a minimum residual benefit.

- *Elimination period*—specifies the elimination period selected by the employer. Some states limit the duration of the elimination period in relation to the benefit period to prevent the issuance of contracts with very long elimination periods and short benefit periods. The rationale is that such contracts provide little consumer value.

- *Benefit period*—specifies the duration of the benefit period selected by the employer. States typically allow LTD benefit periods as short as two years and as long as life, although few modern-day LTD contracts provide lifetime contracts.

- *Amount of benefits*—specifies the formula for determination of benefits. States may require minimum benefits for partial and residual benefits. However, there is little or no limit on the maximum benefit that may be provided, so long as the formula precludes individual selection.

- *Notice of claim*—specifies the time period for filing a claim. Its purpose is to ensure that claims are promptly filed so that the insurer has the opportunity to determine their validity and to administer return-to-work programs early in the disability.

- *Proof of loss*—requires the insured to provide written evidence of disability within a specified period from the date of disability. It ensures that the insurance company obtains adequate information to adjudicate the validity of the claim.

- *Examinations*—grants the insurer the right to require the insured to submit to certain examinations to determine the extent of a disability. It protects the insurer from malingering and/or collusion between an insured and his physician.

- *Exclusions*—sets forth the disabilities that are excluded from benefits under the contract. As noted elsewhere in this text, exclusions have become fairly standardized from policy to policy and are generally limited to disabilities involving ''moral turpitude'' by the insured (such as suicide attempts and substance abuse) or situations beyond the normal scope of one's activities (such as war). Except in large cases, preexisting conditions are usually excluded.

- *Limitations*—describes disabilities for which benefits may be limited to a shorter duration than the normal benefit period. For example, most states allow limitations for subjective disabilities, including psychiatric conditions such as depression, although such provisions are not free from controversy.

- *Rehabilitation*—When the contract conditions the payment of benefits on mandatory rehabilitation, the conditions must be set forth in the contract.

- *Coordination of benefits*—describes reductions in benefits because of the insured's receipt of certain other income during a period of disability. As described in Chapter 8, the states generally allow LTD benefits to be reduced by income sources such as Social Security, workers' compensation, other disability income benefits, other employer-provided benefits, and earned income.

State regulation of contractual provisions is intended to protect consumers and provide a general framework for acceptable policy forms. The marketplace will decide within a wide range of acceptable alternatives whether one insurer's own occupation definition is more favorable than another's, or whether one insurer's mandatory rehabilitation benefit is too restrictive compared to another's.

As a general rule, it is the role of the insurer's legal department to draft the actual contract language to reflect both company philosophy and the constraints imposed by state law. For better or worse, competition in the DI field often focuses on precise contractual language—how disability is defined, what examinations can be ordered, what exclusions and limitations apply. Consequently, the drafting of policy language takes on added importance in the DI insurance field.

The legal department is also typically responsible for filing policies with the various state insurance departments for approval. Because of the variability of state law, managing the approval process for a new contract or rider can be a daunting task.

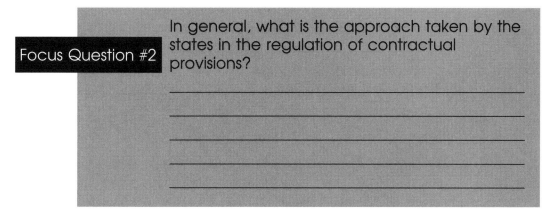

Focus Question #2

In general, what is the approach taken by the states in the regulation of contractual provisions?

Rates

Most states impose some regulation on the rates charged by group insurers. At a minimum, regulators want to ensure that:

- manual rates are adequate,
- rates are non-discriminatory, and
- rates are not excessive.

Within these broad guidelines, there is allowance for considerable price competition, and as a practical matter, experience rating is largely driven by competitive considerations.

Reserves

All states require insurers to maintain certain minimum reserves for the payment of claims, referred to as **statutory reserves**. Statutory reserves typically reflect conservative assumptions about expected claims and interest rates.

Assets and Surplus Values

The states regulate the manner in which insurers value their assets and surplus values on their balance sheets. This is important for evaluating an insurer's solvency on an ongoing basis. Without a standardized, conservative approach to valuation of assets, liabilities, reserves, and surplus, it would be impossible to determine an insurer's financial status in either an absolute or a relative sense. Stocks are usually valued at fair market value, based on their price on the stock exchange in which they are traded. Bonds are valued at their **amortized value**, which reflects not the face value of the bond, but the remaining amount of principal and interest to be paid.

Some assets cannot be carried on the insurer's balance sheet. These **nonadmitted assets** are thought to be of such marginal quality that it would be misleading to include them in the company's net worth. Examples include office furniture and some equipment, as well as premiums or other receivables that are 90 days past due.

Investments

The states also have an interest in the regulation of the types of investments group life and disability insurers can make, and the annual statement must describe the company's investment portfolio in considerable detail. Marketable securities, bonds, and common stocks typically make up the bulk of an insurer's investments, but there is usually a limit placed on the percentage of the portfolio that may be allocated to equities. Also, investment in real estate, while permitted, is usually limited.

Claim Practices

As discussed in Chapter 10, there is considerable regulation of claim practices. At a minimum, insurers are required to make and communicate claim decisions promptly, maintain claim files, explain the reasons for denial of a claim, and provide procedures for handling complaints and appeals about claims handling.

Sales and Marketing Practices

There has been considerable emphasis placed on ethical market conduct by state regulators in recent years. Agents and brokers are required to be licensed and typically must pass a test, pay a licensing fee, and certify that they have not been convicted of a felony or previously had a license denied or revoked. In contracting agents and brokers, insurers typically conduct background checks for criminal violations, ethical misconduct, and financial responsibility. In addition, agents and brokers are prohibited from engaging in a variety of activities including:

- **rebating**—returning any part of the premium to the buyer as an inducement to the sale;

- **twisting**—inducing a policyholder through false or misleading statements to cancel existing coverage and replace it with new coverage;

- **misappropriation**—converting client funds to the agent or broker's own use and benefit; and

- misleading advertising—this includes the use of any letter, brochure, illustration, or other written, verbal, or electronic communication with an applicant or policyholder that is misleading or that misrepresents the features, benefits, or pricing of insurance contracts.

Insurance commissioners have broad powers to investigate complaints against agents and brokers concerning these and other unethical sales and marketing practices. Suspensions, fines, and license revocations are available remedies.

Regulatory Jurisdiction

Group insurance policies often provide coverage to employers and employees in several states. An issue that arises is which state law applies if there is a dispute about an eligible group, a contractual provision, or a claim. In most situations, common law **conflict of laws doctrines** will apply. Under these doctrines, it is generally recognized that the law of the state that has the greatest number of contacts with the group insurance contract controls. Over the years, a majority of courts have concluded that the laws of the state in which the contract is delivered are controlling.

Under another common law doctrine, the **doctrine of comity**, each state recognizes the validity of each other state's laws. Therefore, all states in which insurance certificates are delivered to insureds recognize the validity of the laws of the state in which the insurer delivered the policy to the employer. However, some states have enacted statutes that overturn the doctrine of comity. Under these statutes, insurance provided to residents of the state must conform to the laws and regulations of that state, not the laws of some other state where the policy may have been delivered.

Issues involving regulatory jurisdiction and conflicts of laws can be extremely complex. Although a recent trend toward uniformity in state insurance laws has gone a long way toward minimizing the differences among the states, it remains the case that litigation can turn out differently depending on which state's laws apply.

State regulation of group DI insurers is comprehensive and pervasive. While compliance with state laws can be expensive and time consuming, it is also essential to maintaining public confidence in a poorly understood and often undervalued product.

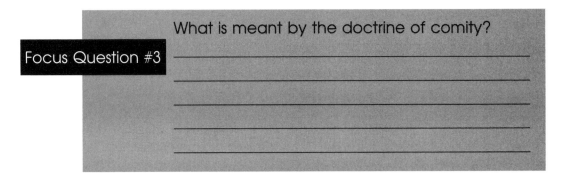

What is meant by the doctrine of comity?

Focus Question #3

▶▶ FEDERAL REGULATION

As mentioned earlier, regulation at the federal level is primarily concerned with non-discrimination in employee benefits and with the protection of funds allocated to employee benefits. This section considers the following major pieces of legislation:

- the Age Discrimination in Employment Act (ADEA),
- the Pregnancy Discrimination Act (PDA),
- the Americans with Disabilities Act (ADA),
- the Family and Medical Leave Act (FMLA), and
- the Employee Retirement Income Security Act (ERISA).

The Age Discrimination in Employment Act

The ADEA prohibits discrimination in all aspects of employment (recruitment, hiring, supervision, promotions, compensation, benefits, and discharges) against individuals age 40 and older. The ADEA applies only to employers with 20 or more employees, although many states have similar laws that apply to smaller employers. For the act to apply, the discrimination must be intentional on the part of the employer. However, intent may be demonstrated through a showing that the impact of an employer's actions resulted in discrimination. For example, an employer that recruits only graduating college students may be vulnerable to a claim of age discrimination on the grounds that the impact of its recruiting and hiring practices is to exclude older individuals from consideration.

In general, the ADEA affects group DI insurance and other benefits by making it illegal to terminate or significantly reduce benefits solely on the basis of age. However, an exception is granted for certain reductions in disability benefits based on age, provided the reductions can be justified on the basis of cost. In reducing a benefit, the employer must use data that accurately reflect the actual cost of the benefit to the employer over a reasonable period of time. Basically, this means that if an employer pays the same premium for benefits provided to employees age 65-69 as is paid to employees age 60-65, the reduction in benefits must be based on the actual cost of benefits for employees age 65-69.

Obtaining such data can be difficult, but the **Equal Employment Opportunity Commission (EEOC)**, the agency charged with enforcement of the ADEA, has agreed to allow the use of estimated costs obtained from home office and consulting actuaries. Many insurance companies believe that a 20 percent reduction in benefits for employees age 65-69 is a good rule of thumb.

Reductions in both STD and LTD benefits at older ages based on cost are specifically authorized under the ADEA. Alternatively, an LTD plan can reduce the duration of the benefit period at older ages. Thus, while it was once common practice for the benefit period of group LTD contracts to cease at age 65, most common today is a benefit that extends to age 65 for disabilities occurring before a certain age (for example, age 55), with employees incurring disabilities after the specified age receiving benefits for a scheduled period of time.

It should be mentioned that where an employer sponsors voluntary benefits, the employer can require larger contributions from older employees rather than reducing benefits. However, the proportion of benefits paid for by the employer must be the same for all age groups. Thus, if an employer pays 25 percent of the premium for employees under age 60, it must pay 25 percent of the premium for employees age 60 and older.

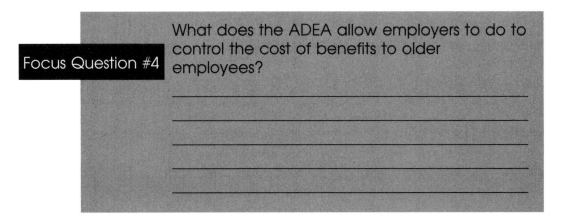

Focus Question #4

What does the ADEA allow employers to do to control the cost of benefits to older employees?

The Pregnancy Discrimination Act

It was common in the past for group DI policies to exclude or limit benefits for disabilities associated with pregnancy and childbirth. However, the PDA, enacted in 1978, requires that women affected by pregnancy, child-birth, and related medical conditions receive the same treatment as any other disabled employee, including the receipt of disability benefits. The act applies only to employers with 15 or more employees, although many states have similar laws that apply to smaller employers.

As a result of the act, uninsured sick leave plans, group STD plans, and group LTD plans no longer exclude pregnancy and related medical conditions from coverage.

The Americans with Disabilities Act

The ADA, enacted in 1992, contains sweeping provisions mandating fair treatment of disabled individuals in a variety of contexts, including public accommodations, public services, telecommunications, and employment.

Title I of the ADA, dealing with treatment of disabled individuals in employment, applies to employers with 15 or more employees. The act prohibits discrimination on the basis of disability with respect to all aspects of employment, including compensation and benefit arrangements. Disability is defined by reference to a person's inability to perform certain activities, such as caring for oneself, performing manual tasks, walking, seeing, hearing, speaking, breathing, and learning. The EEOC, which is charged with enforcement of the ADA, has issued regulations that indicate that epilepsy, cancer, diabetes, arthritis, hearing loss, vision loss, AIDS, and emotional illness can qualify as disabilities. Also, an individual who has completed a drug or alcohol rehabilitation program is subject to the ADA's protection.

A major consideration for group insurers is that the ADA requires employers to offer disabled employees access to insurance coverage on the same basis as other employees. This means that employees meeting the definition of disability under the ADA cannot be excluded from coverage under a group DI insurance plan on the basis of their disability. However, the ADA does allow an exclusion for preexisting conditions, and EEOC guidelines recognize that certain coverage limitations are permissible, including limitations for certain disabilities. As you recall from Chapters 8 and 9, it is common for LTD policies to limit the benefit period for disabilities caused by mental illness, alcoholism, and drug abuse to 12 to 24 months. And as was discussed, some cost-containment options go beyond the usual limitations and offer riders that limit other special conditions to the same 12- to 24-month period. These special conditions might include the following:

- mental illnesses, except for those with organic causes, schizophrenia, dementia, delirium, and amnesia syndrome;
- musculoskeletal and connective tissue disorders of the neck and back, with a fairly long list of exceptions for neck and back disorders for which standard medical tests produce objective data substantiating the presence of a condition that could cause disability;
- carpal tunnel syndrome;
- chronic fatigue syndrome;
- environmental allergic illness;

- fibromyalgia;
- myofascial pain syndrome; and
- alcohol, drug, or chemical abuse, dependency, or addiction and resulting mental illness.

As you might expect, these limitations have been the subject of some controversy and have even resulted in litigation. The contention of the plaintiffs bringing the lawsuits is that these limitations on their face discriminate against the disabled. However, the courts have generally disagreed. As the Fourth Circuit Court of Appeals has stated in the case of *Harold Lewis v. K-Mart Corporation et al.:* "Our federal disability statutes ensure that disabled persons are treated evenly in relationship to nondisabled persons. Our federal disability statutes are not designed to ensure that persons with one type of disability are treated the same as persons with another type of disability." Based on this case and others, limitations in benefits for certain types of disabilities are likely to continue.

The Family and Medical Leave Act

Enacted in 1993, the FMLA requires employers with 50 or more employees within a 75-mile radius to grant employees up to 12 weeks of unpaid leave per year for the following reasons:

- for the birth or adoption of a child;
- to care for a child;
- to care for a child, spouse, or parent with a **serious health condition**; and
- for the worker's own serious health condition that makes it impossible to perform a job.

A serious health condition is defined as one that requires continuing treatment from a health care provider. The regulations of the FMLA also provide that a serious health condition requires at least three days' absence from school, work, or regularly scheduled activities. However, pregnancy and treatment for certain chronic conditions, such as asthma and diabetes, fall into the category of serious health condition, even though treatment may last for less than three days. Also included in the definition of serious health condition are problems that are not ordinarily incapacitating, but for which a person is receiving ongoing multiple treatments (for example, radiation or chemotherapy for cancer, kidney dialysis, and physical therapy for severe arthritis). Specifically excluded from the definition are common colds, flu, upset stomach, and routine dental problems.

Although the employer is under no obligation to continue salary or wages during the employee's absence, the act requires employers to continue to provide medical and dental benefits. And the employer must return the employee to his old job (or an equivalent) when he returns.

A consideration with the FMLA is its integration with STD and LTD plans. A serious medical condition that qualifies an employee for FMLA leave may not qualify as a disability under the employer's group plan. On the other hand, an employee who suffers a sickness or injury is often unsure about whether the resulting inability to work will last through the elimination period under the employer's group plan and/or whether the disability meets the definition under the contract. To obtain the protection and benefits under the act, should the employee file for leave immediately? If the employee files for leave under the FMLA, also files a disability claim, and later is determined to be eligible for disability benefits, should the FLMA days be restored to the employee?

In practice, the answers to these questions are likely to vary from employer to employer. However, an integrated disability management approach is becoming increasingly popular. Under this approach, an employee absence is treated the same regardless of the reason. In all cases, the effort is to return the employee to work as soon as possible, taking advantage of all available benefits including FLMA leave, uninsured sick days, and benefits under STD and LTD plans.

The Employee Retirement Income Security Act (ERISA)

ERISA was enacted in 1974 to protect the interests of employees in pension and **welfare benefit plans**. The definition of welfare benefit plan includes any plan, fund, or program established by an employer that provides the following benefits:

- medical, surgical, or hospital care or benefits;

- benefits in the event of sickness, accident, disability, death, or unemployment;
- vacation benefits;
- apprenticeship or other training programs;
- day-care centers;
- scholarship funds;
- prepaid legal services; and
- holiday and severance pay plans.

There are three major exceptions to the definition of welfare benefit plan:

- compensation for work performed under other than normal circumstances (including overtime pay and shift, holiday, and weekend pay);
- compensation for absences from work because of sickness, vacation, holidays, military duty, jury duty, sabbatical leave, or training programs to the extent such compensation is paid from the general assets of the employer; and
- group insurance programs under which (1) no contributions are made by the employer; (2) participation is completely voluntary for employees; (3) the sole function served by the employer is to collect premiums through payroll deduction and remit the amount to the insurer; and (4) no consideration is paid to the employer in excess of reasonable compensation for administrative services actually performed.

Because most group DI insurance plans are paid for in whole or in part by the employer, they are considered welfare benefit plans under ERISA. And because most voluntary worksite plans involve at least some employer contribution, these plans also often fall within ERISA's grasp. The only DI plans that appear to escape the requirements of ERISA are completely voluntary plans paid for solely with employee contributions. These plans are exempt from ERISA, even if the employer deducts the employee's premium payment from payroll.

If a group or voluntary worksite plan is subject to ERISA, there are a variety of requirements. The most important of these are described below.

Written Plan

All welfare benefit plans must be in writing. The plan must set forth its funding policy, a procedure for amending the plan, and the basis on which payments are made to and from the plan.

Trust

If a plan is uninsured, a trust must be established for the investment and management of plan assets. The trustee of the trust is subject to requirements of **fiduciary responsibility**. Essentially this means that the trustee must invest assets prudently, ensure that conflicts of interest are avoided in the operations of the trust, and ensure that the trust does not engage in a variety of transactions, referred to as **prohibited transactions**.

Summary Plan Description

Each plan participant must receive a **summary plan description (SPD)**. The SPD must be written in language understandable to the average plan participant and must contain information about the plan, including the following:

- the name of the plan;
- the name, address, and telephone number of the plan administrator;
- the name and address of the plan sponsor;
- the type of plan;
- the sources of contributions;
- eligibility requirements;
- circumstances resulting in disqualification from participation;
- the benefits, rights, and obligations of participants;
- claim procedure and appeals procedure for denied claims; and
- a statement of the participant's rights under ERISA, including the right to examine plan documents, make copies of plan documents, and obtain a summary of the plan's annual financial report.

The Health Insurance Portability and Accountability Act (HIPAA) imposes additional requirements on SPDs. Those requirements applicable to group DI insurance include disclosure of the following:

- whether the plan is self-funded or whether it is insured;
- the name and address of the insurer, if the plan is insured;
- cost-sharing arrangements, including sharing of premiums; and
- annual or lifetime caps or other limits on plan benefits.

Annual Reports

Welfare benefit plans subject to ERISA must file an Annual Report (Form 5500) with the Department of Labor. This report must be made available to employees on request, and in addition each participant must receive yearly a Summary Annual Report that includes the plan's assets and liabilities or a description of the insurance contract funding the plan.

Small employer plans—those with fewer than 100 participants—are exempt from the requirement to file Form 5500 and furnish a Summary Annual Report. To qualify for this exemption, benefits must be paid solely from the employer's general assets, or benefits must be paid for through insurance contracts, the premiums of which are paid for solely by the employer, or by contributions by both employer and employee, provided the employer forwards the employee's contributions to the insurer within three months of receipt.

Even small employer plans must provide SPDs to employees.

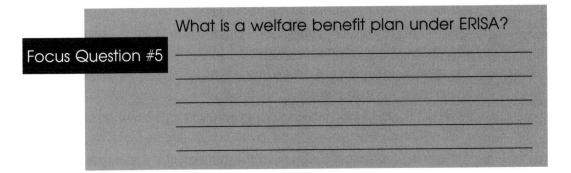

Focus Question #5

What is a welfare benefit plan under ERISA?

▶▶ SUMMARY

Group DI insurance is subject to regulation at both the state and federal levels. The states have the authority to impose requirements on insurers regarding the conduct of business, allowable contractual language, and the manner in which products are marketed and sold. A major thrust of state legislation and regulation is consumer protection. State statutes relating to insurance often begin by establishing the office of the insurance commissioner and charging it with the regulation of insurance practices so that buyers are adequately protected from insurer insolvency, faulty product design or pricing, and unethical sales and marketing practices.

At the state level, the focus is on:

- the formation and licensing of insurers,
- insurance company operations, and
- regulatory jurisdiction.

Regulation at the federal level is primarily concerned with non-discrimination in employee benefits and the protection of funds allocated to employee benefits. Major laws with which group insurers must contend include:

- the Age Discrimination in Employment Act (ADEA),
- the Pregnancy Discrimination Act (PDA),
- the Americans with Disabilities Act (ADA),
- the Family and Medical Leave Act (FMLA), and
- the Employee Retirement Income Security Act (ERISA).

Key Terms

Amortized value
Articles of
    incorporation
Bylaws
Conflict of laws
    doctrines
Doctrine of comity
Equal Employment
    Opportunity
    Commission (EEOC)
Fiduciary responsibility
Misappropriation

Non-admitted assets
Prohibited
    transactions
Rebating
Serious health
    condition
Statutory reserves
Summary plan
    description (SPD)
Twisting
Welfare benefit plan

▶▶ REVIEW QUESTIONS

1. Compare and contrast the focus of state regulatory legislation with that of federal regulatory legislation.

2. Discuss unethical sales and marketing practices targeted by the laws and regulations of most states.

3. Group DI insurance contracts often contain limitations or exclusions for certain subjective and other disabilities. What argument would you advance that such provisions are contrary to the ADA? What counter-arguments would you advance that the law does not prohibit these provisions?

4. What challenge is posed to employers and group DI insurers by the FMLA?

5. What key ERISA requirements must be met by employer welfare plans with more than 100 employees?

▶▶ ANSWERS TO FOCUS QUESTIONS

Focus Question #1—The formation and licensing of insurers, insurance company operations, and regulatory jurisdiction.

Focus Question #2—As a general rule, state laws do not specify the length of probationary periods, the language that must be used in defining disability, the duration of elimination periods, or the duration of benefit periods. Instead, it is left to market forces to determine the specifics of such features. However, state laws do regulate what provisions must be contained in contracts and often provide a range of acceptable alternatives.

Focus Question #3—Under the doctrine of comity, each state recognizes the validity of each other state's laws. Therefore, all states in which insurance certificates are delivered to insureds recognize the validity of the laws of the state in which the insurer delivered the policy to the employer. However, some states have enacted statutes that overturn the doctrine of comity. Under these statutes, insurance provided to residents of the state must conform to the laws and regulations of that state, not the laws of some other state where the policy may have been delivered.

Focus Question #4—In general, the ADEA affects group DI insurance and other benefits by making it illegal to terminate or significantly reduce benefits solely on the basis of age. However, an exception is granted for certain reductions in disability benefits based on age, provided the reductions can be justified on the basis of cost. In reducing a benefit, the employer must use data that accurately reflect the actual cost of the benefit to the employer over a reasonable period of time. Basically, this means that if an employer pays the same premium for benefits provided to employees age 65-69 as is paid to employees age 60-65, the reduction in benefits must be based on the actual cost of benefits for employees age 65-69.

Focus Question #5—The definition of welfare benefit plan includes any plan, fund, or program established by an employer that provides the following benefits:

- medical, surgical, or hospital care or benefits;
- benefits in the event of sickness, accident, disability, death, or unemployment;
- vacation benefits;
- apprenticeship or other training programs;
- day-care centers;
- scholarship funds;
- prepaid legal services; and
- holiday and severance pay plans.

►► ANSWERS TO REVIEW QUESTIONS

1. Group disability income insurance is regulated at both the state and federal levels. By virtue of the McCarran-Ferguson Act of 1945, the states have the authority to impose requirements on insurers regarding the conduct of business, allowable contractual language, and the manner in which products are marketed and sold. A major thrust of state legislation and regulation is consumer protection. State statutes relating to insurance often begin by establishing the office of the insurance

commissioner and charging it with the regulation of insurance practices so that buyers are adequately protected from insurer insolvency, faulty product design or pricing, and unethical sales and marketing practices.

Federal law is less concerned with the operation of insurance companies and more concerned with the regulation of employee benefit plans, which are often funded with insurance products. The thrust of these laws is the protection of employees against discrimination in the provision of benefits and the protection of employee funds from mismanagement, fraud, or embezzlement.

2. Agents and brokers are prohibited from engaging in a variety of activities including:

   - rebating—returning any part of the premium to the buyer as an inducement to the sale;

   - twisting—inducing a policyholder through false or misleading statements to cancel existing coverage and replace it with new coverage;

   - misappropriation—converting client funds to the agent or broker's own use and benefit; and

   - misleading advertising—this includes the use of any letter, brochure, illustration, or other written, verbal, or electronic communication with an applicant or policyholder that is misleading or that misrepresents the features, benefits, or pricing of insurance contracts.

3. An argument against these limitations and exclusions is that on their face they discriminate against individuals with certain types of disabilities and should therefore be illegal under the ADA. On the other hand, it can be persuasively argued that the ADA requires equal treatment of disabled and non-disabled individuals, but does not require that all disabled individuals be treated equally.

4. A consideration with the FMLA is its integration with STD and LTD plans. A serious medical condition that qualifies an employee for FMLA leave may not qualify as a disability under the employer's group plan. On the other hand, an employee who suffers a sickness or injury is often unsure about whether the resulting inability to work will last through the elimination period under the employer's group plan

and/or whether the disability meets the definition under the contract. To obtain the protection and benefits under the act, should the employee file for leave immediately? If the employee files for leave under the FMLA, also files a disability claim, and later is determined to be eligible for disability benefits, should the FLMA days be restored to the employee?

5. ERISA welfare benefit plans must meet the following key requirements:

- *Written plan*—All welfare benefit plans must be in writing.

- *Trust*—If the plan is uninsured, a trust must be established for the investment and management of plan assets.

- *Summary plan description*—Each plan participant must receive a summary plan description (SPD).

- Annual reports—Welfare benefit plans subject to ERISA must file an annual report (Form 5500) with the Department of Labor. This report must be made available to employees on request, and in addition each participant must receive a summary annual report.

» 14

Tax Considerations

»» OVERVIEW

Although taxes are rarely a driving force in the purchase of group or voluntary worksite disability income insurance, taxation of these products cannot be ignored. For better or worse, income taxes have been a part of our economic landscape since 1913 and show no signs of going away.

While there are other eligible groups, tax issues most often arise in the context of employer-sponsored group and voluntary insurance. Employers want to know whether group insurance premiums or amounts withheld from employees' payroll to purchase voluntary DI insurance are deductible. Employees want to know if they must pay taxes on premiums paid by an employer on their behalf, and whether premiums they pay out of pocket or through payroll deduction are tax deductible. They also want to know how benefits are taxed—in today's tax environment, where the highest individual income tax rate for married couples filing jointly is 35 percent (2003), a tax-free DI benefit can be worth that much more to a disabled individual.

Objectives

After reading this chapter and completing the accompanying exercises, you will be able to:

- explain the tax considerations of employers that sponsor group and voluntary worksite DI insurance plans, and
- explain the tax considerations of employees who participate in group and voluntary worksite DI insurance plans.

▶▶ THE EMPLOYER'S PERSPECTIVE

With respect to group or voluntary worksite DI insurance plans, the key question employers want answered is whether premiums paid on behalf of employees are tax-deductible. A secondary question is whether amounts withheld by an employer from an employee's salary or wages for payment of premiums under a voluntary plan are deductible to the employer.

As a general rule, Internal Revenue Code (IRC) Section 162 allows a deduction for all "ordinary and necessary" business expenses including "reasonable compensation." It is generally recognized that premium payments for employee benefits, such as group DI insurance, are deductible to the employer.[1]

Where the employer pays a DI insurance premium directly to the insurer on behalf of employees, the premium is usually deductible as reasonable compensation in the form of an employee benefit. Where the employer makes payroll deductions for payment of premiums on behalf of employees, the wages or salary from which the premiums are paid is straight compensation. As such, these amounts are also deductible to the employer.

This deduction can make a big difference in the **after-tax cost** of group insurance for an employer. Consider, for example, an employer in a 40 percent corporate tax bracket. If a $50,000 group DI insurance annual premium were *not* deductible, the after-tax cost would be $50,000. But assuming the premium *is* deductible, the after-tax cost is reduced to only $30,000. The after-tax cost is calculated by multiplying the employer's premium by the reciprocal of the employer's tax bracket (1 minus 0.4 equals 0.6). Because the premium is deductible, the employer avoids paying taxes on the premium and saves $20,000 (in a 40 percent tax bracket) in taxes by doing so.

An issue that sometimes arises is whether group insurance premiums paid by an employer on behalf of **owner-employees** or **self-employed individuals** are tax deductible.

Focus Question #1

What is the general rule regarding deductibility of DI insurance premiums paid by an employer on an employee's behalf?

_____

_____

_____

_____

_____

The issue of owner-employees comes up in connection with employers that are organized as corporations. It is often the case, especially with smaller employers, that owners of the business also work as employees. As a general rule, group insurance premiums paid on behalf of owner-employees are deductible as reasonable compensation just as they are for other employees.

However, if the corporation is an **S corporation**, a different rule applies. An S corporation is subject to restrictions on the number and types of shareholders. In return for complying with these restrictions, the corporation is not taxed on its income. Instead, it merely serves as a conduit for passing profit and loss through to shareholders. If an employee owns 2 percent or less of the corporation's stock, DI insurance premiums paid on her behalf are generally deductible. On the other hand, if the employee owns more than 2 percent of the stock, premiums paid by the employer for DI insurance are *not* deductible.

Similarly, if an individual is a self-employed sole proprietor or partner, DI insurance premiums paid on her behalf are not deductible by the business.

It is worth noting that the tax rule denying deductibility of DI insurance premiums for shareholders owning 2 percent or more of an S corporation, sole proprietors, and partners differs from the rule that applies to deductibility of employer-paid premiums for **medical care insurance**. Medical care insurance is defined under IRC Section 213 as insurance for hospital, surgical, and medical expense reimbursement—the definition does not include disability income insurance. In 2003, health insurance premiums paid by an S corporation for shareholders owning 2 percent or more, by a sole proprietorship for the owner, and by a partnership for partners are 100 percent deductible.

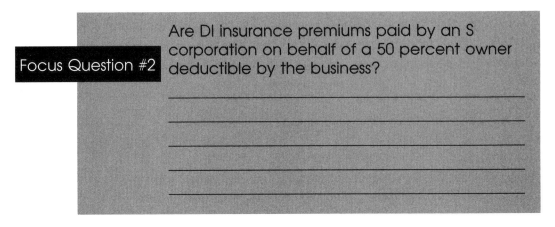

Focus Question #2

Are DI insurance premiums paid by an S corporation on behalf of a 50 percent owner deductible by the business?

State Taxation

In addition to federal income taxation, most states levy income taxes on employers and self-employed individuals. The variability in the way the 50 states tax business entities and provide for deduction of compensation and benefits makes it difficult to generalize about whether employer-paid DI insurance premiums will be deductible or not in calculating state income taxes. The most common approach is for a state to follow the federal law closely and allow business entities to deduct the same items against taxes at the state level as are allowed at the federal level.

➤➤ THE EMPLOYEE'S PERSPECTIVE

The employee has three questions concerning taxation of group or voluntary worksite DI coverage:

- Are premiums paid by the employer for such insurance includable in income?

- Is any portion of the premium contributed by the employee (by payroll deduction or otherwise) deductible by the employee?

- How are DI insurance benefits taxed?

Tax Treatment of Premiums

As a general rule, premiums paid by an employer on behalf of an employee for either group or individual DI insurance are not included in the employee's income.[2]

However, if an individual is a 2 percent or more shareholder of an S corporation, a sole proprietor, or a partner in a partnership, the individual effectively ends up paying taxes on the amount of business revenue applied to the payment of DI insurance premiums. As discussed above, these business entities are not allowed to deduct DI insurance premiums paid on behalf of self-employed individuals. Consequently, the premium expense does not reduce the taxable income of the business reported on an owner's Form 1040.

If a DI insurance plan calls for an employee contribution, through payroll deduction or otherwise, the law is clear. No deduction is allowed for the employee's share of the contribution.

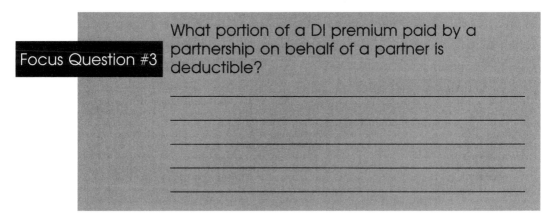

Focus Question #3

What portion of a DI premium paid by a partnership on behalf of a partner is deductible?

Tax Treatment of Benefits

The tax treatment of benefits received under a group or voluntary worksite DI plan depends on how premium payments were structured. It is helpful to distinguish between three types of plans:

Employer Pays All (Non-contributory)

In some plans, the employer pays the entire premium. As discussed above, the employee is entitled to exclude from income the premium paid by the employer on her behalf. Because the employee pays no tax on the premium, any disability benefits paid under the policy are included in the employee's income.

A tax credit is available to offset the tax on DI benefits, but this credit has limited applicability:[3]

- First, the credit is available only to individuals who meet the definition of disabled under Social Security. As you recall, Social Security requires that an individual be unable to engage in any gainful work because of a disability that has lasted or is expected to last at least 12 months or to result in death. Basically, Social Security requires total and permanent disability.

- Second, the maximum amount of the credit is limited to the lesser of the taxpayer's taxable disability benefits or a set dollar amount. The dollar amount is $750 for singles, $1,125 for married individuals filing jointly, and $562.50 for married individuals filing separately.

- Third, the maximum credit is reduced to the extent that adjusted gross income (AGI) exceeds $7,500 (singles), $10,000 (married filing jointly), and $5,000 (married filing separately). The reduction is equal to 7.5 percent of income over the adjusted gross income limit. Furthermore, the credit is reduced by 15 percent of any tax-free amount received as a pension, an annuity, or a disability benefit from any government program, including Social Security. Just taking the first reduction into account, the credit is phased out entirely for a married couple filing jointly when AGI exceeds $22,500.

Employee Pays All (Fully Contributory)

Under a plan where the employee pays the entire premium, either via payroll deduction or out of pocket, benefits are entirely tax-free.[4]

Employer and Employee Both Pay (Contributory)

In some plans, the employer pays a portion of the premium and the employee pays the balance out of pocket or via payroll deduction. In this case, the portion of the benefits attributable to the employee's share of the premiums is tax-free, while the portion attributable to the employer's premium payments is taxable, subject to possible offset by the IRC Section 22(b) credit discussed above.[5]

In determining the percentage of the premium paid by employer and employee, for a group DI plan the employee's contributions for the previous three years are considered. For individual policies, only the current year's employee contribution is considered.[6]

If DI insurance benefits are taxable income, the insured may ask the insurance company to withhold income taxes as benefits are paid. If no tax is withheld, the employee is liable for reporting the benefits on her Form 1040 and paying the tax out of pocket.

In addition, to the extent that DI insurance benefits are includable in an insured's income, they are subject to Social Security and Medicare taxes during the last month the employee works prior to disability and for the first six months of disability.

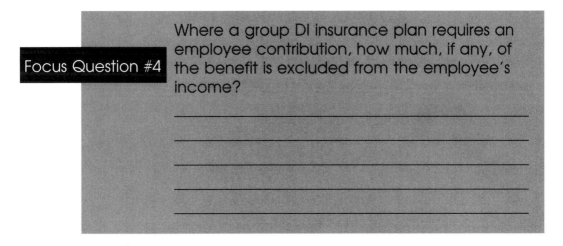

Focus Question #4

Where a group DI insurance plan requires an employee contribution, how much, if any, of the benefit is excluded from the employee's income?

State Taxation

Most states consider an individual's income to be the amount of income reported on the federal Form 1040. In these states, state taxation of DI benefits follows federal law. In a few states, individuals pay no state income taxes at all. In the remaining states, there is considerable variability in the way insurance and retirement benefits are taxed, and some states exclude disability and sick-pay benefits from income, or they offset taxes on such income with a credit.

▶▶ SUMMARY

Taxes are rarely a driving force in the purchase of group or voluntary worksite disability income insurance, but taxation of these products cannot be ignored.

As a general rule, premiums paid by an employer are tax-deductible for the employer, while employee contributions are not deductible for the employee. On the other hand, premiums paid by an employer on an employee's behalf are generally not included in the employee's income.

The taxation of benefits depends on the type of plan. If the employee pays the entire premium with after-tax dollars, the entire amount of the benefit is tax-free. If the employer plays the entire premium, the benefits are taxable to the employee. If both parties pay a portion of the premium, the portion of the benefits attributable to employee premiums is tax-free, while the portion attributable to employer contributions is taxable.

Key Terms	After-tax cost	S corporation
	Medical care insurance	Self-employed individual
	Owner-employee	

▶▶ REVIEW QUESTIONS

1. Acme, Inc. is in a 40 percent corporate tax bracket. It pays a $100,000 annual group DI insurance premium. What is its after-tax cost for the premium? How did you arrive at your answer?

2. Explain the difference in the rules for the deductibility of health insurance premiums and DI insurance premiums for self-employed sole proprietors and partners.

3. Explain how the Section 22(b) credit gets reduced.

➤➤ ANSWERS TO FOCUS QUESTIONS

Focus Question #1—Where the employer pays a DI insurance premium directly to the insurer on behalf of employees, the premium is usually deductible as reasonable compensation in the form of an employee benefit. Where the employer makes payroll deductions for payment of premiums on behalf of employees, the wages or salary from which the premiums are paid is straight compensation. As such, these amounts are also deductible to the employer.

Focus Question #2—If an employee owns more than 2 percent of the stock, premiums paid by the employer for DI insurance are not deductible.

Focus Question #3—No part of the premium is deductible.

Focus Question #4—The benefits attributable to the employee's share of the premiums is tax-free, while the portion of the benefits attributable to the employer's premium payments is taxable, subject to possible offset by the IRC Section 22(b) credit.

➤➤ ANSWERS TO REVIEW QUESTIONS

1. The after-tax cost is $60,000. It is calculated by multiplying the employer's premium by the reciprocal of the employer's tax bracket (1 minus 0.4 equals 0.6).

2. The tax rule denying deductibility of DI insurance premiums for shareholders owning 2 percent or more of an S corporation, sole proprietors, and partners differs from the rule that applies to deductibility of employer-paid premiums for medical care insurance. Medical care insurance is defined under IRC Section 213 as insurance for hospital, surgical, and medical expense reimbursement—the definition does not include disability income insurance. In 2003, health insurance premiums paid by an S corporation for shareholders owning 2 percent or more, by a sole proprietorship for the owner, and by a partnership for partners are 100 percent deductible.

3. The maximum credit is reduced to the extent that adjusted gross income (AGI) exceeds $7,500 (singles), $10,000 (married filing jointly), and $5,000 (married filing separately). The reduction is equal to 7.5 percent of income over the adjusted gross income limit. Furthermore, the credit is reduced by 15 percent of any tax-free amount received as a pension, an annuity, or a disability benefit from any government program, including Social Security. Just taking the first reduction into account, the credit is phased out entirely for a married couple filing jointly when AGI exceeds $22,500.

NOTES

1　Treas. Reg. Section 1.162-10(a); Rev. Rul. 58-90, 1958-1 CB 88; Rev. Rul. 56-632.

2　IRC Section 106.

3　IRC Section 22(b).

4　IRC Section 104.

5　Treas. Reg. Section 1.105-1(c).

6　Treas. Reg. Section 1.105-1(d).

Key Terms

Key terms are indicated in the text by boldface and this symbol ▣ in the margin. Key terms are introduced, defined, and explained on the pages listed below.

Index

Frequently Asked Questions About the HIAA Examination

What material does the examination for the HIAA course *Disability Income Insurance: Group and Worksite Issues* cover?

The 14 chapters of the textbook titled *Disability Income Insurance: Group and Worksite Issues.*

Is information from tables and figures covered in the exam?

Yes, information from the tables and figures found in the 14 chapters is covered.

How many questions are on the exam, and how much time do I have?

There are 75 questions. You have two hours.

What is the format of the questions of the exam?

All questions are multiple choice.

EXAMPLE *All of the following are eligible employees for group DI insurance EXCEPT:*

    a) managers
    b) part-time employees
    c) owners
    d) union employees

(The correct answer is b.)

Some questions are multiple-option multiple choice.

EXAMPLE   *The rationale for return-to-work programs includes:*

I.   *They ensure compliance with state laws.*
II.   *They benefit employees.*
III.   *They lower employer costs.*

a. *I and II only*
b. *I and III only*
c. *II and III only*
d. *I, II, and III*

(The correct answer is c.)

A few questions are application questions. These require you to determine which of the facts given in the question are relevant and then apply your knowledge to reach a conclusion.

EXAMPLE   *Janine seriously injured her neck in an accident at work in January 2003. She receives $1,800 per month in workers' compensation. Her highest earnings year was 2002, and her average monthly earnings for that year were $3,000. Based solely on her PIA, she is entitled to $1,000 of disability benefits from Social Security. How much will Janine actually receive in Social Security disability benefits?*

a. *Nothing*
b. *$600*
c. *$1,000*
d. *$1,200*

(The correct answer is b.)

You should be able to answer the question by applying your knowledge of the rules for Social Security disability benefits. (Janine's total benefits—Social Security and workers' compensation—can be no more than 80 percent of her average monthly earnings, or $2,400.)

If I can answer all the focus questions and review questions, will I be able to pass the exam?

Not necessarily. The focus questions, review questions, and key terms are intended to direct the student to the most important information and ideas, but they do not cover everything that might be asked on the exam.

I have a lot of experience in insurance. Can I pass the exam without reading the textbook or studying?

Possibly, but you should be aware that the examination is based on the most common practices in the insurance industry. What your company does may differ. The safest approach is to read the textbook and see if you know the material. This will go very quickly if you already have a lot of knowledge.

HIAA's Courses and Professional Designations

For more than 40 years, the Health Insurance Association of America's Insurance Education Program has offered current, comprehensive, and economically priced courses for professionals seeking to advance their understanding of the health insurance industry. Since 1958, more than 500,000 people have enrolled in these courses. Many enrollees are employees of health insurance companies or managed care organizations, but consultants, third-party administrators, agents, brokers, and other health insurance professionals also study with us. In addition, an increasing number of noninsurance professionals, including health care providers, economists, consumer advocates, and government officials, are taking HIAA courses to gain a better understanding of the operations of our industry and to advance their careers in their own fields.

Courses include:

- The Fundamentals of Health Insurance (Parts A and B)
- Managed Care (Parts A, B, and C)
- Medical Expense Insurance
- Supplemental Health Insurance
- Disability Income Insurance (three courses)
- Long-Term Care Insurance (four courses)
- Health Care Fraud (three courses)
- Customer Service for the Health Care Environment
- HIPAA Rules, Requirements, and Compliance (three courses)
- Medical Management (six courses)
- Certified Senior Advisor

The completion of HIAA courses leads to widely respected professional designations:

- Health Insurance Associate (HIA®)
- Managed Healthcare Professional (MHP®)
- Long-Term Care Professional (LTCP)
- Health Care Anti-Fraud Associate (HCAFA)
- Disability Income Associate (DIA)
- Disability Healthcare Professional (DHP)
- Medical Management Associate (MMA)
- HIPAA Associate (HIPAAA)
- HIPAA Professional (HIPAAP)
- Healthcare Customer Service Associate (HCSA)
- Eldercare Health Professional (EHP)

The HIA designation has been in existence since 1990 and is currently held by more than 18,000 professionals. The MHP, offered for the first time in 1996, is held by more than 5,500 designees. The other HIAA designations have been introduced in recent years.

For more information, visit our Website (www.insuranceeducation.org) or call 800-509-4422.

▶▶ Other Books from HIAA

▶▶ On Disability Income Insurance:

Disability Income Insurance: A Primer

Many people are unaware of the consequences of preretirement long-term disability. Contrary to popular belief, government programs such as Social Security, Medicare, and Medicaid do not provide adequate coverage. This book explains the benefits of disability income (DI) insurance, describing government- and employer-sponsored plans and offering an in-depth exploration of individual DI insurance, including its evolution, application, contracts, underwriting, and claims administration. The *Primer* serves as an introductory textbook for the first of three courses in DI insurance leading to the designation of Disability Income Associate.

Disability Income Insurance: Advanced Issues

The second book in the disability income insurance series examines the role of standard policies in providing basic coverage and explores a variety of ways of structuring disability income programs to meet the needs of lower, mid-tier, and higher-level employees. Readers will gain practical knowledge about the role of business overhead expense insurance in the protection of business profits, as well as the transition of ownership when disability strikes a key person. The tax implications of the choice of various planning tools are considered from both employer and employee viewpoints. The text also provides a disability income blueprint for individuals to consider in planning for retirement, long-term care needs, and estate accumulation and distribution.

▶▶ On Health Insurance:

The Health Insurance Primer: An Introduction to How Health Insurance Works

This book, together with *Health Insurance Nuts and Bolts*, serves as a complete introduction to the health insurance field. The authors assume no prior knowledge and begin by explaining basic concepts and terminology, but they progress to an in-depth examination of such topics as the various kinds of health insurance, health insurance contracts, underwriting, and sales and marketing. *The Health Insurance Primer* is an excellent choice for beginners in health insurance.

Health Insurance Nuts and Bolts: An Introduction to Health Insurance Operations

The introduction to the basic facts and concepts of group and individual health insurance begun in *The Health Insurance Primer* continues in *Health Insurance Nuts and Bolts*. Topics include managing the cost of health care; policy issue, renewal, and service; claim administration; pricing health insurance products; government regulation; and fraud and abuse.

Medical Expense Insurance

For those who have a basic understanding of the concepts and functioning of health insurance, this book provides more specific information on medical expense insurance, the most common kind of health insurance in America. The text begins by describing the two coverages that provide health insurance to most Americans: group major medical insurance and individual hospital-surgical insurance. Subsequent chapters discuss the following topics: marketing and sales, pricing, contract provisions, underwriting, policy administration, claim administration, and industry issues.

Supplemental Health Insurance

This book is intended to provide those who have a basic knowledge of health insurance and supplemental health insurance with more specific information on the major supplemental products in the marketplace. In addition, the gaps in health coverage that led to the need for additional insurance are discussed for each product. Topics include Medicare supplements, hospital indemnity coverage, specified disease insurance, accident coverage, dental plans, specialty plans, and the supplemental insurance market.

▶▶ On Health Care Fraud:

Health Care Fraud: An Introduction to Detection, Investigation, and Prevention

This book provides an orientation in how health care fraud is perpetrated and what is being done to combat it. It looks at how some of the most common fraudulent schemes operate, how these schemes are detected and investigated, and the laws that can be brought to bear against them. Fraud perpetrated by health care providers, consumers, and others is included, and fraud involving not just medical expense insurance but also managed care and disability income insurance is covered.

Insurance Fraud in Key Products: Disability, Long-Term Care, MedSupp, Drug Coverage, & Others

While the first book in HIAA's fraud series focuses on medical expense insurance, this text looks at a range of health insurance products: disability, long-term care, dental, behavioral health, prescription drug, and Medicare supplement insurance. It also introduces the reader to fraud in related coverages, such as life insurance and property/casualty insurance. For each of these, common fraudulent schemes are examined, and legal and investigative issues are explored.

Health Care Fraud: Legal Issues

The third volume in HIAA's series on health care fraud focuses on enforcement activity. It examines the roles of state governments and the federal government in fighting fraud, and looks at the statutes and other tools available to government agencies. Private sector enforcement activity is also discussed, with an emphasis on legal issues such as compliance and privacy. Finally, there is an exploration of how the public and private sectors can work together to combat fraud.

▶▶ On Long-Term Care Insurance:

Long-Term Care: Understanding Needs and Options

This book provides an introduction to the field of long-term care and long-term care insurance. It begins with an explanation of what long-term care is, who needs it, and how and where it is provided. It then looks at various ways of paying for long-term care and the limitations of each. It examines long-term care insurance, describing how it works and why it is often the best solution to the problem. Finally, it discusses the ways salespeople and insurance company personnel can bring this solution to the people who need it.

Financing Long-Term Care Needs: Exploring Options and Reaching Solutions

This book examines in detail the various ways that people finance long-term care. It covers in depth a variety of financing options, including personal savings, reliance on family members, government programs, reverse mortgages, annuities, and long-term care insurance. It also looks at the role of long-term care insurance in estate and business planning.

The Long-Term Care Insurance Product: Policy Design, Pricing, and Regulation

Long-term care insurance (LTCI) is a relatively new, and still evolving, product. This book looks at this evolution, focusing on the innovations insurers have made to better meet consumer needs and the impact of regulation, especially HIPAA. It also provides a comprehensive discussion of LTCI policy provisions, including benefit eligibility, benefit amounts, inflation protection, elimination periods, policy maximums, nonforfeiture, renewal, lapse, and others, as well as an explanation of how the premium is calculated.

Long-Term Care Insurance: Administration, Claims, and the Impact of HIPAA

This book provides an overview of long-term care insurance administration. It looks at practices and procedures in several administrative areas, including underwriting, issuance, premiums, policy maintenance, policyholder services, and reporting. It describes the LTCI claim process and the steps insurers take to control claim costs and hold down premium prices. And it examines the impact of the Health Insurance Portability and Accountability Act of 1996 (HIPAA).

►► On HIPAA:

HIPAA Primer: An Introduction to HIPAA Rules, Requirements, and Compliance

This is the basic textbook designed for all students who want to develop a strong, baseline knowledge of the Health Insurance Portability and Accountability Act of 1996 (HIPAA) and its impact on the health care system. The *Primer* complements the HIPAA workbooks, helping readers fully understand the Privacy Rule—what it is, what its key components are, and whom it affects. It presents an overview of all the key parts of the administrative simplification provisions.

HIPAA Action Items for Insurers

This book provides easy-to-understand guidelines that will help insurers interpret the HIPAA Privacy Rule and implement compliance action tasks. From appointing a privacy official to training staff, this resource will prove its worth as managers get compliance efforts underway. Included are industry-specific case studies and templates for creating compliance documents such as the privacy notice, business associate agreement, and authorization.

HIPAA Action Items for Home Care Providers

The Health Insurance Portability and Accountability Act (HIPAA) is here to stay, and home care providers must comply with HIPAA's Privacy Rule. This practical guide cuts through information overload and gives readers a jump-start on compliance efforts. The first in a series of innovative HIPAA compliance texts and courses, this workbook helps health care providers and others in the health care continuum organize compliance efforts and explain HIPAA to staff, patients, and business associates.

►► On Managed Care:

Managed Care: What It Is and How It Works (Second Edition)

Completely updated and expanded by Peter R. Kongstvedt, MD, the foremost authority in the managed care industry, this exciting new edition provides readers with a solid grounding and clear understanding of managed health care. Written in a clear and concise style that provides the fundamentals for practitioners and students, the book includes learning objectives and an extensive glossary of key managed health care terms. It serves as the textbook for the course Managed Care, Part A.

Managed Care: Integrating the Delivery and Financing of Health Care, Part B

Part B of HIAA's managed care series covers operational issues and problems. Topics include the governance and management structure of managed care organizations; selective medical provider contracting; network administration and provider relations; marketing and member services; claims administration; financing, budgeting, and rating; legal issues; accreditation; and regulation.

Managed Care: Integrating the Delivery and Financing of Health Care, Part C

Part C of this series examines current issues in managed care, operations and problems in specialized areas of managed care, and the role of managed care in government health benefit programs. Topics include public and private purchasing groups; consumers and physicians; managed care for pharmacy, dental, behavioral health, and vision benefits; and managed care for federal employees and military personnel, in the Medicare program, and in state government programs.

Dental Benefits: A Guide to Dental PPOs, HMOs, and Other Managed Plans (Revised Edition)

Written for benefit plan sponsors, dentists, administrators, and dental students, this expanded and updated reference by Donald S. Mayes provides the ''nuts and bolts'' of dental benefits. It clarifies managed dental plans and explains how they differ from other health plans. By using this book as a tool, readers will be able to objectively evaluate dental plans. This book serves as the text of an elective course in the managed care program.

▶▶ On Medical Management:

Medical Management: An Overview

This book is intended for those who work in the health insurance industry, and also for educators, providers of health care services, and others who seek more knowledge about the evolution of managed care. Readers will explore historical perspectives and early models of managed care; gain insight into legislative and regulatory requirements that affect the industry; learn about accreditation and certification; find out why and how health care benefit plans are developed; and discover current and future trends.

Medical Management: Utilization Management

The purpose of utilization management is to determine whether health care services are medically necessary and appropriate. A balancing act among professionals who work for health plans, hospitals, and other entities, it is centered on the needs of the patient to ensure the right provider, treatment, and site for delivery of services. This book examines the many aspects of utilization management to give students a thorough grounding in goals, programs, processes, staffing, and other key issues. It is recommended for medical management staff within hospitals, health systems, HMOs, insurance companies, and PPOs; third-party administrators; utilization, quality, case, and disease management professionals; and medical call center managers and staff.

Medical Management: Call Centers

This book presents an overview of the "telehealth" industry—from standard centers that serve health plan members to more sophisticated systems that provide access to registered nurses who can assist patients with specific health problems. Students are given practical pointers on "nuts and bolts" issues—such as steps to take in establishing a call center, how to select vendors, and what to expect with regard to hiring and training employees. They also gain insight about service and quality, the impact of legal and regulatory requirements, and trends in the use of electronic communications by health care consumers. The book is recommended for those who have an interest in medical management and want to learn more about the key role of call centers in integrated care management systems.

Medical Management: Case Management

Case managers help clients and families navigate health care delivery systems and manage their own health care needs. Practitioners come from many disciplines—they are nurses, social workers, rehabilitation counselors, and physicians—and collaborate with other key stakeholders to achieve quality, cost-effective outcomes. This book imparts a clear understanding of the basic concepts of case management, the background of the professionals who provide these services, and how case management processes and services function. It is intended for those working in the health insurance industry and allied fields who want to learn more about case management and where it fits in today's health care system. The book is also recommended for professionals who are interested in becoming case managers.

Medical Management: Disease Management

Disease management is described as a *system* of coordinated health care interventions in which patient education and self-care are key components. This book takes a practical systems approach to the subject. It is recommended for students at all levels—from beginners exploring the concept of disease management to managers of full-scale operations. The book is designed as a basic guide for practitioners, program administrators, educators, and other professionals who want to understand the evolution and current practice of disease management.

Medical Management: Quality Management

Providing the right health care at the right time in a way that produces the most favorable patient outcomes is the objective of quality management. This book covers the essentials, helping students understand why quality management is important, how programs are implemented, and who the key stakeholders are. Intended for a wide audience—employees of health plans and medical groups, regulators, purchasers of health care services, educators, and consumers—the book introduces students to the fundamental framework of quality management. Its primary aim is to provide an overview of the programs, processes, and procedures used by health care organizations to ensure the delivery of quality services.

▸▸ On Customer Service:

Customer Service Strategies for the Health Care Environment

In an easy-reading style, this text focuses on practical ways to create a customer-driven organization. It also covers accreditation issues. Readers learn how accreditation surveyors identify and review customer service initiatives, review assessment guidelines, and find solutions to common customer service problems. The book features many valuable resources that can be used for self-study or for training staff and developing quality customer service programs.

**THESE BOOKS MAY BE ORDERED
BY CALLING 800-828-0111.**

The HIAA Insurance Education Program

Gregory F. Dean, JD, CLU, ChFC, LTCP
Executive Director

Joyce C. Meals
Assistant Director

Leanne Dorado
Manager of Education Operations

Kevin Gorham
Fiscal Manager

La'Creshea Makonnen
CE Credit Manager

Yolaunda Janrhett
Registration Coordinator

Matthew Grant
Internet Coordinator